19

PELICAN BOOKS

SEX AND GENDER

Barbara Lloyd is Reader in Social Psychology at the University of
Sussex. She was educated at the University of Chicago, Boston
University and Northwestern University in Evanston, Illinois, where
she took a Ph.D. in Social Psychology. She came to England in 1964 and
taught at Birmingham University before joining Marie Jahoda's Social
Psychology group at the University of Sussex in 1967. Since coming to
England she has studied cognitive development in English and Nigerian
children and has recently completed training as a psychotherapist. She
is the author of *Perception and Cognition: A Cross Cultural Perspective*,
Nyansongo: A Gusii Community in Kenya (with R. A. LeVine), and is
co-editor of *Universals of Human Thought: Some African Evidence* (with
John Gay) and of *Cognition and Categorization* (with Eleanor Rosch).
She is on the editorial board of the *British Journal of Social Psychology*
and the *Journal of Child Psychology and Psychiatry*, and is one of the
editors of the Developing Child Series published by Fontana and
Harvard University Press.

She is married to Peter Lloyd, Professor of Social Anthropology
at the University of Sussex, and has two children, a teenage daughter
and a young son.

John Archer was educated at the University of Wales where he gained a
B.Sc. in Zoology and at the University of Bristol where he took a Ph.D.
in Psychology. He was a Research Fellow at the University of Sussex,
where he studied hormones and behaviour in animals. Since 1975 he has
been a lecturer and Senior Lecturer in Psychology at Preston Polytechnic
and has carried out research on gender differences in school children as
well as continuing research on animal behaviour. He is a member of the
Council of the Association for the Study of Animal Behaviour and is on
the editorial board of two animal behaviour journals. His other books
are *Exploring Sex Differences* (co-edited with Barbara Lloyd), *Animals
under Stress* and *Exploration in Animals and Humans* (co-edited with
Lynda Birke).

Sex and Gender

John Archer and Barbara Lloyd

Penguin Books

Penguin Books Ltd, Harmondsworth, Middlesex, England
Penguin Books, 625 Madison Avenue, New York, New York 10022, U.S.A.
Penguin Books Australia Ltd, Ringwood, Victoria, Australia
Penguin Books Canada Ltd, 2801 John Street, Markham, Ontario, Canada L3R 1B4
Penguin Books (N.Z.) Ltd, 182–190 Wairau Road, Auckland 10, New Zealand

First published 1982

Copyright © John Archer and Barbara Lloyd, 1982
All rights reserved

Made and printed in Great Britain by
Richard Clay (The Chaucer Press) Ltd, Bungay, Suffolk
Filmset in Monophoto Plantin by
Northumberland Press Ltd, Gateshead, Tyne and Wear

Contents

Preface

One impact of the women's movement of the 1960s was a reawakening of concern about the psychology of women and about sex differences in psychological research. The first wave of interest among psychologists, in the late 1960s and early 1970s, was often characterized by attention to biological explanations. At this time the influence of the women's movement was also being felt in anthropology and sociology. It was only later in the 1970s that social psychologists became interested in comparing the behaviour of men and women.

The impact of social scientists, and the contrast between their approach and that of more traditional psychologists of the early 1970s, are reflected in the change of both explanations and terminology. The study of differences between men and women has moved from biological explanations to a consideration of the importance of broader social processes. The term 'sex differences' was originally used in a vague sense by psychologists to indicate both socially derived distinctions between men and women and their biological differences. Recently this usage has been called in question, and increasingly the term 'gender' is being used when referring to socially derived distinctions, leaving the term 'sex' for biological differences. Our title and usage reflect this change.

In entitling our book *Sex and Gender*, we are extending its concerns beyond those of earlier, more strictly psychological, accounts of 'sex differences', although we do not ignore the topics found in them. This change in emphasis means that the issues involved in describing, measuring and explaining sex (or gender) differences have become complex. We begin by considering these issues in the first two chapters. In Chapter 1 we look at some commonsense beliefs about the nature of men and women, and consider the way in which these have influenced psychological accounts. We then consider the nature of research strategies used to study sex and gender, and establish our usage of the two terms. In Chapter 2 we present three different approaches to the study of gender differences. We begin by drawing demographic portraits of men and women, since these produce views which, on the surface, appear to be very objective. We then consider how psychological testing provides a description of the abilities of men and women. We conclude with studies of stereotyping, which bring us back to commonsense beliefs. In the remaining chapters we consider a range of topics which are of central importance in the discussion of sex and gender differences: physical attributes, sexuality, aggression and power, mental health, the family, intelligence and achievement, the development of gender differences, and social change.

We are indebted to Julia Vellacott, who first suggested that we write a book about sex differences. This project has led us back to old problems and into new fields, and has ultimately helped us to consider the boundaries of the area known as the psychology of sex differences. Along the way many people have given generously of their time and expertise. In particular we thank Neil Berry, Lynda Birke, Glynis Breakwell, Ernest Brown, Mervin Glasser, Ken Gledhill, Carol Jacklin, John Lazarus, Mike Scaife, Bill Scott, Mary Sissons and Helen Weinreich-Haste. Special thanks are due to Peter Lloyd.

CHAPTER I

Commonsense Views and Psychological Research

Commonsense Views of Men and Women

Everyone has ideas about the nature of men and women, and knows in a commonsense way what they are like. If this were the whole story, we, and the biological and social scientists whose research we report, would be wasting our time. But it is not. Commonsense views are only a part of the story, but they are an important place to begin because they have had a major influence on the scientific study of sex and gender.

Commonsense views about differences between men and women were more widely accepted before the challenges of the modern feminist movement modified public consciousness. Since awareness of the prejudice inherent in commonsense notions has tempered contemporary images, we shall look at the popular culture of an earlier decade to find a typical example. It comes from 'A Hymn to Him' in *My Fair Lady*, the musical version of Shaw's *Pygmalion*. This may or may not appeal to you aesthetically; but whatever your reaction, bear with us, since it provides a clear example.

Henry Higgins is puzzled. After achieving a social triumph at a ball, Eliza Doolittle disappears. Higgins laments:

> *Women are irrational, that's all there is to that!*
> *Their heads are full of cotton, hay and rags!*
> *They're nothing but exasperating, irritating, vacillating,*
>   *calculating, agitating, maddening and infuriating hags!*
> *Why can't a woman be more like a man?*
> *Men are so honest, so thoroughly square;*
> *Eternally noble, historically fair;*
> *Who, when you win, will always give your back a pat!*
> *Why can't a woman be like that?*

And so it goes on through several more verses. Rather than consider all of these, let us use the eight lines above to extract some general principles.

The first principle is that men and women differ fundamentally. Most comparisons take the form of a dogged pursuit of their differences; our common humanity is either deliberately ignored or so tacitly assumed as to have much the same effect.

The second principle is that men are superior and women their inferiors. Henry Higgins provides a clear example of this. He leaves us in no doubt that women are not a patch on men; in these lines he contrasts women's emotionality with men's steadfastness. In other verses he comments negatively on women's intelligence, conformity, vanity and sensitivity to slight. You may wish to say that this is just a song – one man's view of the opposite sex. Nevertheless, with the exception of writings from the women's movement, it is difficult to find comparisons which err in the opposite direction and present women in an overwhelmingly positive light. This is hardly surprising, since commonsense views reflect the respective places of men and women in society, and in most cases men exert more power and have greater status in public life than women.

Rather than provide further examples of commonsense views from plays, films and novels (Ellman, 1968), we shall use these two principles – that men and women differ fundamentally and that the differences involve female deficiencies – to analyse further everyday notions about physical, intellectual and emotional differences between men and women. We then go on to consider the roles of the two sexes in society, commonsense explanations of them and possibilities for change.

The commonsense emphasis on categorical differences appears to be grounded in recognition of anatomical and functional differences in reproduction. This leads to the assumption that other physical, intellectual and emotional differences have the same non-overlapping distributions. If we return to the lines from *My Fair Lady*, we can see that men and women are seen as totally different in their actions and mental make-up. Women are described as emotional and illogical ('irrational' is Henry Higgins's word), while men, by implication, are stoical and sensible.

Although it is no longer believed that men are intellectually superior to women, it is still widely held that the two sexes think differently and have a natural bent for different intellectual activities. The preponderance of boys and men studying pure science, mathematics, engineering and architecture, and the concentration of girls and women in biology, the arts and language studies, support this view. Not only are sciences and engineering seen as the special domains of men, but they are viewed as more complex and difficult. Boys and girls have different skills, and those of males are superior. Old ideas do not die easily.

Is it merely coincidence that the two sexes are regarded as fundamentally different both in physical form and in mental characteristics, or are mental and physical differences linked in some way? One common assumption is that bodily characteristics influence mental ones, but no effort is made to explain the nature of the influence precisely. In Victorian times the idea that women are the weaker sex was generalized from physical to mental traits. They were regarded as intellectually inferior, and reasons were sought in terms of the biological knowledge of the day (Burnstyn, 1971; Gould, 1978). At present the hormonal changes associated with the menstrual cycle, pregnancy, childbirth and the menopause are often implicated in women's alleged emotional lability, and the lack of hormonal change with the reputed stability of men.

The search for correlations between physical attributes and mental traits is one everyday way of explaining sex differences. Another is to consider the functions of men and women in biological and social spheres. In this way it is assumed that since only women bear and suckle infants, they must also be responsible for child care. But not all role assignments are based on categorical sex differences. It is often argued that because women are, on average, smaller and less muscular, this precludes them from a variety of strenuous and demanding occupations such as bricklaying or coalmining. This argument is often disguised as an attempt to protect women from strenuous and dangerous physical pursuits.

Until fairly recently there was little need to seek an explanation either for the coincidence of particular physical and mental traits in men and women, or for the consequences of physical traits as seen in sex-specific roles. The traditional explanation according to both Jewish and Christian religious belief was that God had created woman to be the helpmate of man, but not his equal. It was 'the natural order' of things. As our society has grown more secular, biological ideas such as evolution and genetic inheritance have come to replace the deity in sustaining the natural order. But this is not unique to our own society. In Tchambuli culture, where sex roles appear to be the reverse of those of our own society, the explanation for this division is also sought in biological forces (Mead, 1950).

At present there is a competing and fairly widespread view which sees the social environment as the source of differences between the sexes. Even physical differences, it is suggested, reflect the positive encouragement of boys and men to take part in sports and body-building activity, and the restriction of girls and women to less demanding physical pursuits. The process whereby social values are differentially inculcated is commonly described as conditioning. The term does not denote the technical procedures first described by Pavlov, but is used in everyday speech to describe how people are influenced by society. According to the conditioning view, sex differences in temperament and ability are seen not in terms of female inadequacy and weakness, but as the result of societal (male) pressures which have resulted in female subservience and under-achievement.

Acceptance of this type of explanation has produced a reaction from those who seek to defend traditional values. For many people interested in the social issues of our time, biological research and theory are seen as a way of explaining why contemporary society has created social problems through its neglect or disregard for human nature. Books which have caught the popular imagination include *On Aggression* (Lorenz, 1966), *The Naked Ape* (Morris, 1967) and *The Territorial Imperative* (Ardrey, 1967). In these the inevitability of man's aggression, his particular view of women as sex objects and the legacy of his prehistory as a hunter are stressed.

These popular accounts of differences do not exist in a vacuum, but are closely connected with ideas about the desirability of change. For those who believe that the roles of men and women reflect their evolutionary origins, the natural place for women is in the home, looking after children. Emotional traits such as patience, tenderness and sensitivity are seen as fitting them for their role as home-makers and mothers. It follows that drastic changes would be both undesirable and doomed to failure.

However, existing differences and even those traits which suit women to the care of children would be seen from the conditioning perspective as susceptible to change. This explanation, focusing on an upbringing which from an early age thrusts dolls into girls' arms and encourages competitiveness in boys, would see any change as yet another pattern to be produced by learning.

In everyday thinking, these two views and outlooks for change are associated with conservative and egalitarian ideologies. The conservative ideology sees present-day roles as part of the natural order and change as disastrous. As the popular novelist Barbara Cartland puts it, 'All this striving and clawing into a man's world will eventually end in tears.' The implication seems to be that either women will not succeed or that, if they do succeed, change will only bring unhappiness in its wake.

The egalitarian view stresses the inequality in present-day differences between men and women and seeks to put this right through social change. The belief that differences reflect learning supports the possibility of change. Sex discrimination can thus be modified through legislation and education. Although the egalitarian position based on belief in the possibility of change is typically that of feminists, there are a minority who see the problem of male power as residing in biology. Men are regarded as more aggressive by nature and always liable to take it out on anyone weaker.

By and large, feminist writers question commonsense notions about men and women. They challenge both the emphasis on differences and the belief that those traits ascribed to men are more desirable. Descriptions of differences are seen as myths which support the subjugation of women, and men and women are seen as being more similar than popular beliefs would indicate.

Commonsense Influences on Psychological Research

Commonsense views have had a major influence on psychological research. They have led to an emphasis on differences, and they have guided the discovery, characterization and explanation of these differences.

A parallel with the commonsense view which presents men and women as fundamentally different can be seen in psychological research. Psychologists often look for differences between men as a group and women as a group, without taking into account the wide range of variation between individuals of the same sex. The main criterion for deciding that there is a significant difference between two groups is not the magnitude of the difference alone, but whether it would be expected to occur very often by chance. Significance is a measure of reliability, not of magnitude. It enables differences which are small in magnitude but statistically significant to appear important when the variation within groups is low or the samples are large. The widespread use of significance-testing in psychology has led to the use of the term 'sex difference' to refer to average differences which vary greatly in absolute magnitude.

The publication policy of psychology journals increases the emphasis on differences and the neglect of similarities. They accept more readily reports in which statistically significant differences have been recorded, and it is difficult to publish results in which no significant differences have been found. As a result, there is no way to estimate the under-reporting of findings of no difference (Maccoby and Jacklin, 1974; Lloyd, 1976).

Although we have shown the way in which psychological research strategies support the pursuit of differences, there are some hopeful signs of change. Tresemer has drawn attention to the need for estimates of the degree of overlap in the performances of men and women (Tresemer, 1975; Sherman, 1978). Such a procedure would enable a distinction to be made between different magnitudes of sex difference. It may be useful to think of these as lying on a continuum or scale, with at one end those characteristics on which every member of one sex is different from every member of the other, such as the genitals, and at the other end characteristics which men and women share to an equal degree, such as intelligence. In between would be measures on which the sexes partially overlap. Although most psychological measures are of this sort, by referring to them as sex differences it is implied that they show little overlap.

Tresemer has suggested several statistical ways to measure or express the degree of overlap between the sexes. One is the percentage of one sex that exceeds the mean or average score of the other. Another is the percentage of one sex that overlaps the other. Unfortunately these measures are not in current use and we are unable to report findings in this manner.

Intellectual performance provides an example of how such measures might be used. On average, men attain higher scores on tests of spatial ability (see Chapters 2 and 8). Although the magnitude of the sex difference usually goes unreported, where the information is available it is usually the case that about 25 per cent of women's scores are above the mean value for men (Lambert, 1978). Tresemer has described it as a medium to large difference, given the relative magnitude of effects usually found in studies of sex differences. But, as Figure 1.1 shows, there is a considerable degree of overlap between men's and women's scores.

Although few of the studies we report are amenable to the precise analysis which Tresemer advocates, we try to keep in mind the magnitude of differences which we are reporting and the degree to which men and women are similar. For example, in Chapter 3 we consider not only the typical course of physical development for men and women, but also the range that can occur within each sex as a result of variations in

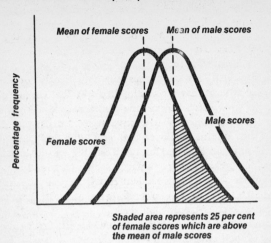

Spatial performance scores

Figure 1.1. Diagram of Percentage Distribution of Male and Female Spatial Performance Scores, Showing Degree of Overlap

normal and abnormal development. At present most psychologists, like ordinary people, look for and exaggerate the magnitude of differences between men and women.

The second commonsense principle, that women are shown as inferior to men, has also been reflected in psychological studies. Fortunately the influence of this belief has waned, and it is primarily when we look back over research of earlier decades that we detect its strong influence. Attempts to prove women's intellectual inferiority have given way to research on specific intellectual abilities, achievement, motivation and emotionality.

Although psychologists no longer set out to show that women are inferior, the influence of commonsense views is apparent in the choice of what to look at and in the borrowing of words from everyday speech to describe it. This occurs in at least two ways: the first is that psychologists actively seek to measure differences described in ordinary language – for example, that men are more aggressive or women more fearful; and the second is that they use everyday terms to describe differences reported in psychological research. These differences may have been encountered fortuitously, actively sought in theory-guided investigations or derived from surveys of published findings.

Accidental findings of sex differences arise because psychologists regularly test both male and female subjects. In analysing their data, they may happen to find a difference in the performance of the two sexes. Since journals encourage the publication of significant differences, these are likely to be reported and an explanation, or at least a label, will be attached to them.

In theory-guided research, measures apparently unrelated to commonsense notions may be labelled in a way that transforms them into characteristics which support the commonsense view. The work of Herman Witkin (1967) on cognitive style (see Chapter 8) is an example of this. Witkin developed two tests – the Embedded Figures Test (EFT) and the Rod and Frame Test (RFT) – to measure the extent to which people perceive a particular visual stimulus as part of its surroundings or as an independent entity. In many studies it was found that men are more able to separate the stimulus from its background than women (Maccoby and Jacklin, 1974). Witkin has argued that these perceptual differences represent wider differences in people's approaches to their environment – their cognitive style (Witkin *et al.*, 1962). Furthermore, a person who tends to separate the stimulus from its background is called 'field independent', whereas someone who tends to perceive the stimulus as part of its environment is called 'field dependent'. This choice of terms implies an active, independent type of person and a passive, dependent person. Men typically show field independent responses, whereas women show field dependent behaviour on the EFT and RFT. This is important in view of Witkin's claim that the measures reflect a difference in the way men and women approach the world (McGuinness, 1976). Had Witkin used different descriptive labels, such as 'context sensitive', the social implications of the research would have been different. As it is, his results, labelled as they are, support the commonsense view of women as inferior to men.

The influence of commonsense terms can also be seen in reviews of the published literature. Since the research evidence on sex differences is large and fragmented, there is much reliance on such summaries. Large numbers of varied findings are organized and collated. There are many examples and we have chosen only two. Firstly, Garai and Scheinfeld (1968) described a miscellaneous collection of measures on which women performed better than men, and then labelled them 'clerical abilities', implying that women naturally possess characteristics which suit them for one of the major female occupations in our society. Secondly, Gray (1971a) described as 'fearfulness' a similarly heterogeneous category of measures on which women showed higher scores, thereby not only confirming the commonsense view of women's greater emotionality but also identifying it with an undesirable quality. It is understandable that reviewers of sex differences need to generalize and to label their findings, but nonetheless it is apparent that the identification and naming of these differences is influenced by the commonsense view of the nature of the sexes.

In psychological explanations there are also parallels with commonsense views: explanations are sought in terms either of specific biological processes or of social influences. These are linked to wider social issues in a manner very similar to the corresponding commonsense views.

Current biological explanations include evolutionary arguments, which have been offered in support of conventional divisions of labour and power relations between the sexes. A typical claim is that men possess evolutionary adaptations which enable them to dominate political life (Tiger, 1970). Other biological explanations involve the effects of sex hormones on the brains of men and women. Such theories have been cited by some opponents of feminism to buttress the view that the social roles of men and women have a biological basis, but they have received limited support in psychology (for example, Stassinopoulos, 1972; Goldberg, 1973).

The main alternative psychological explanation, examined in Chapter 9, is that sex differences in temperament and abilities are the result of the different learning experiences of boys and girls (Mischel, 1966). This view is comparable to the commonsense conditioning explanation, and it has been cited in support of the egalitarian view of sex roles.

In commonsense explanations it is implied that since biological processes are natural, they cannot or should not be changed. On the other hand, since experiential effects are seen as having no basis in biology, they are regarded as malleable. Although this widely held commonsense view also influences psychological accounts, it is incorrect. A person's personality or behaviour may be quite resistant to change and yet be the result of influences in his or her early or later environment. Conversely, someone may inherit a predisposition towards a certain type of behaviour but, owing to the modifying effects of the particular environment, may not develop this behaviour. Commonsense reasoning seems to have influenced the interpretation of biological research so that it has misleadingly been used to support particular ideological positions.

Research Strategies

In this section we consider the various research strategies that have been adopted by psychologists studying sex and gender. One prestigious and influential approach is that of reductionism (Rose and Rose, 1974; Waddington, 1977), whereby the various sciences and social sciences are arranged in a series of decreasing complexity, from the social sciences to psychology, physiology, chemistry and physics, and events in a more complex science are explained in terms of a more fundamental science. Reductionism has provided effective solutions to problems in the biological sciences by offering biochemical and physical explanations of biological systems. Impressed by these successes, many psychologists have sought biological and biochemical explanations for psychological phenomena. An added appeal of this approach is the apparent reality of biochemical and biological processes when compared to abstract psychological phenomena (Lloyd, 1976).

Biological reductionism is apparent in many biological explanations for sex differences in psychological processes. The main alternatives are explanations concentrating on the analysis of environmental influences which are acquired through learning. Both these viewpoints are limited: one considers only a person's biological properties, and the other their social environment. A more complete account is provided when a person's individual characteristics are seen in the context of their interactions with the environment. We now consider three approaches which endeavour to do this by viewing the individual as someone who is actively seeking to make sense of the world. These approaches are known as 'cognitive', because they stress the primary role of thought processes.

Kohlberg (1966) has analysed boys' and girls' ideas about sex roles from a cognitive perspective. He argues that these ideas are of a different nature at different ages, and that they undergo a series of transformations which mark the boundaries of discrete stages in the development of understanding about sex roles. Kohlberg's theory, which is considered in more detail in Chapter 9, is concerned with changes in mental constructions through development. Other cognitive approaches address the question of how adults currently structure their understanding of the world. We consider two of these: first, that of ethnomethodology; and secondly, the social-cognitive approach.

The ethnomethodologist is concerned with the way in which a person constructs his or her view of the social world. The starting point is that what we see as objectively 'out there' is a result of our own construction (and this applies whether we are lay people or scientists; see the beginning of Chapter 2). One person's construction may differ from another's, but each is true for them.

The ethnomethodological approach has been applied to sex and gender by Kessler and McKenna (1978). In doing so, they make important points which challenge some of our commonsense notions about men and women. One assumption which is taken for granted, both in everyday life and in most research on sex differences, is that there are two biologically defined classes: male and female. In fact when we meet someone, we do not decide their sex in the same way that a biologist would sex an animal or a person – for example, by genital inspection or by examining chromosome composition. Instead, we mentally construct their sex from a wide range of cues such as dress, way of moving, length of hair, beard growth and breast development. Usually this process occurs quickly and unconsciously; but it has important consequences, since it forms the basis for selecting very different forms of social interaction in the future. Kessler and McKenna analyse the process of construction and look at cases where it is not obvious and where people have to search for the relevant cues, as in the case of transsexuals.

Recognizing the *social* construction of the distinction between man and woman, ethnomethodologists refer to the two categories as 'genders', reserving the term 'sex' for distinctions made on the basis of biological criteria. The reader may feel that the *way* in which distinctions are made between men and women – whether by social or biological attribution – is of little practical consequence, since in most cases the resulting categorization would be the same. Nevertheless, it is of practical importance when we consider marginal cases – for example, the woman athlete who 'fails' a chromosome test, or the transsexual who sees herself as a woman despite possessing male physical features. These cases show that sex does not define gender, and that if a person adopts important aspects of the cross-gender role, he or she will be seen as being of that gender.

Ethnomethodologists recommend that research should move on from studying the *consequences* of having attributed gender to an examination of the attribution process itself. Very little research of this type has been carried out, and most of the research described in our book concerns the consequences of attribution. Nevertheless, we regard the ethnomethodological approach as important because it is concerned with the interaction of people with their environment, and with the mental picture which is constructed from these social encounters. In doing so, it rejects the reduction of social events to biology or to simple environmental units.

The social-cognitive approach is another major departure from reductionist accounts of sex and gender. Like ethnomethodology, its focus is the social context – hence 'social' – and people's attempts to understand this – hence 'cognitive'. Our view of it is derived from the writings of Kay Deaux (1977), Julia Sherman (1978) and others. To explain the social-cognitive approach, it is useful to contrast it with the more traditional view of psychological testing, which we present more fully in the next chapter.

In much psychological research on sex differences, measurements taken from specific tests or observation procedures are used to make generalizations about wider psychological attributes on which men and women are said to differ, such as aggression, emotionality or mathematical ability. Differences in the average scores of men and women on a particular test which involves mathematical reasoning may be described as a sex difference in 'mathematical ability'. It is seen as a stable attribute or trait of individuals. This view, like reductionism, is based on transposing the scientific method from the natural sciences to psychology; in this case, it is precise measurement of an individual's characteristics that are sought. Attempts to apply such rigorous measurement to abstract psychological characteristics, in a manner analogous to measuring physical features, encounter a number of difficulties which the social-cognitive approach highlights. By taking a broader view of psychological testing, both the psychologist and the person taking the test are considered in a wider social context. Both have commonsense views about themselves as men or women, and about the social setting of the test – in particular whether it favours masculine or feminine skills. The emphasis shifts from trying to define and measure general traits to examining how men and women react to the experimenter, and how they perceive the test conditions and requirements. These are seen as interactions which will be strongly influenced by the person's own commonsense view about the social attributes of men and women. These views will exert strong influences on how people perform in the test and will affect psychological measurement.

Different exchanges will occur according to the sex of the experimenter and the subjects of the experiment. One intriguing example of the possible influence of the experimenter's sex on test performance is given by Sherman. She suggests that tests which involve darkened rooms with male experimenters may make female subjects more uneasy because 'such situations have been known to elicit unwanted sexual advances'.

Men and women may have different ideas about how they should behave in a social setting. Deaux suggests that men generally endeavour to be assertive and women to be affiliative in any social situation, and that being a subject in a psychological experiment or test is no exception. These different ideas about appropriate masculine or feminine behaviour can again influence psychological measurements.

Certain tests may be viewed as masculine or feminine. Interest in them and motivation to succeed will differ for men and women. Sherman claims that this point has been neglected in psychological research on sex differences. She cites research which shows that male superiority in one particular 'spatial ability' test is not found if the same test is identified as measuring a more feminine skill. Previous experience, practice and familiarity with test material will also differ for men and women, and this is again related to whether a test is associated with masculine or feminine abilities. Most reviews of sex differences have neglected the issue of unequal practice.

In contrast to the ethnomethodological view, the social-cognitive approach is still concerned with studying the consequences of attributing gender to a person rather than the attribution process itself. Given this important distinction, the two views have many features in common. Both accord a central place to the social meaning and significance of sex differences. At present there is relatively little research aimed at evaluating the effects of commonsense notions about gender on differences in psychological test measures between men and women. What evidence there is suggests that ideas about gender roles directly and indirectly affect psychological sex differences (Sherman, 1978). We believe that this line of inquiry will prove to be more profitable in the future than both the current emphasis on differences in psychological traits and the predominantly reductionist explanations which are usually offered to account for them.

Sex or Gender?

We now return to the issue of terminology, which was raised in connection with the ethnomethodological approach. Kessler and McKenna refer to men and women as the two genders, since the usual way in which the two are distinguished is on the basis of social criteria. The term sex is restricted to cases where the distinction is made on the basis of biological criteria. Domestic animals, newborn infants and Olympic athletes are divided into two *sexes*; but when we are introduced to a stranger, a *gender* is attributed to us on the basis of a variety of bodily and behavioural cues. Since this is the way in which men and women are usually distinguished, both in everyday life and in psychological research, it follows that most of the differences between men and women which we describe in this book are based on this distinction. We shall therefore refer to these differences as 'gender differences' throughout the remainder of the book. Only when we refer to biologically based distinctions, particularly in Chapter 3, shall we refer to sex differences. In practical terms the distinctions may appear trivial, but it is important to specify whether we are referring to sex or gender in cases of abnormal sexual differentiation (see Chapter 3) and when we consider societies in which there are more than two genders, such as the Omani, described in Chapter 4.

A distinction between the terms sex and gender is becoming increasingly widespread in psychology. We have adopted the ethnomethodological definition, which depends on the nature of the attribution processes. We have used this criterion instead of a commonly used alternative which uses 'sex differences' to refer to biological features and 'gender differences' for social attributes. We believe that this distinction is often difficult to make in practice, and furthermore it implies that differences between men and women are *either* biologically produced *or* socially determined. We have already indicated the limitations of this view, which is derived from commonsense explanations and from the reductionist approach. Adopting a distinction based on attribution poses fewer problems. When attribution is derived from social criteria, whatever differences are subsequently found between men and women are called gender differences. In fact, biological differences would be expected to contribute to gender differences, but they would be mediated through an interaction with the environment according to a person's mental concepts – or commonsense ideas about men and women.

CHAPTER 2

Men and Women: Three Views from the Social Sciences

In Chapter 1 we explored the influence of commonsense ideas on psychological studies of men and women. Here we begin by considering commonsense ideas about the nature of scientific investigation; we then trace the influence of these ideas on the evaluation and credibility of three different ways of studying men and women.

A balanced picture of the scientist in popular imagination would include the demoniacal Mr Hyde as well as the dedicated Dr Jekyll toiling in the laboratory to improve the lot of the human race. We are not concerned with the darker side but with the popular idealization of science, which sees it as a straightforward, reliable, public procedure involving discovery by the ingenious scientist of 'facts' residing in the outside world. The distinguished biologist C. H. Waddington (1977) has caricatured this view of science, calling it the 'Conventional Wisdom of the Dominant Group' – a clumsy phrase to which he attaches the evocative mnemonic 'COWDUNG'.

But is science as objective as naive opinion assumes? Waddington, as his choice of initials suggests, thinks it is not. He emphasizes that scientific knowledge is obtained by the scientist making observations, a process which he describes as an active interchange between the observer and the objects of his study. The process is similar to that used every day in making sense of the world. According to Waddington, the distinction between scientific and non-scientific knowledge is only one of degree. In a scientific investigation the observations are made in a controlled and organized fashion (as experiments or surveys) in order to minimize the effects of observer bias and to ensure that the measurements could be replicated by other scientists. Observations which form the basis of everyday generalizations are less systematic, and little effort is made to control sources of bias. It is difficult to know whether other observers would come to similar conclusions under these conditions.

Adopting Waddington's view, we realize that scientists may try to limit the effects of observer bias but that scientific studies cannot be completely objective. Scientists inevitably see the world through the filter of their own culture and their particular experiences in it. Our society's notions about the nature of men and women are an inevitable lens through which scientific findings are distorted. The mechanics of particular kinds of investigation make some appear more objective and more credible than others. In this chapter we contrast three different ways of seeking and presenting knowledge about men and women. We begin by examining demographic accounts. At first glance these appear to rely only on simple counting and to be very objective. Next we consider the results of psychometric testing, the application of standard tests and procedures to provide descriptions of the skills and abilities of men and women. Finally, we report the explicit study of common-sense notions in the social psychological investigation of stereotypes.

The Demographic Approach: Mr and Ms Average

The demographic 'facts' about men and women are statistical averages taken from various government reports (*General Household Survey*, 1976; *New Earnings Survey*, 1978; *Population Trends*, 1977; *Social Trends*, 1977 and 1979). Early sociologists, including Durkheim, shared the commonsense view of these official statistics as providing objective evidence. Fluctuations in the number of suicides were once compared with the movement of mercury in a thermometer. It was believed that these fluctuations could be used to study social forces, just as the rise and fall of mercury could provide valid information about a host of scientific processes. Contemporary critics point out that whereas the calibrated scale of the thermometer provides a more reliable measure than unaided sensory experience, official statistics do not have a straightforward relation to social phenomena. In order to compile the numbers of people committing suicide, it is necessary to determine in each instance whether a person took his own life while of sound mind. Attitudes towards suicide affect such judgements, and suicide statistics are compiled only after such judgements of ambiguous events have been made. Critics have argued that the meaning of the statistics remains ambiguous unless the judgemental processes are understood (Douglas, 1967).

We have already argued that total objectivity in terms of the detachment of the observer from the object of study is impossible, so it is hardly surprising to learn that official statistics are neither totally objective nor theoretically neutral. But there are different degrees of subjective involvement and observer participation. The census and social surveys are designed to minimize the influence of the people administering the questionnaire, and in surveys the choice of individuals to be included in the sample is carefully scrutinized. Such investigations aim to limit the role of the observer to an almost mechanical one of collecting and tabulating figures. Similarly, when the figures are published there are usually few comments, and the statistics are often presented as raw material for others to use and interpret.

Despite precautions in the administration and tabulation of census and survey results, decisions must be made at the beginning of an investigation about the categories to be included and the particular questions to be posed. An obvious bias in the statistics which we present is the categorization of adult men and women in the work force. According to the Department of Employment, girls become 'women' at 18 years of age while boys only become 'men' at 21. As the statistics are examined, other choices which make the picture presented by them less than totally objective will become apparent. These include problems of judgement in the classification of crimes and in the report of reasons for unemployment.

The simplest question we can ask of census statistics is, 'How many men and women are there?' At first the answer appears straightforward. More boys than girls are conceived and born, but at every age male mortality is greater than that of females. Given the experience of our own society, it is surprising to learn that in parts of Asia women die earlier than men (El-Badry, 1969). We will look first at figures for the United Kingdom and then at comparable statistics for Ceylon (Sri Lanka), India and Pakistan.

In the 30–45 year age group the numbers of men and women are approximately equal in the United Kingdom (5·0 million and 4·9 million respectively). Yet when we consider all ages up to 45, we find that there are 1,043 men for every 1,000 women, and after 45 the ratio is different, reflecting the younger ages at which men die. Among people over the age of 45 in the United Kingdom, there are only 812 men for every 1,000 surviving women.

Statistics confirm impressions that there are many lonely old women. The figures in Table 2.1 can be described as follows. Among people in their early 60s, women outnumber men slightly, but by the age of 75 there are four women for every three men. Among those living to 84, women outnumber men two to one, while women predominate more than three to one among those surviving to 85 and beyond. Another way to look at these figures is to note that in England and Wales the current expectation of life at birth is an average 69·5 years for males and 75·7 for females.

Table 2.1. Elderly People by Age and Sex

(Thousands)

Age	Female	Male
60–64	1,568	1,381
65–74	2,844	2,154
75–84	1,560	773
85 +	393	128

Based on Table 3.8 in *Social Trends, No. 9* (1979).

Census statistics from Ceylon, India and Pakistan provide a challenge to the view that on average women can expect to live longer than men and that over the age of 45 there will be more women surviving than men (El-Badry, 1969). It depends on which part of the world you live in, and in Ceylon, India and Pakistan, containing a fifth of the world's population, a female has a lower life expectancy than a male. Ceylon had the smallest difference in male and female expectancies, 61·9 and 61·4 years respectively, according to the figures for 1960–62. The gap is larger in India – 41·9 years for men and 40·6 for women in 1951–60, while in Pakistan males have a life expectancy of 49·6 years compared to a female average of 46·9 years.

These figures are so strikingly different from those to which we are accustomed that it is interesting to consider the explanations which have been offered to account for them (El-Badry, 1969). Two factors have been identified in all three countries. One is the greater mortality of females, particularly in the years of child-bearing but also in infancy and childhood. The second, but minor, factor is a general tendency to undercount females. These explanations stand in sharp contrast to those put forth in our own society, where the greater incidence of coronary heart disease among men has been implicated in the consistently higher male death rate. Those very traits which we shall later consider as part of the masculine stereotype – aggressiveness and competitiveness – have been shown to increase the risk of coronary heart disease (Waldon, 1976). A lesson that we can learn from this brief excursion into comparative demography is that where you look may influence what you find.

What do our statistics say about the households in which male and female children grow up, about their education, careers and other life prospects? Let us start with households. By definition these include at least one adult and one dependent child. According to the 1976 figures, 88 per cent of all households included an adult female and an adult male, and 12 per cent were single-parent households. It probably comes as little surprise to learn that the overwhelming majority of single parents were women (only one sixth were men).

Who are the heads of these single-parent households? The largest group of women living alone with children are divorced (30 per cent), but equal proportions (20 per cent in each case) have never married, are widowed or are legally separated. The remainder are married but living apart from their husbands (10 per cent). Since men remarry more often than women after divorce, there are more divorced women – of the 969,000 divorced people remaining unmarried in England and Wales in 1976, only 405,000 were men. This difference, and the likelihood of children staying with their mothers, partly account for the greater number of single female heads of households.

What do heads of households do for a living? We compare the socio-economic backgrounds or broad occupational categories of male and female heads of households in Table 2.2. In making this comparison, demographers generally regard men as the head of a household whether they are living with an adult female or as a single parent. Table 2.2 shows that children growing up in male-headed homes are better-off economically; male heads of households are from professional, managerial and skilled manual groups much more often than female heads are.

Table 2.2. Socio-economic Standing of Household Heads Expressed as a Percentage of Total

	Female: unmarried	Female: married	Male: single and two-parent
Professional	—	—	5
Employers and managers	2	—	14
Intermediate and junior non-managerial	13	26	14
Skilled manual	3	—	32
Semi-skilled and personal service	8	8	11
Unskilled	4	3	3
Economically inactive	63	57	20
Never worked	7	6	—

Based on Table 2.5 in *Social Trends, No. 9* (1979).

Female heads of households are more likely to be unskilled, economically inactive or never to have worked (there are no men recorded in the latter category). These figures reflect the higher occupational status of men and underscore the obvious financial advantage to children of growing up in a male-headed household.

We shall return to gender differences in occupations after first looking at education. The educational statistics tell two different stories. Those based on attainment at the time people leave school, presented in Table 2.3, show few substantial differences between the sexes. All A-Level passes have been combined, and this presentation hides a small difference: 60 per cent of males but only 47 per cent of females obtained three or more A-Level passes.

Table 2.3. Academic Attainment of 1977–8 School Leavers in England and Wales

	Percentage of totals	
	Female	*Male*
A-Level passes	14·5	16·6
5 or more O-Level GCE or CSE	10·3	8·1
1–4 higher-grade O-Level GCE or CSE	28·5	24·9
1 or more other grade	32·1	33·9
No GCE or CSE	14·6	16·4

Based on Table 4.7 in *Social Trends, No. 9* (1979).

The destinations of school leavers, presented in Table 2.4, show more marked differences. In a 1972 survey of highly qualified people, defined as individuals with at least a first degree, men outnumbered women three to one. Table 2.4, published seven years later, shows that women are gaining ground, although they are still outnumbered two to one. If we count training as teachers and nurses, we could conclude that more girls than boys continue their education after leaving

Table 2.4. Destinations of School Leavers 1975–6

(Thousands)

	Degree courses				Other full-time		
	University	*Polytechnic*	*Other*	*Teacher training*	*education*	*Employment*	*Total*
Females	15·6	2·1	0·7	7·5	61·3	256·4	343·6
Males	27·1	4·3	0·4	1·9	35·0	295·4	364·1

Based on Table 4.12 in *Social Trends, No. 9* (1979).

secondary school and, in this sense, obtain a higher qualification. The initial judgement about what is a high qualification changes the conclusions we can draw from the figures.

A further issue is the occupational destination of the hundreds of thousands of school leavers who do not go on to full-time education. We must rely on 1977 figures, as these statistics were not provided in the 1979 edition of *Social Trends*. Table 2.5 shows that gender differences are even greater than those appearing in further education. Only a small proportion of girls enter apprenticeships, and a similarly small proportion of boys take up clerical employment.

Table 2.5. 16-year-olds Entering Different Classes of Employment; United Kingdom, 1974

	Percentages	
	Female	*Male*
Apprenticeships	6	43
Professional	1	2
Clerical	40	7
Other work with over 12 months' training	6	10
Work with 8 weeks' to 12 months' training	12	7
Other	34	32

Based on Table 5.26 in *Social Trends, No. 8* (1977).

Once in employment, the prospects for a young man or a young woman are again quite different. Both in manual and non-manual full-time employment, men on average earn more than women. According to 1978 figures, full-time male manual workers earned £78.40 per week, while women averaged £48.00. Male non-manual workers averaged £99.90, whereas women averaged £58.50. The argument that men may work more hours than women and hence earn considerable overtime pay can only account for part of these differences (among manual workers men averaged 44·2 hours a week and women 37·4). If we examine hourly pay rates, we obtain a better comparison: among manual and non-manual workers, men averaged almost 40 per cent more per hour than women.

Before leaving the realm of statistical averages, let us look at people who are not working and at criminals. Table 2.6 shows that of those who are not working, most men are retired and most women are keeping house.

Another set of figures which tends to confirm common expectations are replies to a question asking why people in Great Britain left their jobs in 1976. Among unemployed people over 16 years of age who had

Table 2.6. Major Activity for Economically Inactive

	Weeks shown as percentage	
	Female	Male
At school or college	3	12
Permanently unable to work	4	12
Retired	19	71
Kept house	71	1
Other	3	5

Based on Table 6.24 in *General Household Survey* (1976).

previously worked, over half of the men reported being sacked or made redundant (Table 2.7). The most common reason given for unemployment by women was domestic commitments, including pregnancy.

Table 2.7. Reasons for Unemployment Offered by Previously Employed

	Female	Male
Made redundant or sacked	27	53
Dissatisfied with last job	21	23
Ill health	14	16
Last job temporary	10	4
Retired	—	3
Domestic reasons, pregnancy and others	32	9

Based on Table 6.21 in *General Household Survey* (1976).

The temporary nature of the last job also distinguished women from men, but other reasons were offered with almost equal frequency by both genders.

The final set of figures which we present show gender differences in indictable offences (Table 2.8). For all categories, men are convicted of more offences than women. Over 80 per cent of indictable offences committed by women fall into the category of theft and handling stolen goods, yet this category accounts for only 54 per cent of the offences committed by men. Violence against other people is almost ten times as common an offence among men as among women, and criminal damage is even more common for male than for female offenders. Many of the differences which appear as neat statistics will be considered at greater length in later chapters.

Although we have used official statistics to provide a concise, quantitative comparison of men and women, it is important to remember the complex and often ambiguous judgemental processes which lie behind this precise presentation. In the chapters which follow we sometimes take these findings at face value and seek to account for them, but at

Table 2.8. Persons Found Guilty of Indictable Offences, 1977

	(*Thousands*)	
	Females	*Males*
Murder, manslaughter, infanticide	—	0·3
Violence against persons	4·1	38·1
Sexual offences	0·1	9·2
Burglary	3·4	79·6
Robbery	0·2	3·1
Theft and handling stolen goods	80·2	242·0
Fraud	5·0	17·5
Criminal damage	3·6	46·4
Other	2·0	8·9
All indictable offences	98·6	445·1

Based on Table 14.8 in *Social Trends, No.* 9 (1979).

other times we challenge their veracity. For example, in Chapter 3 we consider explanations for the shorter lifespan of men, but in Chapter 5 we question the reporting of violent crime among women. Even though the evidence presented in the preceding pages comes from official reports and appears to be objective, it too must be subjected to critical evaluation.

The Psychometric Approach: What Psychologists Measure

The picture of men and women which emerges from the psychometric assessment of individual differences is neither complete nor completely objective. Standardized tests were developed to meet practical needs. One of the pioneers in the field, Alfred Binet, set out to find a way to identify those French children who would not benefit from a normal state education; once identified, special provisions could be offered to cope with their learning inadequacies. Research psychologists too have devised tests, but these do not aim at predicting success in practical situations – instead they have been designed to assess the validity of different psychological theories.

Psychometricians assume that individuals differ on a variety of characteristics, that these differences can be defined and measured objectively, and that the scores obtained are related to other aspects of the individual's behaviour. Each of these assumptions entails judgements in test construction. Characteristics are sought along which individuals do indeed differ, but at the same time they must be psychologically meaningful dimensions. Our understanding of human behaviour would be advanced little by counting hairs on people's heads, but differences in the rate at which people tap a key might provide clues about motor skills or even persistence. Judgements about what is worth measuring involve the definition of concepts and the inter-relations of different types of behaviour. Even the construction of objective tests and measures involves psychological theorizing.

Individual differences are exploited in the construction of standard-ized tests, but theoretically motivated experimental measurement of sensory processes and learning has not focused on individual differ-ences. It is hardly surprising to discover that many gender differences on standardized tests and procedures have been reported, but that there is little evidence for differences between men and women from studies of perception and learning. The conclusion that we find we are looking for is further strengthened by noting that some intelligence tests, such as the Stanford–Binet Scale, were deliberately devised so that overall scores showed no consistent differences between males and females. This was achieved by carefully balancing those sub-scales on which one gender performed better with other sub-scales on which the other gender excelled. Despite difficulties in test construction, the introduction of standardized tests enabled more objective selection than previous reliance on interviews, teachers' judgements and other in-formal selection methods. Given these caveats, the obvious question 'How intelligent are men and women?' turns out to be complex and difficult to answer. The commonsense concern with natural differences versus conditioning leads to two different sorts of questions. One can be posed as 'How much native wit do men and women possess?' while the other can be stated as 'How much has each gender learned?' Psychological studies have moved away from this formulation ever since it became clear that natural endowment, learning and even experience with being tested all affected performance (Vernon, 1969).

The psychometric emphasis on individual differences makes it dif-ficult to compare men and women, even when we realize that test performance is multiply determined. The vast body of reports on individual differences contains comparison across age, social class, cultures, orders of birth and race. Differences between men and women might cut across any of these or co-vary with them. Perhaps more limiting is the unevenness of available results. Reports are heavily biased towards certain age groups, primarily the captive audiences of school pupils and university students. In addition they are most often of white, middle-class people (Maccoby and Jacklin, 1974).

Difficulties do not end with the collection of original data. The classic summary of Maccoby and Jacklin from which we begin has been criticized both for making more of the evidence than one reviewer believed was justified (Fairweather, 1976) and for overlooking evidence which another psychologist believed indicated further important differences between men and women (Block, 1976a, 1976b). Since their review, which dealt primarily with research carried out between 1966 and 1973, further evidence has accumulated, and this modifies their major conclusions slightly (Wittig and Petersen, 1979).

We begin by considering the picture which Maccoby and Jacklin constructed on the basis of their understanding of the results of many standard intelligence tests. In looking first at measures of general intellectual abilities, we cannot be too surprised that few clear differences are reported. We saw earlier that intelligence tests were originally constructed to provide similar overall scores for males and females.

A summary table of results, comparing the scores of males and females on intelligence tests, is one way to present a picture of psychometric gender differences. Maccoby and Jacklin (1974, Table 3.1) compiled such a table with forty-six entries. We do not reproduce it here as there are few surprises. Although a variety of different tests were used, no clear gender differences emerged. Only three studies reported results from testing people over the age of twenty-one. Two of these show no significant differences, although a third reports that the Intelligence Quotients (IQs) of men improve more than those of women when tested at intervals over a 38-year period (Kangas and Bradway, 1971). As the study was concerned more with change than with absolute levels of IQs, its results, based on the performance of only forty-eight people, give but a limited picture of gender differences in general intelligence.

It is worth pausing to consider the two tests from which these results were derived. The Stanford–Binet Scale (S–B) and Wechsler Adult Intelligence Scale (WAIS) are, like most intelligence tests, made up of a variety of items. The S–B is scored only to yield a composite IQ, whereas the WAIS yields separate verbal and performance IQs. Consistent gender differences have been reported on particular subscales and not on composite IQs.

The measure of verbal IQ on the WAIS is based upon scores in answering 29 general information questions, understanding 14 comprehension items – for example, proverbs – defining 40 words, solving 14 arithmetic problems and remembering strings of digits. The performance IQ is based upon the ability to say which part is missing in 21 incomplete pictures, to translate a digit-symbol code, to reproduce a variety of designs using red-and-white-sided blocks, to arrange pictures in a series so that they tell a coherent story and to assemble objects.

Even a brief examination of the sub-tests which contribute to the two WAIS IQ scores indicates the variety of abilities which are required to produce high scores. In order to solve arithmetic problems, both computational skills and verbal understanding of the questions are necessary. Such is the variety of tasks that it is difficult to describe all the abilities which these tests are measuring. It is likely that males are good at some things and females at others, but composite scores which are based on the combination of many sub-tasks mask these gender-related differences.

Factor analysis is a complex statistical technique which psychometricians have used to analyse the different abilities which their tests measure. Specifically, they examine the relationships between a large variety of tests or even among test items. From the matrices yielded by these measures of relationship, factors are identified. A factor identified as spatial ability has consistently revealed differences between men and women, showing a clear male advantage. This means that on some tests the average performance of males is only reached or exceeded by 20–25 per cent of females (Harris, 1978).

Again it is useful to look specifically at the kinds of tests which are used to measure spatial ability. One extensive review of gender differences in spatial ability organizes empirical results under six headings: recall and selection of shapes; mental rotation and identification; geometric and mathematical skill; chess; sense of direction; and auditory perception, including spatial elements in music (Harris, 1978). This presentation includes mathematical skill under the heading spatial ability. Maccoby and Jacklin report it separately as one of three well-documented gender differences in intellectual ability. They find a male superiority in mathematical ability, which they describe as beginning in early adolescence. Although Maccoby and Jacklin list spatial and mathematical abilities separately, they recognize that mathematical performance may reflect spatial skill. The relative importance of spatial and verbal processing in problem-solving may account for the failure to find clear gender differences in tests of mathematical ability.

Examining tests which consistently show a male advantage in spatial

ferences. Results from the United States are more consistent with our preconceptions, as a female superiority was reported when children aged from 5 to 8 were tested with verbal items from the Stanford–Binet Scale.

Although Maccoby and Jacklin suggest that a female advantage emerges in adolescence, the results are not consistent. The few studies of adults are contradictory, some reporting a male superiority and others a female advantage, particularly in verbal reasoning and vocabulary (Bayley and Oden, 1955; Blum *et al.*, 1972). The evidence for a female superiority in verbal abilities is not as convincing as that which has been marshalled to show a male advantage in spatial skills.

The picture which emerges from the examination of careful tests of intellectual functioning is one of limited differences between men and women. Stereotypes cannot be readily reinforced by this evidence.

The Social Psychological Study of Stereotypes: Commonsense Beliefs

Turning to the social psychological study of stereotypes, we gain a new perspective. Psychologists who study stereotypes employ precise quantitative methods in order to describe socially shared beliefs. The process which they investigate, the assignment of traits according to group membership, is one of everyday life. We noted in Chapter 1 that the commonsense approach to gender differences is based upon this attribution of abilities and characteristics according to gender.

In early social psychological research on stereotypes, people were given long lists of adjectives and asked to choose those which applied to particular racial or ethnic groups (Katz and Braly, 1935). Similar techniques have been used to study gender stereotypes (Williams and Bennett, 1975). It is assumed that these methods reflect the stereotyping process itself: that people make sense of their social world by categorizing other individuals according to easily observable characteristics which signal age, gender or race, and by then attributing other adjectives or traits on the basis of group membership (Secord and Backman, 1964). The relationship between group membership and other traits is difficult to explain and may appear arbitrary. A black might disclaim being superstitious (Katz and Braly, 1935) just as a woman would take issue with being seen as frivolous (Williams and Bennett, 1975), although in the popular imagination both these relationships appear valid.

A more precise relationship between the process of categorization and the contents or traits invoked in forming stereotypes has recently been proposed; it focuses on intergroup relations rather than on the characteristics of isolated groups (Doise, 1978). Beliefs about the nature of particular groups are held to reflect the relations which exist between these groups. If the conflict between men and women for education or jobs were to increase, we might expect that the traits assigned according to gender would provide sharper contrasts between men and women. Here we look at a more static view reflecting social psychologists' efforts to provide an objective appraisal of commonsense notions of gender.

The most extensive research on gender stereotypes has been undertaken at universities in the United States. We start by comparing three American studies and consider the view of men and women which emerges from them. We then look briefly at a study of English students.

We begin with a straightforward study, that of Williams and Bennett (1975). They asked university students to indicate which adjectives from a list of 300 were typically associated with either men or women. The students were able to categorize over 90 per cent, or 272, of the adjectives as belonging to either women or men. There was considerable agreement about this assignment among female and male students. Tables 2.9 and 2.10 show those adjectives which were agreed upon by 75 per cent of all students (males and females combined). This established 30 adjectives describing women and 33 describing men. They are presented with an evaluative classification of each adjective – positive, negative or neutral – which had been developed in an earlier study (Gough and Heilbrun, 1965).

Table 2.9. Adjectives Associated with Women, with Evaluative Classification

Affected	–	Feminine	o	Prudish	–
Affectionate	+	Fickle	–	Rattle-brained	–
Appreciative	+	Flirtatious	o	Sensitive	o
Attractive	+	Frivolous	–	Sentimental	o
Charming	+	Fussy	–	Soft-hearted	o
Complaining	–	Gentle	+	Sophisticated	o
Dependent	o	High-strung	o	Submissive	o
Dreamy	o	Meek	o	Talkative	o
Emotional	o	Mild	o	Weak	–
Excitable	o	Nagging	–	Whiny	–

Based on Williams and Bennett (1975).

Table 2.10. Adjectives Associated with Men, with Evaluative Classification

Adventurous	+	Disorderly	−	Realistic	+
Aggressive	o	Dominant	o	Robust	o
Ambitious	+	Enterprising	+	Self-confident	o
Assertive	o	Forceful	o	Severe	o
Autocratic	o	Handsome	o	Stable	+
Boastful	−	Independent	+	Steady	o
Coarse	−	Jolly	o	Stern	o
Confident	+	Logical	+	Strong	o
Courageous	+	Loud	−	Tough	o
Cruel	o	Masculine	o	Unemotional	o
Daring	−	Rational	+	Unexcitable	o

Based on Williams and Bennett (1975).

Williams and Bennett's results are similar to gender stereotype findings presented about thirty years ago (Komarovsky, 1950) and reported repeatedly since then (for example, Ellis and Bentler, 1973; Rosenkrantz *et al.*, 1968). Investigators often find that greater value is ascribed to male attributes, and these tables support a similar conclusion. Fifteen adjectives in each list have either positive or negative connotations. Of the adjectives associated with women, 5 are positively valued whereas 10 are negatively valued. The values attached to the masculine stereotype are the mirror-image, 5 negative and 10 positive.

Judgements of typical masculine and typical feminine traits provide a very familiar picture – and so they should, since 'commonsense' beliefs are used to make judgements about typical women and men. But there are also a few surprises. Adjectives such as coarse, disorderly, jolly and severe are not usually found among the attributes of the masculine stereotype. On the feminine list, appreciative, complaining and sophisticated are unexpected. Williams and Bennett asked students to choose from a very extensive list of adjectives and gave them instructions which suggested that each adjective could be attributed either to a typical man or a typical woman. These procedures may have contributed to the unexpected findings.

The two studies which we consider next – those of Sandra Bem, who developed the Bem Sex Role Inventory, and of Janet Spence, who devised the Personal Attributes Questionnaire – differ from the simple choice approach which we have just examined. Bem asked students to indicate which traits were desirable, and Spence asked which were typical and also which were ideal. Both of these questionnaires are in a tradition of research which aims to locate individuals along a dimension of masculinity–femininity, but they are innovative in that masculinity and femininity are seen as separate dimensions and not as opposite ends of a single scale.

Bem (1974) asked university students to rate the desirability of 400 traits in order to find 20 adjectives characteristic of women and 20 adjectives characteristic of men. Table 2.11 presents the adjectives she found to be feminine and masculine. Some adjectives were not specifically applied to women or men, although they were rated as generally more or less desirable. Twenty of these undifferentiated but clearly desirable or undesirable adjectives were included in the inventory in order to determine an individual's tendency to exaggerate in a positive or negative direction.

Table 2.11. Traits from the Bem Sex Role Inventory Classified by Dimension

Feminine	Masculine	Socially desirable and undesirable
Affectionate	Acts as a leader	Adaptable
Cheerful	Aggressive	Conceited
Childlike	Ambitious	Conscientious
Compassionate	Analytical	Conventional
Does not use harsh language	Assertive	Friendly
Eager to soothe hurt feelings	Athletic	Happy
Feminine	Competitive	Helpful
Flatterable	Defends own beliefs	Inefficient
Gentle	Dominant	Jealous
Gullible	Forceful	Likeable
Loves children	Leadership abilities	Moody
Loyal	Independent	Reliable
Sensitive to others' needs	Individualistic	Secretive
Shy	Makes decisions easily	Sincere
Soft-spoken	Masculine	Solemn
Sympathetic	Self-reliant	Tactful
Tender	Self-sufficient	Theatrical
Understanding	Strong personality	Truthful
Warm	Willing to take a stand	Unpredictable
Yielding	Willing to take risks	Unsystematic

Based on Bem (1974).

Spence and her co-workers developed their Personal Attributes Questionnaire (Spence *et al.*, 1975) from an earlier test of sex role stereotyping (Rosenkrantz *et al.*, 1968). They asked university students and other groups of people to select items which described either a typical woman and man or an ideal woman and man. Judgements of a typical man and woman were more extreme and resembled other reports of stereotypes. People made less polarized judgements in describing their ideal woman and man, and this suggests that there is a potential for change. Although people recognize that current sex roles are polarized and report this in their typicality judgements, their ideal ratings are less polarized, which implies that at some future time they would wish to see the roles of women and men less polarized.

Fifty-four dimensions along which ratings of typical women and men showed clear and statistically significant differences comprised the final questionnaire. The less extreme ratings of ideal woman and man were used to identify those items which could apply to both men and women and those which were specific to one gender. The 13 dimensions along which ideal men and women were described differently comprise the sex-specific items. The other 41 dimensions did not reveal significant differences in the descriptions of the ideal, but on 18 of them both women and men were rated at the feminine end of the continuum – these items were labelled female-valued items. On the remaining 23 dimensions both the ideal woman and the ideal man were placed at the masculine end of the continuum. These were labelled male-valued items. Variables from the Personal Attributes Questionnaire are presented in Table 2.12 with the female-valued, male-valued and sex-specific items grouped together.

In comparing these three studies, we begin by looking at the sex-specific items from the Personal Attributes Questionnaire (Table 2.12) since these showed masculine–feminine polarization even of ideal ratings. In the future people would expect to see these differences between men and women. None of the 7 female entries from the 13 sex-specific items appears either in the list of adjectives associated with women according to Williams and Bennett or in Bem's list of feminine traits. The sex-specific male items, in conjunction with the other two lists, yield a clear masculine stereotype. Even in an ideal world the male role is more consistently specified. 'Aggressive' and 'dominant' are found on all three scales. 'Loud' appears here and also in Williams and Bennett's list (Table 2.10).

Comparisons with the 18 female-valued and 23 male-valued items show additional overlaps with the other two studies. Once more these are greater for the masculine stereotype. 'Ambitious' and 'independent' appear on all three lists, while 'acts as leader', 'athletic', 'competitive'

Table 2.12. Personal Attributes Questionnaire Items

18 FEMALE-VALUED ITEMS

Aware of others' feelings	Enjoys music and arts	Likes children
Considerate	Expresses tender feelings	Neat
Creative	Gentle	Strong conscience
Devotes self to others	Grateful	Tactful
Does not hide emotions	Helpful to others	Understanding
Emotional	Kind	Warm to others

23 MALE-VALUED ITEMS

Active	Knows ways of world
Acts as leader	Makes decisions easily
Adventurous	Not easily influenced
Ambitious	Not excitable in minor crisis
Competitive	Not timid
Does not give up easily	Outgoing
Feels superior	Outspoken
Forward	Self-confident
Good at sports	Skilled in business
Independent	Stands up under pressure
Intellectual	Takes a stand
Interested in sex	

13 SEX-SPECIFIC ITEMS

Female	*Male*
Cries easily	Aggressive
Excitable in major crisis	Dominant
Feelings hurt	Likes maths and science
Home-oriented	Loud
Needs approval	Mechanical aptitude
Need for security	Sees self running show
Religious	

Based on Spence *et al.* (1975).

and 'makes decisions' are also included in Bem's masculine dimension. Altogether, 6 of Bem's masculine traits appear among the 23 male-valued items in Table 2.12. An additional 2 male-valued items – 'not excitable' and 'self-confident' – are found in the Williams and Bennett list. 8 of the 23 male-valued items are to be found in previous lists.

2 of Spence's female-valued items occur in precisely the same form on Bem's feminine dimension: these are 'gentle' and 'understanding'. 'Expresses tender feelings' and 'likes children', as well as 'warm to

others', are very similar to descriptions in Bem's feminine category. This lenient comparison produces a 5-item overlap with Bem's list. As there are only 18 female-valued items in the Personal Attributes Questionnaire, the proportion of overlap calculated in this manner is slightly larger for female items (28 per cent) than that for the male-valued items (24 per cent). 'Gentle' appears in the Williams and Bennett list, but only 'emotional' adds a new item of overlap and brings the total across the three measures to 6; the male stereotype appears slightly clearer.

A distinction suggested by the sociologists Parsons and Bales (1955) in relation to the family provides a dichotomy which characterizes these descriptions. They summarize the traits ascribed to women as being indicative of emotion and an expressive dimension, while they see the traits which describe men as being concerned with action or an instrumental dimension. This view of the family echoes commonsense judgements and stereotypes of masculinity and femininity, and is not without its critics.

We can now ask how the composite pictures of women and men yielded by these three measures compare with results from an English study. The traits listed on two or more scales to describe women are: 'affectionate', 'emotional', 'feminine', 'gentle', 'likes children', 'tender', 'understanding' and 'warm'. The list of traits associated with men includes: 'acts as leader', 'aggressive', 'ambitious', 'assertive', 'competitive', 'dominant', 'forceful', 'good at sports', 'independent', 'loud', 'makes decisions easily', 'masculine', 'self-confident' and 'not excitable'.

How do these views compare with those of English students? A heterogeneous group of people attending Open University summer schools were asked to rate their own gender and the opposite gender along 21 dimensions (Burns, 1977). In addition they were asked to rate their own gender as they imagined a member of the other gender would rate it. This study, which asked students to give three different viewpoints, is complex, and we report only a part of it. The perception of each gender as seen through their own eyes and their view of the other gender group is similar to the procedures used in the American studies. The widest discrepancies were found between a gender's view of itself and its beliefs about the other gender's view of it, but we cannot pursue these as there is no counterpart in the three American studies.

Women perceived women as showing 'affection', 'expressing anger verbally', 'somewhat creative' and 'taking things personally'. Men saw women as 'showing affection' and 'taking things personally' – here they agree with women's judgements about women – but men also saw women as 'crying easily', 'somewhat kind' and 'warm'. Superficially it appears that English women and men were in less agreement than Americans, but it should be noted that in Williams and Bennett's study judgements of own and other gender were combined without indicating any discrepancies. Students were only asked to indicate whether an adjective was associated with a woman or a man, while English students were required to locate women and men at points on each of 21 dimensions. This may in part explain the differences between the attributes which English students used in describing women and the American list – 'affectionate', 'emotional', 'gentle', 'feminine', 'likes children', 'tender', 'understanding' and 'warm'. 'Taking things personally' and 'cries easily' may be aspects of 'emotionality', but 'somewhat creative' and 'expressing anger verbally' are new dimensions of a feminine stereotype arising from the English findings. 'Creative' appears as a female-valued trait though not as a sex-specific attribute in Table 2.12.

Each of the approaches which we have considered provides information about the nature of men and women. Can we say that one is more scientific or objective, indeed more credible? Even our cursory examination of these three methods of investigation suggests that in each there is an aim to reduce bias and provide replicable results but that none is without problems. The answer must surely be no; we cannot say that one of these descriptions portrays men and women more faithfully than the others.

In demographic and psychometric research, the definition of concepts is a source of ambiguity which can lead to reliance on intuitive commonsense notions. Although social psychologists use our everyday terms in studying stereotypes, their results vary according to the questions they ask. Terms which are applied to men and women in descriptions of their roles as these are currently enacted in society appear with different values attached to them when people are asked to describe their view of roles of men and women in the future – how they would ideally see them.

Although the need for such attention to detail may at times appear fiddling if not positively boring, it is a necessary part of every scientific investigation. It is one characteristic which distinguishes scientific discourse from naive understanding. We believe it distinguishes scientific discourse on the nature of gender, yet that discourse remains sensitive to the influences of commonsense. In the absence of clearly specified theory, ambiguity in defining our dimensions or describing our results leads us to fall back on our intuitive, commonsense understanding of men and women.

CHAPTER 3

Physical Sex Differences: Evolution, Development and Cultural Significance

In the first two chapters we introduced the issues which are important for understanding the scientific study of sex and gender, and showed how differences between men and women had been studied from three diverse points of view within the social sciences. We turn now to more detailed examinations of specific topics. We begin in this chapter by looking at physical differences. We first consider the evolutionary origin of sex and the bodily forms of the two sexes, then physical development in boys and girls, and finally the elaboration and cultural use of physical sex differences – their contribution to gender.

Evolution: Where Did Sex Begin?

As recently as one hundred years ago, many people were apparently satisfied with the Adam and Eve answer to the question of the origin of the two sexes. But the general acceptance of Darwin's theory of evolution, which forms an essential foundation for modern biology, has eroded the credibility of religious sources. Currently we look instead to evolutionary biology to answer questions about the origins of sex.

While science may be able to compete with religion in terms of credibility, it cannot do so in the certainty of the answers it offers. There is still much about the evolution of sex and sex differences which has yet to be explained. The current theories of evolutionary biologists do, however, provide an intriguing and rather different way of looking at this very familiar subject.

Before we can ask about the origins of sex and of the bodily forms of the two sexes, we must ask a further question: 'What is sex?'

What is Sex?

The reader may be thinking that the answer to this question should be clear enough, at least for the human species; but this is not so. In our discussion of the ethnomethodological approach in Chapter 1, we noted that human beings tend to identify a person as a man or a woman by constructing their gender from a variety of cues, including physical attributes such as physique, beard growth and breast development. But from the wider perspective of the evolutionary biologist, who is familiar with a whole range of animal species, these physical differences between men and women – which help us to assign gender – are not sufficiently widespread in the animal kingdom to be useful in answering the general question 'What is sex?'

Even the feature which many men and women regard as *the* essential difference between them – possession of a penis or a vagina – is not one which can be used for defining sex over a wide range of animal species, even if we were to confine our discussion to those animals in which fertilization takes place internally. In birds, for example, the male does not have a penis. In fact, mammals are the only animal group in which the male does possess a true penis, although a comparable male appendage which is inserted into the female body – an 'intromittent organ' – is present in many other forms of animal life where there is internal fertilization. For example, there are paired bony projections called claspers in male cartilaginous fish such as sharks and dogfish.

The existence of a chromosomal difference between men and women is fairly widely known, particularly as this distinction is the one used for defining the sexes for the purposes of professional sporting competitions. Competitors in women's Olympic athletic events have to undergo a sex test, which is an assessment of their sex chromosomes. Every human being, and indeed every animal, starts life as a single fertilized egg cell. In the nucleus of the human egg cell there are forty-six chromosomes: forty-four – twenty-two pairs – called autosomes, and two sex chromosomes. The latter are both relatively long and are identical in females (designated XX); but in males one of them is an incomplete structure carrying little genetic material (the Y chromosome), thus leaving many genes on the longer X chromosome unpaired.

All the cells in a woman's body except the egg cells contain two X chromosomes, and all the cells in a man's body except the sperm cells contain one X and one Y chromosome. In the germ cells – the egg and sperm cells – only half the chromosomes are present, so that female cells all contain one X chromosome, and male cells contain either an X or a Y chromosome. These pair up to form either XX or XY in the fertilized eggs, in roughly equal proportions. Usually there are slightly more males than females at conception in most mammals; but this difference declines with age, owing to relatively greater male mortality at all ages.

Although the Y chromosome has practically no functional genes, the X chromosome has a number of them, including those responsible for fifty-seven varieties of unwelcome conditions such as colour blindness and haemophilia. Most of these harmful genes are 'recessive', meaning that if they are paired with another of a different type, they will not be expressed. In the female the possession of two X chromosomes usually results in these harmful genes being overridden; in the male they are much more common, because the Y chromosome is ineffective in counteracting them, since it possesses practically no functional genes. Characteristics such as colour blindness, which result from the expression of these recessive genes, are termed sex-linked.

A straightforward procedure is available to determine whether a cell contains more than one X chromosome, and thus to identify the genetic sex of a person. Cells from the mouth are prepared and stained. A distinctive spot of colour called the Barr body indicates more than one X chromosome – a female. This test has been used to sex Olympic competitors.

But even chromosomally defined sex is not a general enough characteristic to answer the question 'What is sex?' for all animals. The possession of two X chromosomes may be an adequate defining characteristic for the female sex in mammals, but this is not the case for fish, amphibians and birds: in these animals the female has the shorter chromosome and the male two longer X chromosomes. In some animals sex is determined not by chromosomal differences but by their environment. In the red fish *Anthias squamipinnis*, for example, the absence of a male in the immediate surroundings causes the female to undergo a sex change. But if a male can be seen – even in an adjacent fish tank – this reversal is inhibited by his presence (Simpson, 1976).

Can we define sex in a general way, one which will satisfy the wider viewpoint of the evolutionary biologist? The answer is that we can. Fundamentally, sex is defined in terms of the gametes or germs cells which an animal produces. If an animal produces a gamete which contains food and is immobile, it is called an egg cell and is defined as female. One which contains no food resources and is mobile is called a sperm cell and is defined as male.

Why Did Sex Evolve?

Having provided a general definition of male and female in terms of the unequal size of their germ cells or gametes, we now consider why this size arrangement developed – in other words, why sex evolved. To answer this we consider two more specific questions. One is why sexual reproduction evolved at all. The second is why the two types of gametes are located in different individuals (males and females) in some species, whereas in others, such as snails and earthworms, they both occur in the same individual (hermaphrodites).

Why sexual reproduction evolved at all has puzzled evolutionary biologists. There are several consequences of sexual reproduction which might put a sexual animal at a disadvantage compared with an asexual one. Asexual reproduction involves the budding or cloning of a genetic 'carbon copy' from the parent individual, whereas in sexual reproduction only half of the parents' genetic material is passed on to each offspring. Twice as much time and energy has to be expended in order to pass on the same amount of genetic information in a sexual process. There is also the risk that a sexual parent might mix his or her genetic material with that of a genetically disadvantageous individual, thus producing poorer offspring than by an asexual process. Mating itself involves a number of 'costs', such as the expenditure of time and energy in courtship and copulation, and increased risks from predation, over-eager mates and infectious diseases (Daly, 1978).

Since sexual reproduction involves these disadvantages, why did it evolve at all? The reason seems to be that mixing the genetic material from two individuals – which occurs during sexual reproduction – results in far greater individual variation in the resulting offspring, and this variation is highly advantageous if a species is to adapt to a changing environment (Maynard Smith, 1971). Since asexual reproduction only results in the formation of individuals who are genetically identical to their parents, it cannot produce sufficient variation for the organism to adapt to changing conditions. Although sex is both risky and costly, it has provided a way in which organisms have continually been able to produce sufficient variety in their offspring to increase the chances of their survival in changing environments.

According to this explanation, the usefulness of sexual reproduction is confined to certain fairly restricted circumstances, occurring when an organism produces a large number of offspring which are likely to inhabit rather different environments from those of their parents.

Although this may provide an explanation for the origin of sexual reproduction, it is clear that not all sexually reproducing animals exist under such circumstances today. Birds and mammals, for example, produce relatively few offspring, and sexual reproduction may actually be maladaptive in these circumstances; but the animals, having lost the pre-adaptations necessary for reverting to asexuality, continue to reproduce sexually (Williams, 1975).

The second question about the evolution of sex is why two different-sized gametes – eggs and sperms – have arisen. If the important aspect of sexual reproduction lies in the fusing of genetic material, why are two different-sized germ cells necessary? In many one-celled organisms sexual reproduction does take place through the fusion of two identically sized gametes. But in most many-celled organisms gametes of unequal size – male and female – are produced.

Parker and his colleagues (1972) discuss the possible origins of different-sized gametes from same-sized gametes. They suggest that there are two opposing selection pressures acting on gamete size in many-celled organisms: the first is that individuals can increase their number of fertilizations by producing many small gametes rather than few large ones; the second is that the provision of a large food store in the fertilized egg cell – zygote – increases its chances of surviving to maturity. (In a one-celled organism a large food reserve is unnecessary, since it does not have to develop into a much larger organism.) Parker and his colleagues used a computer simulation to demonstrate that the only stable evolutionary response to the two selection pressures is the production of two different gamete sizes, each of which is a response to one, but not both, of the selection pressures.

It is suggested that small-sized gametes – spermatozoa – originated as a response to selection for high productivity; but these gametes lack adequate food reserves, and hence they can only produce viable offspring if they fuse with larger, food-carrying, gametes – ova or egg cells. The smaller gametes would quickly develop adaptations which would enable them to be more successful in fusing with the larger gametes than these would be in fusing with one another. Once this happened, the larger gametes would begin to lose their initial motility, and there would be selection for increased motility among the smaller gametes, resulting in the characteristically active spermatozoa (Parker *et al.*, 1972).

The third question concerning the evolution of sex is why different-sized gametes are produced by different individuals, males and females.

Since we ourselves belong to a species in which there are two sexes, we tend to regard separate sexes as the natural order of things. Although this arrangement does occur throughout the animal kingdom and in a number of plants, many organisms are hermaphrodites: that is, each individual is capable of producing both types of gamete. In most hermaphroditic species cross-fertilization occurs, thus providing the mixing of genetic material that seems to account for the evolutionary success of sexual reproduction. Why, then, are not all animals cross-fertilizing hermaphrodites? There appears to be no clear answer to this question. There is, however, one fairly obvious advantage of two sexes over hermaphrodites: in the latter, each individual must maintain two sets of gonads and reproductive ducts, both of which are complex and expensive in terms of energy expenditure (Williams, 1975). Identifying the particular circumstances under which hermaphrodites would have an advantage over two separate sexes is a particularly difficult problem, and a convincing theoretical explanation for the occurrence of hermaphroditism has yet to be offered (Ghiselin, 1974; Williams, 1975).

Evolution of Sex Differences in Animals

Sexual dimorphism is the term used to refer to differences in anatomy, physiology and behaviour between males and females of the same species. It is a phenomenon which is widespread throughout the animal kingdom, and of course occurs in the human species. If there is only one fundamental difference between males and females – that of gamete size – why have such a wide variety of other differences evolved? Why, for example, do the sexes of many vertebrates differ in size and other physical characteristics? Why are many male birds more brightly coloured than their females? Why do cocks but not hens crow? And why do men but not women develop beards, and women but not men develop breasts?

The usual evolutionary explanation for sexual dimorphism is derived from Charles Darwin's speculations on the subject in *The Descent of Man, and Selection in Relation to Sex*, first published in 1871. Darwin suggested that there are two selection pressures determining which individuals produce the most offspring: the first of these is competition between males for females, and the second is selection by females of certain male characteristics in preference to others. The first type, male competition, has been used to explain the origin of the complex antler development of the male deer. Large antlers are assumed to be the result of successful competition with other stags for access to fertile females. The second type of selection, female choice, has been used to explain the origin of the elaborate tail of the peacock. This time it is assumed that females choose males with the most elaborately developed tails.

One of the most influential modern views of sexual selection is that of Robert Trivers (1972). Although published a century after Darwin's work, it is still mainly concerned with male competition and female choice. Trivers suggests that these types of sexual selection can be viewed as consequences of the different-sized gametes in the two sexes. He suggests that since the female provides all the food reserves for the fertilized egg, the male's contribution to the offspring is much less in time and energy than that of the female. Trivers argues that the number of offspring a female can produce is limited by her ability to produce egg cells, since a relatively large amount of energy is necessary to produce the food reserves in these cells; on the other hand, no such limit operates in the case of the male. His reproductive success will not be limited by gamete production but by his ability to fertilize the egg cells of females – that is, by his access to fertile females. Trivers infers from this that the ways in which the two sexes can maximize their reproductive success will be different: males by mating with as many females as possible, and females, who require only one successful mating to fertilize their eggs, by choosing the male with the best genetic endowment, or males who will make good parents if parental care is involved. The result is competition among males for access to females with un-fertilized eggs, and selection by females of genetically fit males – the two forms of sexual selection originally envisaged by Darwin.

If Darwin's view of sexual selection and Trivers's argument sound notoriously like a familiar view of human conduct, of males trying to sow as many wild oats as possible and of females remaining coy and choosy, this is not surprising. Such a view of human conduct – some would say 'human nature' – has clearly influenced both views of animal nature, and they provide a further example of scientific thinking reflecting commonsense notions prevalent in society at large.

Irrespective of the source of Trivers's inspiration, are his assumptions about the relative contributions of the male and female in gamete production correct? Some of our colleagues, including Janson-Smith, Lazarus and Birke, have convinced us that they are not necessarily correct, for the following reason. Female animals produce a certain number of egg cells – many or few, depending on the species – each with its store of food. But the male sheds a far greater number of sperm cells, together with their accompanying fluid. Only if one compares the energy expended in producing *one* egg cell with that expended in producing *one* sperm cell is Trivers's assumption obviously correct. But since males produce far more sperm cells than females produce egg cells, males may make up in numbers what they omit in terms of food resources. The relative contribution of male and female to the total amount of gamete production is not a simple matter of assumption, as Trivers suggested. It would require empirical measurement, and is likely to vary from one animal species to another.

This objection to Trivers's assumption is not a crucial one for his whole theory, since he uses his point about the relative contribution of the sexes to the fertilized egg as a basis for considering a much wider range of possible differences in the contribution of males and females to reproductive processes. Using a term borrowed from economics, Trivers regards each parent as 'investing' in its offspring: the greater the investment, the greater the chance that the offspring will survive to perpetuate themselves – and hence their parents' genes. Trivers defines 'parental investment' as any contribution by a parent which increases an offspring's chances of surviving and reproducing itself while also reducing the parents' ability to produce future offspring. Some examples of parental investment are the energy expended in gamete production and activities such as feeding and protecting the young. The total range of possible activities which this description covers is very difficult to combine and quantify in a single value, and this difficulty limits the usefulness of Trivers's subsequent speculations. We can say, however, that features such as giving birth to live young, production of enclosed eggs, and lactation all represent high degrees of parental investment.

Trivers suggests that the (supposedly) smaller contribution of males to gamete production will result, if there are no other factors involved, in males competing for access to females. But he also extends this argument by suggesting that the sex which makes the lower parental investment will compete for access to the sex which makes the greater parental investment. This more general point does not depend on his initial assumption about gamete production being correct, since 'parental investment' is a wider concept. It provides a reason for either sex competing for access to the other or showing mate choice. Trivers contends, however, that the usual case will still be that of male competition and female choice, basing his argument partly on the usual investment imbalance at fertilization leading to a subsequent imbalance in parental investment. Whatever the logic of this assumption – and it can be convincingly disputed (for example, Dawkins and Carlisle, 1976) – many animal sex differences do seem to fit Trivers's predictions. For instance, Trivers's theory predicts that male competition, and hence sexual dimorphism, will be most marked in animals where there is practically no male parental investment – that is, no paternal care or protection. In such cases, the difference in reproductive success between individual males will also be greatest, and so will the mortality difference between the sexes. There are many examples which fit these predictions: in the elephant seal, for example, the males are considerably larger than the females, male competition is pronounced, and a success-ful male can hold a 'harem' of about forty females, whereas an un-successful one obtains no females.

Trivers's theory also predicts that when the male's investment approaches that of the female, competition between males will be lessened, and so will sexual dimorphism in size, aggressiveness and mortality. This occurs in most birds – which are monogamous, forming relatively permanent pairs – and as predicted show relatively small sex differences.

Trivers's theory goes on to suggest that in cases where male parental investment is the higher, females will possess typically 'male' charac-teristics such as bright plumage, larger size and aggressiveness. This occurs in some wading birds, where the male is the sex which incubates the eggs and shows parental behaviour, whereas the female is poly-androus, mating with several males.

Thus parental investment and sexual dimorphism do appear to be related in the way in which Trivers suggested. This does not necessarily mean that sexual dimorphism has always evolved as a consequence of prior differences in parental investment, since parental investment refers to an assortment of activities which may have arisen either relatively early or relatively late in evolutionary history. One would expect, therefore, that there will be cases where sexual dimorphism has arisen prior to or independently from sex differences in parental invest-ment, and that Trivers's theory can only provide a partial explanation for sex differences in animals.

There are indeed cases of sexual dimorphism which Trivers's theory cannot explain. For example, in many mammalian species the female is slightly larger than the male, and it has been suggested that this is more common than is generally supposed (Ralls, 1976, 1978). Trivers's theory would predict that where the female is the larger sex, there should be greater parental investment by the male than the female, as in polyandrous wading birds (Jenni, 1974). However, in mammals where the female is larger, the male does not make any appreciable contribution to parental care; nor is the larger size of the female accompanied by typically 'male' characteristics, as it is in female polyandrous birds. Ralls also cites examples from other groups of animals: in the guppy, the female is larger than the male, but the male is still the more aggressive and brightly coloured sex. These two features can be explained in terms of parental investment, but we should still have to offer another type of explanation for the larger female size.

What, then, is the explanation for large females? Ralls (1976, 1978) offers several possibilities, but there is really very little evidence on the subject. The first possibility is the 'big mother' hypothesis: simply that big mothers make better mothers – 'better' in this context meaning that they will leave more surviving offspring. It is known that larger size is associated with greater reproductive success in women and in domestic ewes, but both these examples come from species in which the male is larger than the female. Ralls suggests that under certain conditions – for instance, where there was the possibility of prolonged food shortage – the benefits of large size would become more pronounced and might result in the female becoming larger than the male.

A second possibility is that males and females may reduce competition between the sexes by feeding from different food sources. This has been suggested to account for some sex differences found in birds (Selander, 1972). Ralls suggests that the same process might in some cases produce large females, but at present this remains purely hypothetical.

A third possibility, again lacking concrete examples for its support, is that certain resources, such as food or nesting sites, may be more crucial to females and hence lead to competition between females, resulting in large size in the same way that this is produced by competition in the male.

Whatever the explanation might be, it is clear that Trivers's theory cannot explain Ralls's large females. Ralls's suggestions are not particularly convincing as explanations for large female size, but they do represent a departure from the tradition of explaining sexual dimorphism solely in terms of male competition and female choice. Changes resulting from selection pressures on the female for efficient mothering, female competition, and specialized adaptations in the two sexes for different types of food foraging tend to take the focus of attention away from the male.

Evolution of Human Sex Differences

We can never be certain about the evolutionary origin of human sexual dimorphism. There is no shortage of opinions on the subject, simply because it is so difficult to demonstrate that any particular one is incorrect (for example, Freedman, 1964; Morris, 1967; Tiger, 1970; Hutt, 1972a; Goldberg, 1973; Morgan, 1972). What we shall attempt to do here is to relate some of these views to the general theories discussed in the previous section.

First, there are the possibilities raised by Darwin's discussion of sexual selection and by Trivers's theory. Darwin (1871) suggested that the larger average size, strength and muscular development of men, and the greater male aggressiveness (see Chapter 5) could all have originated as a result of male competition. Trivers (1972) suggests that higher male mortality (Madigan, 1957) may also have originated in this way. (But see also the section on demography in Chapter 2.) Tanner (1970) attributes men's beards to a similar origin, in terms of their intimidating appearance. Darwin (1871) suggested that these masculine features, including beards, originated partly through female choice.

An alternative explanation for the greater average size, strength and musculature of men is that these features are adaptations for cooperative hunting of big game. This 'hunting hypothesis' is used to explain a range of masculine psychological characteristics such as the existence of all-male groups and male dominance (Tiger, 1970), and throwing accuracy and spatial ability (Kolakowski and Malina, 1974). In the 'hunting hypothesis', only selection pressures on the male are considered (Slocum, 1975). Many views of human evolution are of this type, and cooperative hunting is often cited as the driving force in making us the intelligent creatures we are today (for example, Washburn and Lancaster, 1968; Alcock, 1975). But male hunting is only one side of the coin. In most present-day hunter–gatherer societies, the women do not sit around at home while the men hunt the meat: there is a division of labour in food-finding, men hunting animals and women gathering plant food – and women usually contribute more to the bulk of the diet than men do (Martin and Voorhies, 1975). Thus, if men show adaptations for a hunting existence, women should also show adaptations for plant-gathering. The division of labour into hunting and gathering might have arisen as a way of reducing competition between the sexes for food-finding; we have already considered Selander's explanation of this adaptation in other animals.

As we have seen, there are several theories to account for the evolution of male features; but there has been less speculation about the female, and what has been offered usually emphasizes the male. Women show a number of features which make them unusual compared to other female primates: for instance, female sexual interest is less clearly related to the stage of the human menstrual cycle, and there are no external visual signals of sexual receptivity in women. In addition, the mammary glands develop into their adult form at puberty rather than during the first pregnancy, and body hair has been lost to an even greater extent than in the human male.

The standard explanation for prolonged female sexual interest is that it promotes long-term relationships between the sexes (for example, Morris, 1967; Napier, 1971). In our closest living relative, the chimpanzee, there is practically no association between members of a mated pair other than for copulation (Lawick-Goodall, 1971). Although human sexual acts can be as transient as this, there is usually some form of prolonged association between human sexual partners. Sexual interest and activity throughout the female cycle would have contributed towards prolonging the length of time that mated pairs remained together, but other psychological characteristics such as the capacity for exclusive emotional attachments and sexual jealousy would also be required for any more permanent associations to have arisen. Whatever adaptations the human species possesses in this respect, these certainly operate inefficiently compared, for example, with those that produce true monogamy in birds. The term 'pair bonding', derived from research on birds, has been used to refer to human partners; but it is perhaps a misnomer, since in humans the so-called bonds are often heavily dependent on cultural sanctions. The usual reason given for prolonged sexual relationships in human beings is that they provide a favourable environment for child-rearing (for example, Morris, 1967; Crook, 1972).

Other female characteristics, such as the breasts, body-hair loss and the rounded figure, were attributed by Darwin (1871) to male choice. This idea was extended and popularized by Desmond Morris, who viewed the human female as consisting largely of a collection of adaptations for sexually arousing the male, or, as he puts it, for 'making sex sexier'. This explanation reflects both our society's definition of women as 'sex objects', and our values as far as these characteristics are concerned. Morris suggested that both prolonged sexual interest and attractiveness in the human female promote long-term relationships.

While we agree that prolonged sexual interest might have this effect, increased attractiveness is a different matter, and it could just as readily disrupt long-term relationships by resulting in more promiscuous sexual activity.

Another difficulty with Morris's explanation is the emphasis on male choice of females. In our discussion of sexual selection in animals, we pointed out that where there is selection by one sex due to choice of attractive features in the other, this is usually made by the sex investing more in the offspring, which in most species, including human beings, is the female. As Jewell (1976) says: 'Regardless of whether our ancestors were polygamous or monogamous, it is difficult to imagine that any fertile woman, however ill-favoured, would have remained unmated or even suffered any reduction in fertility on this account. The promiscuous habits of men would have guaranteed fertility!'

Despite these criticisms, many people have been convinced by Morris's arguments, probably because it is difficult to account for some human female features in any other way. Women's breasts are unique in that they develop before they are required for lactation, they are conspicuous and they contain a large amount of fatty tissue, features which cannot be easily explained in terms of their adaptive value in milk production (although they could be adaptations for supporting the milk-producing and -dispensing tissue of the breast). The obvious erotic significance of the female breast in our culture, and in many other cultures (Short, 1976), makes Morris's theory appear attractive in the absence of a convincing alternative.

Current explanations of the female form in terms of male choice overlook the importance of adaptations for ensuring survival, efficient reproduction and good infant care in less affluent and well-fed times than our own. The female breasts may have originally occurred as part of a general increase in fatty deposits in the female, so as to enable her to survive periods of food shortage. The female has to provide food for herself and for her infant when she is pregnant or lactating. This will entail a much greater food requirement than for the male, who has only himself to feed. It is also important for the female to produce a constant supply of milk in spite of hard times, and the fatty tissue in the breast would help to achieve this.

Other features of the human female are more obviously adaptations for reproduction: for example, the wider pelvis to accommodate the infant's head which has increased in size during the course of evolutionary history.

Some aspects of human sexual dimorphism have clear reproductive functions common to all the mammals. The mammalian penis, for example, arose as an adaptation for efficient internal fertilization, and similar organs have developed as a result of parallel evolution in several other animal groups. Internal fertilization is a prerequisite for another characteristic of mammalian reproduction, that the young develop inside the mother and are born alive rather than enclosed in an egg. This is called 'viviparity', and it has resulted in specializations of the female reproductive organs to house the foetus (the uterus), to allow nutrient and waste-product exchange between the embryo and the mother (the placenta) and to transport the full-term foetus to the outside world (the vagina).

Milk production appears to be of more ancient origin than viviparity, since it occurs in primitive egg-laying mammals such as the spiny ant-eater (Sharman, 1976). In fact the mammary glands may have decreased in importance during the course of mammalian evolution, yielding part of their function of feeding the developing young to the placenta.

To sum up, there are several hypotheses which might account for the evolutionary origins of human sexual dimorphism: intrasexual competition, female choice, hunting and gathering specializations, male choice, and adaptations directly or indirectly related to reproductive functions in the female.

The Development of Physical Sex Differences

In humans there are not only the obvious physical sex differences in reproductive organs, secondary sexual characteristics and physique, but also some less obvious differences in physiological processes (Glucksmann, 1974). In this section we consider how these differences arise in normal development, describe certain abnormalities and discuss the normal variations in the developmental process which can lead to within-sex differences. The issue of within-sex variation reflects our concern with the extent to which male and female characteristics show overlapping distributions, which we discussed in Chapter 1.

We first describe the three 'sex hormones' which feature prominently in accounts of sexual development. The main hormone produced by the testes is testosterone; this, together with hormones of the same general type, but produced in other parts of the body, are called androgens. The main hormones produced by the ovaries are oestrogen and progesterone; the hormones of the same general type are referred to as oestrogens and progestogens respectively. Except during pregnancy, both types of 'female' hormone show cyclical changes in their output from the ovary: this produces the oestrous cycle (in most mammals) and the menstrual cycle (in primates). Both involve periodic release of an egg and changes in behaviour towards males. The menstrual cycle is distinguished by monthly vaginal bleeding, caused by the shedding of the uterine wall.

These so-called 'male' and 'female' hormones are not confined to their respective sexes. The ovaries and testes each produce all three hormones, and the adrenal glands, situated above the kidneys, secrete androgens in both sexes. The ovaries and the adrenal glands of women produce androgens which affect hair growth under the arms and in the pubic region (Glucksmann, 1974); the testes produce a small quantity of oestrogens, but at present there are no known physiological effects.

The Developmental Process

Prenatal Development. There is no difference in male and female development during the first 6 weeks after conception. At this time the embryonic sex organs, or gonads, are identical in the two sexes. The Y chromosome of the male is crucial for ensuring that the embryonic gonad will develop into a testis, and this occurs by enlargement of the inner part of the embryonic gonad at about 6 weeks of age. In the female, no gonadal development occurs at this time: instead, at about 12 weeks the outer part of the embryonic gonad develops into an ovary, and this development is completed during the sixth or seventh month of pregnancy. At that time the ovaries will contain all the 300 to 400 egg cells which will be released during the woman's future life, and also an additional 100,000 which will not be used (Money and Ehrhardt, 1972).

During early development we all possess the rudimentary internal ducts for our own and for the opposite sex. At about 3 months after conception those for our own sex enlarge, whereas those for the opposite sex degenerate. This process depends, in the male, on the secretion of two hormones from the testis: the first, testosterone, causes enlargement in the male, or Wolffian, ducts, which develop into the vasa deferentia, epididymis and seminal vesicles (see Figure 3.1); the second, factor X, or Mullerian-inhibiting substance, causes the female, or Mullerian, ducts to degenerate (Simpson, 1976). The testis functions early in development, and testosterone synthesis has been reported in the human foetal testis at 8 to 10 weeks after conception, only 2 to 4 weeks

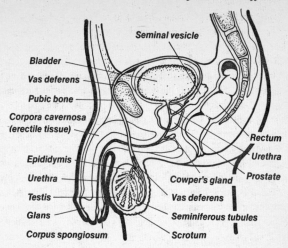

Figure 3.1. The Male Sexual and Reproductive Organs: Side View. From Hyde (1979).

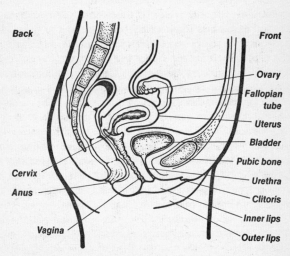

Figure 3.2. Internal Sexual and Reproductive Organs of the Female: Side View. From Hyde (1979).

after testis development has begun (Reinisch, 1976). In the female, the absence of these two hormones results in degeneration of the Wolffian ducts and development of the Mullerian ducts to form the oviducts, uterus and vagina (see Figure 3.2).

The final step in sexual differentiation is the development of the external genitals. Both male and female organs develop from a single undifferentiated structure: the presence of testosterone during the third and fourth months of pregnancy causes the formation of a penis and scrotal sac, whereas the female clitoris and labia develop if testosterone is absent (Money and Ehrhardt, 1972).

The crucial importance of the presence or absence of testosterone for normal sexual differentiation in mammals was first realized in 1947, following publication of animal experiments performed by Alfred Jost. He demonstrated that castration of the male rabbit foetus early in life resulted in the development of female reproductive structures (Jost, 1972). Research which followed showed that sexual development was similar in human beings and in other mammals.

The adrenal glands of male and female developing foetuses secrete small amounts of androgens, as do the adult glands. Since masculine development is dependent on the presence of androgens in the foetus, these adrenal androgens could be expected to produce some degree of masculinization in female foetuses. Research on rats and on rhesus monkeys has implicated the hormone progesterone in protecting the female foetus from the possible masculinizing effects of foetal andro-gens, since progesterone is produced in much greater quantities by female foetuses than by male foetuses (Resko, 1975; Shapiro *et al.*, 1976). At present, it is not known whether these findings can be extended to other mammals, including humans.

In rats and mice, androgens from the foetal testes affect the develop-ing brain of the male in a way that influences both the physiology and the behaviour of the adult animal. These influences range from the facilitation of masculine sexual behaviour to non-sexual activities such as fighting and playing (Archer, 1975; Olioff and Stewart, 1978). Several writers have suggested that testosterone may affect human brain development in a similar manner (for example, Hutt, 1972a; Goldberg, 1973), but more recent studies indicate that the findings from rats and mice do not extend to primates, the group to which human beings belong (Resko, 1975; Herbert, 1976; Gray and Drewett, 1977).

Another theory about human behaviour, derived from studies of rodents, is that of Dorner (Dorner *et al.*, 1975). He suggests that low levels of testosterone during foetal development predispose human males to become homosexual. This assertion is based on a particular finding in rats, namely that testosterone affects areas of the foetal brain that later influence adult sexual behaviour. This results in the reduction of female patterns and the enhancement of male sexual behaviour in adult rats (Gray and Drewett, 1977). Dorner claims that a similar process generally occurs in human males, and that insufficient testosterone during development results in what is effectively 'behavioural feminization', which he equates with homosexuality. But the two are rather different. The first refers to a person or animal's preferred role in the sexual act, whether it is active or passive; it is this that is affected by foetal testosterone in rats. The second refers to the choice of sexual partner, and it is this that is the defining feature of homosexuality. If correct, Dorner's theory would also predict that exposure of human females to testosterone during foetal life would result in their showing lesbian preferences when they are sexually mature. Studies of women exposed to foetal androgens indicate that this is not the case (Money and Ehrhardt, 1972).

Dorner's theory, like many reductionist theories, involves unwarranted generalizations from animal studies to complex human behaviour. It seeks to define the psychological and social phenomenon of homosexuality in terms of an abnormality of individual development. In doing so, Dorner supports the view of homosexuality as an illness for which a physical 'cure' should be sought and administered. We consider some alternative ways of viewing homosexuality in the next chapter. For the moment we conclude by noting the lack of firm support from research on human beings.

Development during Infancy and Childhood. Although testosterone is crucial for early sexual development, its level declines just before birth (Knorr *et al.*, 1974). Until recently it was thought that it remains negligible throughout childhood; but it is now reported that male infants show a rise in testosterone during the first six months following birth (Tanner, 1978), although the significance of this is unknown at present.

The most notable sex difference during infancy and childhood is that girls grow faster and reach puberty before boys do. They also stop growing earlier. Individual developmental age can be assessed accurately by measuring bone and tooth development, and by comparing these measures against a set of standards (Tanner, 1970). Girls are shown to be more advanced than boys even before birth, by which time they are, on average, four weeks ahead. This difference is maintained until adulthood, and is reflected in other measures such as those indicating motor coordination (Tanner, 1970). Girls reach puberty before boys: the first outward sign of puberty, increased growth rate, occurs about two years earlier in girls.

The cause of these differences is unknown, but there is evidence that the timing of puberty is affected by prenatal testosterone; thus girls and female rhesus monkeys who were exposed to testosterone during foetal development show delayed puberty (Resko, 1975; Money and Ehrhardt, 1972).

The other physical sex differences found during childhood are generally less pronounced versions of adult sex differences. Girls begin life slightly shorter than boys, and they remain shorter until about eleven years of age, when they overtake boys for about three years as a result of their earlier puberty. Girls also weigh slightly less at birth, and continue on average to be the lighter sex except for a few years around the age of puberty (Tanner, 1970).

Puberty and Adulthood. Most of the well-known physical differences between men and women begin to appear at puberty, triggered by the action of the sex hormones – testosterone in the male and oestrogen and progesterone in the female.

In boys, testosterone produces a number of changes which are similar to its effects in many other male mammals: the voice deepens, sweat-gland activity is increased, body-hair distribution changes, and muscular development is increased, particularly in the neck, chest and shoulders (Glucksmann, 1974). Testosterone also has a number of less well-known physiological effects: for instance, it promotes growth in the skeletal system, and it increases the size of the heart and lungs, the capacity of the blood to carry oxygen, and the body's ability to neutralize the waste products of muscular exertion.

In girls, the rise in oestrogen levels leads to breast development, fat redistribution, and the beginning of the menstrual cycle. The growth of pubic and axilla (underarm) hair is produced not by oestrogen but by adrenal androgens (Tanner, 1970). Oestrogen and progesterone show cyclic fluctuations during the menstrual cycle, oestrogen levels rising during the earlier follicular phase, and progesterone during the later luteal phase (progesterone is produced by the corpus luteum, which develops in the ovary after ovulation). Far greater hormonal changes occur during pregnancy, when the levels of these hormones, particularly progesterone, are greatly increased. Thus, in the female, puberty marks the beginning of a series of hormonal changes which have complex regulatory effects on reproductive life, whereas in the male the hormonal changes are of a simpler nature, affecting mainly the production of secondary sexual characteristics.

The bodily changes which begin at puberty are largely maintained during adult life. In men, testosterone levels show a gradual decline throughout the middle or later years. In women, reproductive life ends much more abruptly, between the ages of 45 and 55, when oestrogen levels decline dramatically; it is called the menopause. A variety of bodily reactions may also be experienced, including dryness of the vagina and urethra, 'hot flushes', and symptoms of general discomfort such as insomnia, headaches and possibly depression. These are mostly transient reactions occurring while the hormone levels are declining. In addition, there are longer-term changes which are associated with normal ageing but are exaggerated by some aspect of the post-menopausal hormonal state. These include loss of skin elasticity and greater bone brittleness (Sherman, 1971; Birke and Best, 1980).

Some doctors give synthetic oestrogen – known as hormone replacement therapy (HRT) – to menopausal women, with the aim of preventing the post-menopausal symptoms. This treatment is controversial, because HRT gained its initial impetus from a best-selling book and drug company publicity but has not been subjected to rigorous clinical trials. The physical risks involved with some of the hormone preparations have only recently become known (Gillie and Weitz, 1978).

One sex difference which is supposedly widespread in mammals is a greater average life span in females than in males (Trivers, 1972; Glucksmann, 1974). This occurs in the human species, but, as we have shown in Chapter 2, it is subject to reversal in parts of present-day Asia. Several possible explanations have been put forward for greater male mortality: Trivers (1972), for example, has suggested that testosterone has a number of indirect effects which combine to lower the life expectancy of males, and he cites some (admittedly limited) evidence that castrated male rats and human eunuchs live longer than their normal male counterparts. Whatever the causes of the sex difference in mortality, one important consequence in our society and in many others is that during the later years of adult life women increasingly come to outnumber men of their own age group; another is that women will be more likely than men to have to face the distress and strain of bereavement during the later part of their life. Again, we cannot divorce bodily differences from their social consequences and meaning.

Variations in Development

Having described the typical pattern of development, we now consider
variations in development which produce an overlapping distribution
of physical characteristics in men and women. The reproductive organs
generally show no overlap between members of the two sexes. The
secondary sexual characteristics, which develop at puberty, are more
variable: a woman may be flat-chested or she may develop large breasts,
and a man may or may not develop hairs on his chest. The two sexes
show a degree of overlap on these characteristics, some fat men showing
feminine-looking breast development, and some women having relatively abundant body hair. There is even more overlap in general
features, such as physique, height and rate of development, which vary
widely within each sex.

Variations in development may produce these different degrees of
overlap between the sexes. Since the reproductive organs' characteristics generally show no overlap with one another, it can be inferred
that normal sexual differentiation is a fairly rigid process, not prone to
producing wide variations. There are, however, a small number of
people whose reproductive organs show characteristics of both sexes,
but this results from fairly drastic modifications in the developmental
processes. We consider some of these cases of abnormal development
below.

Since there are fairly wide variations within each sex in secondary
sexual characteristics and in the processes controlling growth and
maturation, we can infer that for these features normal development is
more flexible. Such variations can be produced by a larger number of
smaller and more gradual changes than those producing abnormal
sexual differentiation.

Abnormal Sexual Differentiation. Abnormalities in sexual development
provide a valuable source of information about factors necessary for
normal development, supplementing the information gained by experimental studies of animals. Regrettably, such knowledge is gained as a
result of human suffering, but it has also proved useful in treating some
of the disorders. Abnormal sexual differentiation, perhaps more than
most other disorders, will have complex psychological repercussions.
Gender is among the first distinctions which children make in classifying others in their social world, and it is crucially important for the
developing self-concept. Parents also interact with their infants and
children on the basis of this distinction. Any ambiguity in a person's

physical sex at birth upsets these social processes and will have serious psychological consequences.

The work of John Money and his colleagues on the various clinical conditions involving abnormal sexual development has had considerable impact. Their approach is important because it takes into account the wider social and psychological implications of the disorder when deciding on a possible course of treatment (Money and Ehrhardt, 1972).

Abnormal sexual differentiation can result either from additional or missing sex chromosomes, or from a specific gene affecting a crucial aspect of sexual differentiation, or through abnormal hormonal conditions. Soon after the first successful attempts to stain and view the human sex chromosomes in 1956, a number of possible abnormalities were reported. Some of these corresponded to previously known clinical conditions. For example, women who were previously characterized in terms of Turner's syndrome – first described in 1938 – were found to possess only one X chromosome in each cell, designated XO. Their internal and external reproductive organs appear typically female, this being the result of the absence of the Y chromosome. There are, however, a number of other abnormalities which result from the single chromosome composition, such as short stature and rudimentary and inactive sex organs (Mittwoch, 1973).

Men who were previously described as showing Klinefelter's syndrome were found to possess an additional X chromosome or chromosomes. The XXY constitution is the most common abnormality, although up to three extra X chromosomes or additional Y chromosomes have been recorded. The Y chromosome ensures male development, although the additional X chromosome results in small, inactive testes and in many cases in breast development (Simpson, 1976). A rarer condition occurs in people who possess a normal complement of sex chromosomes and yet develop bodily characteristics of the opposite sex. This is caused by a gene that affects sexual differentiation. The most dramatic examples appear to be men, but the individuals actually have two X chromosomes. Although they occur rarely, such cases are of considerable interest in helping to discover the way in which normal sexual differentiation is brought about. According to our account of sexual differentiation in the previous section, such an occurrence should be impossible, since the presence of the Y chromosome triggers the development of the testes and male differentiation. XX men, although having small testes and signs of androgen deficiency, are otherwise very similar to XY men in appearance. The most likely explanation for their condition is that the part of the Y chromosome which controls male development has moved to another chromosome (Simpson, 1976). Such a gene – which causes testicular development in the absence of a Y chromosome – has been found in mice, and Ohno (1976) has suggested that this is the result of a small piece of the Y chromosome moving to one of the other chromosomes (an autosome). A similar explanation could account for human XX males.

Although there are cases in which male differentiation occurs in the presence of XX chromosomes, the reverse case of complete female differentiation in the presence of XY chromosomes is not known in the human species. XY females occur commonly, however, in the wood lemming and, unlike human chromosomal anomalies, they are fertile. XY female wood lemmings probably possess a gene on the X chromosome which suppresses the male-determining effects of the Y chromosome (Ohno, 1976). They were discovered by Fredge and his colleagues in 1976 and appear to represent a mechanism, unique in mammals, for producing surplus females. The germ cells of XY females all contain X chromosomes, so that for the purposes of reproducing they are identical to XX females. All the offspring produced by a mating between a male and an XY female are female, since all the XY offspring will contain the Y-suppressing gene.

The testicular feminizing syndrome is a clinical condition which causes feminization in the human genetic male, but it does not suppress the effects of the Y chromosome, as occurs in the remarkable case of the wood lemming. Instead, the Y chromosome proceeds to differentiate the testis normally and it produces testosterone, but this has no effect on any of its usual target organs (Mittwoch, 1973; Simpson, 1976). Since most male differentiation results from testosterone action, no male differentiation can occur, and the resulting individuals develop into women. There are, however, some differences from normal female development: in particular, testes are present, although they remain inside the body and produce no sperm. There is also no uterus, since its development has been suppressed by the Mullerian-inhibiting substance secreted by the foetal testis (Mittwoch, 1973). Externally, the only difference from the typical female body lies in the absence of pubic and axilla hair growth, since these are normally controlled by the action of androgens.

Just as a lack of androgenic action feminizes genetic males, so the presence of androgenic action during development can masculinize a genetic female. The adrenogenital syndrome (AGS) is a genetically transmitted condition involving a deficiency of various enzymes necessary for the synthesis of adrenal hormones, and it indirectly leads to the accumulation of large quantities of androgenic substances during foetal development. These produce masculinization of females, the extent of which can be partial or extensive; thus the genital appearance at birth may be typically female with a small degree of clitoral enlargement, or it may appear to be completely male.

In the late 1950s, similar masculinizing effects were reported in the female babies born to mothers who had been treated with synthetic progestogens given to help prevent possible miscarriages (Simpson, 1976). These substances evidently had an additional androgenic effect which had not been realized at the time.

Occasionally a human being develops into a true hermaphrodite, with ambiguous external genitals and both testes and ovaries. Genetically, a hermaphrodite may be XX or XY or have cells of both types, but the developmental origin of the condition is unknown (Simpson, 1976).

These various abnormalities illustrate the complex and precarious nature of the developmental process, and show that the apparent inevitability of the division into physically distinct sexes is one which we take for granted all too often.

Variations in Normal Development. Individual differences in secondary sexual characteristics are well recognized and have been remarked upon since Old Testament times: thus Jacob said to his mother Rebekah, 'Behold, Esau my brother is a hairy man, and I am a smooth man.' The modern counterparts of Esau and Jacob can readily be observed wherever the male body is on view.

Some women may show a relatively marked degree of hair growth, particularly on their legs, arms and face, whereas others have relatively little body hair. But it is more difficult to observe differences in body-hair growth in women than in men (at least in Western societies), since there are social pressures for them to remove all traces of body hair except their pubic hair. Young women may be made anxious about very normal growths by commercial interests marketing hair-removing products, and by women's magazines portraying idealized versions of feminine beauty. Normal variations in development are labelled as unfeminine according to culturally defined norms, which seek to deny or minimize the natural results of the developmental process.

Secondary sexual characteristics develop as a result of the action of testosterone or oestrogen at puberty. There are several possible sources of variability in these characteristics: differences in the sensitivity of the body to hormones, different levels of sex hormones, the overlap of sex hormones in the two sexes, and non-hormonal influences.

Considering the first of these, it is known that individual differences in the sexual behaviour of male rats – which is controlled by testosterone – depend not on differences in testosterone levels but on differing sensitivities to the hormone (Gray and Drewett, 1977). The extreme case of total lack of sensitivity to testosterone – in all parts of the body and at all ages – occurs in the human testicular feminizing syndrome, discussed in the previous section, where the body develops as a female. More subtle variations in sensitivity to androgens could account for some individual differences in body-hair growth in both men and women.

Secondly, the levels of the sex hormones themselves may vary in different people, during both prenatal development and adulthood. Resko (1975) reported a wide range of individual differences in the levels of testosterone found during foetal development in male rhesus monkeys, and he suggested that these differences might produce different degrees of 'masculinization' of the developing brain. A wide range of variation has been found in the testosterone levels of adult men, both between individuals and within one individual at different times (for example, Doering *et al.*, 1974). Body-hair growth is known to be directly related to testosterone levels in young men (Tanner, 1970), so that differences in testosterone secretion are presumably an important cause of the variation in body-hair growth between different men.

Individual differences in sex hormone levels may result from processes largely controlled by a person's genetic make-up. But the environment can also exert important influences on hormone secretion. For example, emotional stress causes marked reductions in the levels of both male and female hormones in human beings and other mammals (Archer, 1979), and in several species of mammal the male responds to the presence of a sexually receptive female with a rise in testosterone secretion (for example, Purvis and Haynes, 1974; Katongole *et al.*, 1971). Measurements carried out on a human male subject also showed that testosterone levels increased during and immediately after intercourse (Fox *et al.*, 1972).

There are, therefore, several possible sources of variation in an individual's sex hormone levels, and some of these may affect bodily characteristics. Indeed there is a remarkable paper, by a male research worker about to leave a remote island, claiming that his beard growth was enhanced by the anticipation of future sexual activity (Anon., 1970). However, although secondary sexual characteristics result largely from hormonal action, they are also affected by other bodily processes: for instance, breast development in both men and women is affected by the total amount of body fat.

Sex hormones also affect physiological processes involved in skeletal growth, muscle development and fat deposition. They are important causes of the greater average height and muscular development of men, and of the more rounded physique of women, although there are many other influences at work here too. However, these features do show more variation within each sex, and more overlap between the sexes, than is the case for secondary sexual characteristics.

We have shown some of the reasons why the sexes overlap in terms of physical characteristics, different degrees of overlap being apparent in different cases. We have also given one example of an attempt to minimize this degree of overlap – the removal of body hair by women.

The Social Meaning of Physical Sex Differences

So far, we have discussed physical sex differences in terms of their evolutionary origins and individual development. But, as we have also indicated, physical sex differences have a significance and meaning in human social life in addition to their interest for the biologist. Social traditions tend to use biological features as instruments of culture (Sahlins, 1977). Gender – the social distinction – involves the elaboration and evaluation of physical sex differences.

There are many ways in which this occurs. For example, physical sex differences provide signals on which to base social distinctions at crucial times in a person's life history – the initial distinction between boy and girl is based on the appearance of the genitals at birth. They provide a rationale for far-reaching differences in social roles between the two genders – for instance, the average differences in size and strength are used as reasons for restricting the entry of women into physically demanding and dangerous occupations. Physical sex differences are also important elements of physical attractiveness and will again be subject to cultural selection and modification, such as their exaggeration by clothes and make-up.

Physical sex differences have important social functions quite unrelated to their original biological function. For example, at birth the human genitals provide the crucial signal for deciding which of two very different life experiences the child will be exposed to, as a boy or a girl (see Chapter 9). The importance of this initial signal is perhaps only realized when one considers the anxiety and distress caused to parents if a baby is born with ambiguous genitals. Money and Ehrhardt (1972) report that 'parents whose minds are in doubt about their baby's authentic sex tend to monitor the child's behaviour with super-vigilance, *looking vainly for signs to resolve their doubt*' (our italics). Until they find such a sign, the parents will not be sure whether to reward traditionally masculine or feminine behaviour, something that is taken for granted with a normal baby.

The physical characteristics produced at puberty are less important for discriminating between the two genders, since this distinction has generally been established once and for all at birth. But they do provide social signals which indicate the completion of male and female physical development. The responses to such signals vary in different cultures: for instance, menarche, the onset of menstruation, may in one culture be used to signify in a positive way the onset of womanhood, whereas in another it may be regarded as private and shameful, and be used to transmit more negative ideas (Sherman, 1971; Birke and Best, 1980).

In modern Western society, most girls know what to expect at menarche, although earlier studies in the United States showed a considerable proportion of girls to be unprepared for menstruation, especially in working-class samples (Sherman, 1971). Although menarche is essentially private in our society, it is often taken to indicate that the girl should have outgrown tomboyish activities of childhood and should begin to act like a woman. In the novel *Kinflicks* by Lisa Alther (1977), the heroine is still a keen football player at the age of thirteen, and her first menstrual period takes her by surprise: 'So unprepared was I for this deluge that I assumed that I had dislodged some vital organ during football practice the previous afternoon.' After embarrassed reassurance that what had happened was indeed normal, her mother adds, 'No more football. You're a young woman now.'

The outward signs of puberty appear more gradually in boys. To define a single point as indicating the attainment of manhood requires much more arbitrary or culturally variable signals, and it is often based on undergoing an initiation ceremony at a particular age rather than on physical development.

A further social use of physical sex differences is to provide a rationale for justifying the different roles of men and women. For example, the greater average size and strength of men is commonly used to justify the restriction of many physically demanding and dangerous occupations and sports activities to men. Thus men predominate in active roles in the army, police and fire services, undertake heavy work in the construction industry, handle heavy lorries and farm tractors; and athletic and sports activities, especially those requiring speed, strength and stamina, have traditionally been the domain of men. Do physical differences between the sexes necessitate the exclusion of women from these activities, or do the physical differences merely provide a convenient justification for our social customs?

On average, men possess a number of physical advantages that potentially enable them to perform better than women in sports in which speed, strength or stamina are important. Men generally are larger, stronger and more muscular than women; they can also carry higher concentrations of oxygen in their blood and are better equipped to deal with the waste products of physical exertion. These are only average differences, however, and, with the exception of height, are all characteristics which can be improved by appropriate training. The argument that because men are *on average* better equipped physically for energetic sports, such sports should be totally reserved for men, ignores both the variable overlapping distribution of physical abilities in men and women, and the potential for improvement as a result of training. The discouragement of women from taking part in traditional sports, at least as serious competitors, would seem to derive mainly from cultural rather than physical considerations, although the latter are often cited as justifications for excluding women from particular sports. In the earlier part of this century, women were not regarded as being at all suited for strenuous athletic events. The first women's races were introduced into the athletic programme of the Olympic Games in 1928 (Keating, 1978), but middle-distance races were regarded as too exhausting for women until comparatively recently, and there are at the time of writing no long-distance races for women in major international athletics competitions.

Various reasons have been given for discouraging or preventing women from participating in sports, and sex differences in physical abilities are only one of these. At one time appeals were made to what seemed to be the natural order: in a Badminton magazine of seventy years ago, women were advised to 'leave the rough outdoor pastimes to those for whom they are naturally intended – men' (Keating, 1978). The same sentiments may still be voiced, but they are now taken less seriously and have been supplanted by the more culturally based, though equally powerful, belief that sports achievements are incompatible with culturally defined femininity. Thus it is regarded as 'undignified' for women to wrestle or box or run in long, exhausting races. Research on attitudes to sport in school children by Anita White, an England hockey captain, showed that most girls ceased fairly abruptly to be interested in sports achievement after they had reached adolescence, at which time sports achievement was viewed as being incompatible with the feminine role (*Sunday Times*, 24 August 1977). By discouraging women from engaging in sports activities, such cultural pressures accentuate the average sex differences in physical abilities, so that the actual differences in sports performances become much larger.

In a rather different way, sex differences in reproductive function are used as the basis for wider differences in social roles. The most obvious of these is the child-care role of women, which is based on the mammalian method of reproduction, in which the female bears and suckles the offspring. We suggest that the mammalian method of reproduction has not so much dictated women's exclusive child-care role as provided the necessary conditions which have resulted in this role being adopted in most human cultures. As a result, women have generally been excluded from other activities, particularly those concerned with public power and status (Rosaldo and Lamphere, 1974; Rosenblatt and Cunningham, 1976).

Our last example of the cultural use of physical sex differences is sexual attractiveness. There are many ways in which a culture can minimize or emphasize sexually attractive bodily features. Our culture in particular emphasizes the physically attractive features of young women – in fact they are used to market almost any type of wide-selling product. Clothes, padding and cosmetics can be used to accentuate physical sex differences, and this is again a notable occurrence in modern Western society compared, for example, with a country such as China. The sex difference in body-hair growth is accentuated by women removing hair from under their arms and from their legs, and differences in complexion are heightened by make-up. The rounded female figure may be accentuated by tight-fitting jeans in younger women, and may be maintained by foundation garments in older women. Women's breasts are made higher and more prominent by a bra, and padded bras are available for making the breasts look larger.

Although the less adorned sex, men have by no means escaped such devices. Height is an important feature for sexual attractiveness in men, and small stature is often a cause of great anxiety. Shoes with built-up soles are marketed with this problem in mind. Emphasis on a muscular physique being attractive to women has diminished in recent years, so that even the old 'Charles Atlas' advertisements now emphasize health and fitness rather than the female admiration of bulging muscles. Men's jackets have traditionally contained padded shoulders, which are an attempt to simulate a more broad-shouldered muscular appearance, an emphasis which is less apparent in more modern jackets.

With the advent of tight trousers and jeans, some men have even tried to accentuate the bulge produced by the male genitals. Elvis Presley is reputed to have had his own way of doing this, but there are now commercially made appliances available. Reputable newspapers may contain advertisements such as this one: 'Fantastic padded pouches! Padded and moulded to add to your masculine outline under tight jeans . . . no one will know your secret!' (*Sunday Times*, 15 January 1978).

In conclusion, there are a number of different ways in which physical sex differences assume cultural as well as biological importance. In other words, they become used, modified and often accentuated as part of our ideas about the real and ideal attributes of the two gender groups. We have concentrated on examples from contemporary Western society, but there are of course other examples available in other cultures.

CHAPTER 4

Sexuality: Psychophysiology, Psychoanalysis and Sociology

We began our detailed examination of sex and gender in Chapter 3 by asking how and why sex evolved. In this chapter we consider the human sexual experience from three different perspectives: those of psychophysiology, psychoanalysis and sociology.

We use the awkward term psychophysiology to denote those classic modern studies of Masters and Johnson and of Kinsey, which aim to provide antiseptic, empirical descriptions of adult sexual behaviour. They seek answers to questions such as 'What are the measurable physiological correlates of orgasm?' and 'In what circumstances do people find sexual satisfaction?'

In examining the psychoanalytic approach, we move from the readily observable world of physiology and conscious experience to explore the meaning of sexual experience in the remote inner world of the unconscious. Here we seek answers to different sorts of questions. We pursue the origins of adult sexual satisfaction in early childhood experiences, and ask how the child's recognition of anatomical sex differences influences adult personality.

In the final section we consider the use of sexuality in defining social roles and the influence of social values on sexuality. To gain a perspective on our own society's definitions of the roles of men and women, we consider the Omani solution. In this closed and traditional Islamic society a third gender role, that of the male transsexual, is important in maintaining the highly contrastive roles of male and female. The Omani acceptance of transsexual behaviour contrasts with our society's treatment of deviance.

The three approaches differ in their modes of study and in the data which they seek to explain. The objective methods of Masters and Johnson provide precise physiological descriptions of sexuality, but they ignore the deeper levels of meaning pursued by psychoanalysis. While the unconscious bears the marks of an ordinary understanding of anatomical sex differences, it interprets them in ways which are not available to commonsense. Whatever its elaborations and complexities, the unconscious is influenced by culture. The discussion of the three Omani gender roles provides a contrast with our own society, which forces us to reconsider our role system based only on male and female roles and to consider sexual alternatives beyond those of adult hetero-sexuality.

The Psychophysiological Measurement of Sexual Behaviour

The studies of Masters and Johnson attracted considerable publicity when they appeared in the 1960s, but public attitudes towards the study of human sexuality had already begun to change with publication of the Kinsey reports more than a decade earlier. Scholarly interest in sexuality is not a twentieth-century creation, but our inheritance of a Victorian morality made even the scientific study of human sexuality controversial and long delayed. Ancient Chinese physicians writing within the Taoist tradition carried out careful observations and offered advice which enabled both women and men to achieve great sexual satisfaction (Chang, 1977). The Talmud, one of the major sources of Jewish scholarship, contains detailed instructions concerning not only sexual satisfaction but also contraception. Love, like food, was con-sidered an important aspect of life.

When it was initially reviewed by the comparative psychologist Frank Beach (1966), the work of Masters and Johnson was compared with the fundamental studies of the digestive system undertaken a century earlier. The delay in studying sexual functioning reflected repressive social attitudes and not a lack of scientific technology. Neither the physiology nor the behavioural aspects of human sexuality were con-sidered suitable for open discussion or even for dispassionate, objective, scientific study. Here we can only discuss highlights of Masters and Johnson's research. Interested readers can pursue further details in their two major works, *Human Sexual Response* (1966) and *Human Sexual Inadequacy* (1970), or in accounts which appear in textbooks on sexuality (for example, Katchadourian and Lunde, 1975).

The Human Orgasm

The four-stage description of the sexual response which Masters and Johnson provide emphasizes similarities rather than differences between men and women and is based upon their observations of 10,000 orgasms, or sexual cycles as Masters and Johnson labelled them. Of these, three quarters were the sexual cycles of women, but this still leaves a sizeable number, 2,500, of observations of men's orgasmic behaviour. Their aim was to provide sound physiological information about sexuality and to dispel myths about women and men which had been maintained through ignorance. In addition to orgasms achieved through heterosexual intercourse in one of three positions, satisfaction by self-stimulation was studied; they also observed women's use of a plastic phallus and in a few cases stimulation of the breasts leading to orgasm. The artificial phallus contained photographic equipment which recorded, for the first time, the internal changes in women which accompany arousal and gratification.

The four-stage description of orgasm applies both to women and to men (see Table 4.1). It is independent of the nature of the sexual activity, autoerotic or heterosexual, as well as the source of stimulation, tactile or psychological. The activities of the sex organs differ according to their anatomical structures, but the mechanisms of arousal are similar: they are vascocongestion and myotonia. The first describes

Table 4.1. Bodily Changes during the Sexual Response

FEMALE	MALE
	Excitement phase
Consistent nipple erection	30% nipple erection
25% sex tension flush	
	Plateau phase
75% sex tension flush	25% sex tension flush
Tension in hands and feet	Tension in hands and feet
Generalized muscular tension	Generalized muscular tension
Hyperventilation	Hyperventilation
Rapid heartbeat (100–160 per minute)	Rapid heartbeat (100–160 per minute)
	Orgasmic phase
Specific muscle contractions	Specific muscle contractions
Hyperventilation	Hyperventilation
Rapid heartbeat (110–180 per minute)	Rapid heartbeat (100–180 per minute)
	Resolution phase
30–40% sweating reaction	30–40% sweating reaction
Hyperventilation	Hyperventilation
Decreasing heartbeat (150–80 per minute)	Decreasing heartbeat (150–80 per minute)

Based on Katchadourian and Lunde (1975).

the filling of the pelvic area with an increased blood and fluid supply, and the second refers to a general and widespread increase in muscle tension.

There are variations in the sources of stimulation which trigger the excitement phase, in its length and in whether tension will increase to reach the plateau phase or dissipate. The vagina rapidly produces a lubricant, the clitoris swells, the cervix and uterus move upwards. One feminist writer and physician (Sherfey, 1973) compares the production of the vaginal fluid in the excitement phase to the rapid appearance of the penile erection. Viewed in this way, both sexes have available observable evidence of sexual arousal.

In the plateau phase there are further changes in both sexes due to vascocongestion. The tip of the penis may increase in size and deepen in colour, and the outer passageway of the vagina narrows. These changes are specific to the structure of each sex. Unlike the erect penis, the erect clitoris tends to disappear into its hood.

The contractions of the orgasmic phase initially occur with a frequency of 1 per 0·8 seconds in both sexes, though only males experience ejaculation. The rate slows down after 5 to 12 contractions in women but after only 3 to 4 in men. Once the orgasmic phase is reached, these responses become involuntary.

In the resolution phase following orgasm, congestion gradually disappears and muscles relax. While women in the resolution phase may react to further stimulation and experience additional orgasms, men experience a refractory period of at least some minutes during which another erection cannot be achieved whatever the nature of the stimulation. The multiple orgasms which Masters and Johnson observed appeared to be identical to earlier ones and were often described by women as feeling more intense.

Masters and Johnson's work drew attention to similarities in the physiological experiences of the sexes. Now, more than a decade after their research first came to popular notice, we all recognize these similarities and may tend to forget that they provided an innovatory perspective. Technical criticism about their description – for example, that it is difficult to separate the excitation and plateau stages – throws no doubt on their major conclusion that functionally men and women experience sexual satisfaction in a similar manner though anatomically they differ.

In addition, there are two other myths which this research programme dispelled. Masters and Johnson put forward the idea of a single orgasmic mechanism in women. As we shall see in the next section, the Freudian view of mature female sexuality places considerable emphasis on the vagina as a source of satisfaction distinct from the clitoris. Their evidence shows that the clitoris not only receives stimulation but is also crucial in transmitting feelings of arousal. The vagina, on the other hand, is relatively lacking in nerve endings and is relatively insensitive.

Another Victorian myth which Masters and Johnson helped to dispel was the notion that morally correct women endured sexual relations whereas only 'fallen' women enjoyed them. In fact, in their early studies observing intercourse with prostitutes they rarely witnessed orgasm. Ordinary women having sexual relations with their regular partners provided the bulk of their evidence of orgasmic behaviour.

Before considering women's and men's reports of their sexual experiences, let us examine some differences which Masters and Johnson reported. Along many dimensions there is considerable overlap in the behaviour of women and men, but men are generally more variable than women in achieving orgasm. Frequency of orgasm over a lifetime is an exception, and here women are more variable. If we think of this dimension as running from never at one end to a very great number at one time at the other end, we find women spread fairly evenly along it. Many women, though perhaps not as many as was thought fifty years ago, have never experienced orgasm. At the other end there are a number of women who experience multiple orgasms, and their rate cannot be matched even by very young men.

The men observed by Masters and Johnson achieved fewer orgasms at any one time and experienced more failures than women. Although three times as many female cycles were observed, only 118 failures to achieve orgasms were recorded for women. In 2,500 male cycles there were 220 failures. Before rushing to conclusions about the sexual natures of women and men, we should note that all participants were volunteers capable of achieving orgasm. Perhaps only women who were particularly sure of their performance offered to participate in the study.

Sherfey (1973), who has drawn heavily on Masters and Johnson's work, argues that the female has an almost limitless capacity for sexual pleasure and would no doubt disagree with our cautious interpretation. In her view, female sexuality is physiologically constituted to outdistance the male, and has been held in check only by the rise of civilization and by male oppression of women in the pursuit of private property and individual ownership. Here we have a view of female sexuality which is the complete opposite of the Victorian ideal. 'Natural' woman is seen as more highly motivated to achieve sexual satisfaction than 'natural' man.

Sources of Sexual Satisfaction

The classic studies of Kinsey, which provide evidence of a cultural patterning of sexuality, give little support to Sherfey's view: men reported achieving far more orgasms. The Kinsey studies provide a new dimension. We have concentrated primarily on the mechanisms or physiology of the sexual response. Kinsey and his colleagues (1948, 1953) examined the array of arousing events and behaviour which leads to orgasm and the conscious factors which affect the experience of sexual satisfaction.

Their first book, *Sexual Behavior in the Human Male* (1948), was based on interviews with 5,300 American men, mostly white. A similar report based on interviews with 5,940 American women was published in 1953. The description of male orgasms as 'sexual outlets' has a quaint ring today, but Kinsey's findings belong to the contemporary scene more than to the Victorian notions of sexual behaviour which they explicitly challenged. Although the Kinsey reports describe men as sexually more active than women, they present no major challenge to the conclusions drawn later by Masters and Johnson. Indeed, the Kinsey data on multiple orgasms in women, which were initially received with scepticism, were buttressed by the later studies.

The array of activities which lead to orgasm were divided by Kinsey into six major categories, roughly equivalent for women and men. These are masturbation, nocturnal sex dreams (or emissions for men), heterosexual petting, heterosexual intercourse, homosexual relations and intercourse with animals of other species. Although slightly more women than men were interviewed, it was men who reported more orgasms. Nonetheless, Kinsey maintained, as did Masters and Johnson later, that physiologically the orgasmic potential and response of the sexes were similar. Let us look at a few aspects of the behaviour of men and women before comparing them.

We begin with the first book, which reported the sexual behaviour of men. Kinsey found very clear effects of age and social class on the sexual behaviour of men. An older commonsense view recognized that men experienced fewer orgasms as they got older, but it was generally assumed that men reached their peak of orgasmic frequency somewhere in their twenties and only began to experience a decline in their forties. A very different picture emerged in terms of the number of sexual outlets per week recorded by Kinsey. On average, males were shown to reach a peak in adolescence, and a decline from this early peak was observable by the late twenties. Kinsey showed that sexual behaviour often continued into the seventies and eighties.

Kinsey used education as a major indicator of social class. Although he sometimes employed a tripartite system, separating those who had attended primary school only, secondary school, and finally college or university, he often grouped together those of primary and secondary education and compared them with people who had had further education. This system is difficult to apply to British society, where until quite recently very few people went on to university. Kinsey's upper level might best be thought of as the professional classes. Kinsey found that lower-level men reported the majority of their outlets in genital intercourse – premarital, marital or extramarital, with prostitutes or in homosexual relations. His upper-level sample reported far more masturbation, petting to orgasm or nocturnal emissions. The upper-level men grew less faithful the longer they were married, while lower-level men showed a reverse pattern.

No doubt one of the most widely discussed findings of the report on male sexual behaviour was the statistic showing that 37 per cent of men had at one time or another engaged in homosexual behaviour. The form in which this result was reported reflects Kinsey's views on the nature of homosexuality. He believed that it was incorrect to describe an individual as either homosexual or not in an all-or-nothing fashion. Instead, he devised a seven-point scale which ran from zero to six. Individuals who reported never having achieved sexual gratification with persons of their own sex scored zero, and those of exclusively homosexual experience scored six. A great many individuals were to be found at points in between. His definition of homosexuality is problematic. We return to it in our discussion of the social definition of gender and its relation to sexuality.

In his report on women Kinsey noted less clear-cut evidence for the effects of social class and age. The only activity affected by class was extramarital intercourse, which echoed for females the class-determined patterns of infidelity first described for males. A greater incidence of homosexual relations was reported by upper-level than by lower-level women. The effects of age were different and more gradual. Women slowly built up to a peak of orgasmic frequency, which generally occurred in their late twenties and early thirties. It was maintained until their fifties, and only then did it show a gradual decline.

Religion, which had had a negligible effect on men's sexual behaviour, emerged as the most important factor influencing satisfaction for women. Women who described themselves as religious achieved fewer orgasms in any circumstances; in particular, they were less likely to achieve orgasm in heterosexual intercourse. Historical factors, such as date of birth and cultural attitudes influencing socialization, also affected female sexuality. Women born after 1900 reported more orgasms in all contexts. We could say that women were breaking free of the constraints of Victorian values.

Since much of the second volume is concerned with comparisons of women and men, we can only sample the differences between the sexes reported by Kinsey. There are fascinating behavioural differences, such as the female peak of outlets through nocturnal dreams in their forties compared to the male peak in the late teens, and the more pronounced decline in masturbation as a source of satisfaction after marriage for men than for women. But one of the most interesting contrasts is Kinsey's own formulation of the differing natures of female and male sexuality. He saw female sexuality as being based on physical stimulation, while he ascribed the frequency and regularity of male gratification to men's susceptibility to psychological stimulation. Though he was careful to avoid an explanation in physiological terms, Kinsey believed that men were more easily conditioned and thus became susceptible to a variety of psychological stimuli. This view of the differential effects of learning, which presumably accounted for the sharp class differences in male behaviour, overlooked the equally plausible hypothesis that women too were conditionable but that they had been conditioned not to respond with sexual arousal in the same situations which men found stimulating.

Reporting Physiological Arousal

A recent study of university students provides a partial test of the Kinsey hypothesis. These students would be described as sophisticated in terms of the older Kinsey data in that almost 80 per cent of them had had intercourse and 84 per cent of the women reported experiencing orgasm. Heiman (1975) used recently developed devices which recorded vaginal and penile pulse and blood pressure to measure the students' physiological arousal while they were listening to four different kinds of stories.

One group heard romantic stories and another erotic tales. In addition to a control group who heard neither erotic nor romantic stories, a fourth group listened to a mixture of the two. Each student participated in two sessions. With few exceptions, only students listening to erotic or mixed erotic and romantic stories showed evidence of arousal. Women found the stories in which women were the initiators and the main focus the most arousing. Men showed similar but less marked preference for this type of story. The next most arousing story for both sexes featured a male initiator and focused on the female. In physiological terms – that is, pulse rate and blood pressure – it appeared that there was little difference in women's and men's physiological arousal reactions.

Heiman also examined a related question, the recognition of physiological arousal by the two sexes. The students were asked to report any general arousal, specific genital arousal such as erection or lubrication, or more diffuse genital arousal. These self-reports were then compared with the physiological measures. By and large, women were not as accurate as men in reporting their own arousal. It is interesting to note that there were more errors made by those women who experienced arousal to non-erotic stimuli – that is, romantic stories or control stories. It would seem that more sophisticated women may experience and recognize physiological arousal in exciting situations, but they are less willing, perhaps even unable, to report arousal when the nature of the stimulus fails to provide socially accepted support for their sexual feelings. These results suggest that Kinsey's findings may reflect differences in women's and men's reports of their sexual arousal and not in their physiological response to particular stimuli.

Current Reports of Sexual Experience

The Kinsey reports reflect the social attitudes of the 1940s in their use of the term 'sexual outlets' to describe orgasms. *The Hite Report* (1976) is also a product of its time. This book, based on the questionnaire responses provided by 3,000 American women volunteers, contains vivid verbatim accounts of women's masturbation, their feelings at orgasm and their evaluation of various aspects of their sexuality. The promised sequel on male sexuality had not appeared while we were writing, so our account is restricted to women's views of sexuality.

A unifying theme of the various chapters of *The Hite Report* is the assertion of a female potential for sexual satisfaction equal to, if not actually greater than, that of the male. It is possible, of course, that women who hold such views are more likely to volunteer to complete questionnaires about sexuality. The work of Masters and Johnson and the speculations of Sherfey are quoted to support the claim of greater female potential. Rather than looking at *The Hite Report* in detail, we shall examine data provided by 10,000 British women who replied to a questionnaire which *Woman's Own* published in their attempt to assess the applicability of the American findings to the English scene.

These two volunteer samples differ in many ways. The women who sent their replies to *Woman's Own* appear to be rather more inhibited than Hite's American respondents. One example is the woman who ridiculed her own liberation by noting that she found it impossible to show her completed questionnaire to her husband. Another example is age: the American sample ranged from fourteen to seventy-eight years, but the majority of *Woman's Own* replies were from women under thirty who reported frequencies of intercourse at two or three times a week. Over half felt this sufficient, but many voiced their dissatisfaction. At least among younger British women, sexuality appears alive if not completely well. Just over half of the women regularly experienced orgasm in intercourse, but the others admitted to faking it to please their partners or reported feeling dissatisfied.

There are differences too in attitudes towards masturbation. American women may discuss masturbation very explicitly, but the English sample is much more reticent. While 36 per cent said they never masturbated and just over half that they did, the rest simply failed to answer. This semi-public study on a different population sampled by very different techniques still manages to convey a sense of active female sexuality, though it lacks the explicitness of *The Hite Report*. There have been many studies of the conscious experience of sexuality, but we now turn instead to consider explanations of sexuality which speculate about its representation at an unconscious level.

Psychoanalytic Explanations of Sexuality

In considering psychoanalytic explanations of sexuality, we begin by moving back in time as well as altering the level of our attention. By 1905, when Freud first published the classic *Three Essays on the Theory of Sexuality*, he had developed a revolutionary view of the nature of

human sexuality. His theory derived primarily from his clinical experience with psychologically distressed, mainly neurotic, patients and not
from physiological measurements or reports of normal sexual behaviour. To appreciate Freud's view of the inner world, it is necessary
to begin by examining his approach to mental functioning and the
unconscious. We then move on to examine the sources of adult genital
sexuality in infant experiences.

The Unconscious

It is essential to appreciate Freud's theory of mental functioning and
the role of the unconscious in order to understand the *Essays* and the
psychoanalytic view of sexuality. The academic psychology of Freud's
day was a psychology of conscious experience, which was considered
accessible to trained introspective reflection. Normal individuals were
viewed as rational and their thought was believed to obey the rules of
logic. Freud found his way to the unconscious through attempting to
understand the symptoms, fantasies and dreams of his patients.

Most of us recognize conscious thought and would not quarrel with
Freud's view of it as obeying the laws of logic, or secondary process.
Primary process, or unconscious mental functioning, is not readily
accessible or acceptable. A couple of concrete examples should bring
the unconscious into focus. First, let us imagine a hypnotist telling
the person he has put into a trance that when the person wakes up he
will feel thirsty and ask for a cup of tea, though he will have no memory
of the suggestion. The subject wakes and asks for a cup of tea. Though
the suggestion seems forgotten, conscious thought has been modified
by the lingering suggestion. A more homely example is the common
experience when our own unconscious plays tricks – we wish to intro-
duce someone we know to another friend but for the moment the name
is gone, lost in our unconscious or, technically more correct, in our
preconscious. In order to understand the meaning of symptoms and
fantasies Freud set about studying the mental functions of the unconscious, which he found were determined neither by reality, time,
order, morality, nor by the rules of logic. Initially, Freud regarded
dreams as providing special access to these processes; later, the interpersonal relations established during therapy were used to understand
the role of the unconscious in action and experience.

This discussion of sexuality starts with consideration of the unconscious because its crucial role in all mental functioning is often

overlooked by those who attack the psychoanalytic interpretation of sex differences. As Juliet Mitchell (1974) notes, it is by applying only the rules of logic rather than those of the unconscious that many feminist critics distort the theory and find it wanting.

Unless we believe that the infant is born rational, with knowledge of the world, the unconscious and its functions must be seen as primary in the infant. Essentially, the infant is viewed as hedonistic, seeking satisfaction and withdrawing from 'unpleasure' as these are experienced in his or her inner world. Primary processes lead the hungry infant to hallucinate the experience of feeding if the feed fails to arrive when the need is felt. But the hallucination does not satisfy the biological hunger and slowly, out of such failures to find pleasure or escape from unpleasure, the infant begins to recognize the outer world, or reality. In the structural theory, Freud (1923) described the agency which dealt with reality as the ego and that arising from the drives or instincts as the id. Even after the reality principle and the ego are well established, they do not replace the pleasure principle and the id. Feelings and thoughts which are unacceptable to the world of reality, to the ego, do not disappear but are pushed into the unconscious, or repressed, and seek expression in forms unrecognizable to the ego, disguised by the processes of unconscious thought. The dynamic quality of mental life reflects the tension between the ego and repressed feelings and thoughts. It is with this inner world of the unconscious and the id that Freud's explanation of the sexual experience begins.

Psychosexual Development

Freud sought an understanding of adult sexuality in the earliest experiences of the infant. This does not imply that he believed inter-personal, object-oriented (that is, person-oriented), genital sexuality was present in infancy. Rather he considered that the mature hetero-sexual response, whose measurement we examined in the first section, had motivational origins in early sensual experiences. This view of infantile sexuality was unconventional and led to Freud's censure by his medical colleagues, but his work with his patients and their emotional problems guided his theorizing. From his female patients he heard tales of childhood seduction and rape by their fathers; although he initially believed their accounts to be true, he gradually came to view them as fantasies expressing repressed sexual wishes. In neurosis Freud observed the repression of infantile sexual wishes, but in the 'perversions' – sado-masochistic practices, fetishism and homosexuality – Freud believed that he could discern the direct expression of infantile sexuality. In order to understand these far-reaching conclusions to which Freud was led by his clinical experiences, we must examine the nature of this 'polymorphously perverse' infantile sexuality and follow the developmental path which results in adult heterosexuality.

We begin by considering the classic Freudian theory of infantile sexuality and its development, noting in particular similarities and differences in the routes taken by women and men. The theory itself has a developmental history, and we consider some of the changes which have been introduced in the last seventy-five years as the result both of further clinical investigations and of observations of children.

Our account of Freud's use of the term instinct is as concise and incomplete as our statements about mental functioning and the structures of personality. Freud viewed instinct as a concept on the border-line between biology and psychology. Unlike the external stimuli which release reflexes, instincts have their source in the human body, and this makes withdrawal an impractical method for dealing with them. The component sexual instincts have sources of excitation in the erotogenic zones of the lips, mouth and anus as well as in the genitals. Initially they function independently, only becoming organized as adult libido in the course of development. The sexual instincts are the mental representations or symbols of these bodily excitations. The strength of the instinct is determined both by its bodily origins and by its role in the individual's psychological system. The aim of the instinct is satisfaction and, in Freud's system, the reduction of tension. A moment's reflection on the number of ways in which human beings gain sexual satisfaction tells us that sexual aims are achieved through a great variety of objects, both material and interpersonal. It was in infantile sexuality that Freud sought an explanation for this diversity of sexual aims and objects.

Human sexuality is markedly different from that of other animals. Not only are we flexible in terms of aims and objects, but the human female lacks the extreme periodicity of most other mammals. As we noted in Chapter 3, women are sexually receptive throughout most of their adult lives. Freud (1940) drew attention to another difference which he held to be of major significance for psychological development – the latency period. Freud believed that our species experiences a unique sexual moratorium which even the most closely related primates lack; our closest animal relations reach sexual maturity at about five years of age. During the latency period, after the age of five or six, the urgency of sexual interests normally abates and the child's attention can be deployed in other pursuits. The bodily changes which occur at puberty reawaken sexual interest, and with development sexuality reaches its adult genital form.

Freud's earliest descriptions of infantile sexuality reflected his pre-occupation with the essentially bisexual nature of human beings. His study of embryology made him aware of the early parallel development of male and female internal organs. In the original formulations of the oral, anal and phallic stages, Freud (1905) drew no distinctions between the development of girls and boys. The acts of feeding, defecating and urinating, from which each of the component sexual instincts arose, were undifferentiated by sex. In both girls and boys the aim of the oral instinct was sucking, and later biting, and the normal object was the breast. In the anal stage the aim was either expulsion or retention, and the appropriate object was the stool, or faeces. Even the phallic stage was seen as similar: girls, Freud believed, had not yet discovered the vagina and both girls and boys viewed the mother as phallic. The clitoris was held to function as a small penis and was the source of erotic feelings. The aim of phallic fantasies for both boys and girls was penetration. He wrote: 'So far as the autoerotic and masturbatory manifestations of sexuality are concerned, we might lay it down that the sexuality of little girls is of a wholly masculine character ... The leading erotogenic zone in female children is located at the clitoris, and is thus homologous to the masculine genital zone of the glans penis' (1905).

At this point it is useful to return to the interpersonal relationships of the developing child; in focusing on the sexual instincts as they originate in the erogenous zones, we may overlook the social psychological aspects of development. In the *Three Essays* Freud expressed the view that separate male and female sexuality developed only at puberty. Focus on the love relations of the child as well as psychosexual development led to the reformulation of psychological differentiation around the child's recognition of the anatomical differences between men and women.

Freud believed that boys and girls interpreted the difference as a lack in the female. In this way the boy's love for his mother would lead to fear of his father's jealousy and retaliation through castration. In the girl's disappointment at not having a penis, she would abandon her mother who had made her this way and turn to her father, hoping to make up for her loss. In this manner the sexual instincts and love relationships within the family come together in penis envy, fear of castration and the Oedipus complex.

Further work on the Oedipus complex appeared after the original publication of the *Three Essays* and after Freud's final reformulation of his theory of instincts (1923, 1924). The life instincts, or Eros, were seen in opposition to the destructive instincts, or Thanatos. This meant not only that each individual struggled with masculine and feminine trends in the Oedipal conflict, but that for each there was both a positive erotic element and a negative destructive factor. Before we consider this additional complexity, we need to examine Freud's views of masculinity and femininity in greater detail. Freud considered the terms masculinity and femininity difficult and confusing. He delineated three different senses in which the terms were used. We have described one of these, the biological sense, in Chapter 3. In our discussion of stereotypes in Chapter 2, we examined socio-psychological attempts to quantify commonsense understanding of masculinity and femininity. The meaning of masculinity and femininity, crucial in psychoanalytic theory, refers to activity and passivity, but it is only with the development of adult sexuality that this distinction can be made and becomes meaningful for the individual.

We have already noted that in the phallic phase Freud saw both boys and girls as essentially masculine. The aim of their phallic sexuality was active and penetrating. For the boy, the active aim in the Oedipal complex remains the active penetration of the mother, but passive penetration by the father is also a possibility. To further complicate the picture, there are passive aims directed towards the unrelinquished phallic mother, or fantasy mother, and active aims directed towards the father. But typical male development continues the active aim of the phallic stage and directs it towards the female. The other possibilities are repressed and lost in the unconscious. They may return as symptoms or, when repression fails, as those adult practices which Freud labelled perversions.

For the boy, threat of castration leads to the resolution of the Oedipal conflict and the establishment of the super-ego, or moral agency. Freud saw the beginnings of sexual differentiation for the girl in her recognition of her own and her mother's imagined loss of the penis. In his later writings Freud was precise in describing the consequences of the girl's discovery of the anatomical differences. In 1925 he wrote: 'Thus the little girl's recognition of the anatomical distinction between the sexes forces her away from masculinity and masculine masturbation on to new lines which lead to the development of femininity.' For the girl, the castration complex leads to feelings of inferiority and penis envy. It was in order to regain the lost penis that the little girl turned to her father and to fantasies of replacing her mother.

The Oedipal complex for the girl is a secondary development dependent on phallic sexuality, recognition of the anatomical differences between the sexes, castration anxiety and penis envy; but it too gives rise to the super-ego, though in weaker form. Given all these preconditions, it is difficult to appreciate the sense in which Freud saw the Oedipal complex as simpler for the girl than for the boy (1924). Its resolution left the girl with a passive aim – to be penetrated – and at puberty a new source of sexual excitation – the vagina. We have already noted in the first section of this chapter the Masters and Johnson results which show that at a physiological level the clitoris and not the vagina is the main source of pleasure. Freud was describing the psychological experience of pleasure and not just its bodily source. Nonetheless, Masters and Johnson's work has been used to attack psychoanalytic views of female sexuality.

The paths leading to the resolution of the Oedipal complex are different for girls and boys, but the resolution is a major developmental landmark for all children. The incorporation of parental standards in the super-ego provide internal constraints on action. The post-Oedipal child is believed to repress the component sexual instincts – oral, anal and phallic – and is prepared at an unconscious level for sex-appropriate aims and object choices in adulthood. The earlier component instincts are now fused in a mature structure. Repression during latency frees sexual energy for other activities and the sublimated energy can find fulfilment in intellectual and artistic pursuits. Indeed, a certain amount of repression is considered essential for development in the early school years.

Freud's phallocentric theory of infantile sexuality was the target of criticism almost from its inception. Hostility arose not only from those who condemned the very idea of childhood sexuality but also from within the psychoanalytic group. Karen Horney (1924) challenged the notion of penis envy as an inevitable consequence of the girl's discovery of her genitals. Horney suggested that girls were jealous of boys' achievements in being able to urinate a greater distance, see their genitals and more easily manipulate them. She was one of the earliest critics to consider the issues of control and power and the influence of the male position in society on the formulations offered by Freud and other male psychoanalysts. Juliet Mitchell has defended Freud by arguing that he sought to explain our unconscious understanding of sexuality as it developed in a particular milieu. The influence of culture is inevitable. Only if culture and society were to change would your unconscious change too.

Freud (1931) himself was aware of many shortcomings in his account of infantile sexuality. As early as 1905 he acknowledged in the *Three Essays* that he knew more about the sexuality of boys than girls. While he retained the firm conviction that full female sexuality only developed from the castration complex, he urged his analytic colleagues to examine the pre-Oedipal period more closely. He recognized the special importance of the girl's relationship to her mother and the sources of her psychosexual identity in it.

Critics who basically accept the Freudian position on psychosexual development have revised the theory as the result of careful observations of infants. Typical of this approach is the work of Galenson and Roiphe (1977). From the observation of thirty-five baby girls and thirty-five baby boys, they report sex differences in the age of onset of, and behaviour in, genital play within the first year of life. They describe female masturbation and suggest, on the basis of preoccupation and emotional love, the existence of elements of fantasy. This evidence, together with their clinical work with children, leads them to suggest a differentiated sense of sexual identity as early as a year and a half. They also note awareness of anatomical sex differences in the second year. While accepting Freud's views about penis envy and the feminine castration complex, they see these in relation to the two-year-old's fears of the loss of love objects and anal concerns. According to Galenson and Roiphe, it is from the age of two that girls and boys follow very different paths in the psychological development of their inner worlds.

Criticisms of Freud's theory are legion, but we have chosen in the space available to concentrate on an explication of psychoanalytic theory. We conclude with some points raised by the psychoanalyst Roy Schafer (1977), as they allow us to return to the evolution of sex. We present only one of the arguments which Schafer raises in a paper examining problems in Freud's psychology of women. He asserts that in a most curious way Freud turned on his own discovery of the psychological plasticity of human sexuality in terms of its aims and objects and espoused the values of nineteenth- and early twentieth-century evolutionary biology. Accepting these, Freud also posited procreativity and heterosexual genital intercourse as the culmination of development, but he sought an explanation for this in terms of the diverse currents of infantile sexuality. Accordingly, exclusively oral or anal pleasures are considered immature and perverse, while non-procreative homosexual intercourse is labelled an inversion.

We share with Schafer his view of the irony of the situation. We owe to Freud and the insights of his clinical investigation our vision of human psychosexual development as being free from biological imperatives, yet Freud's own deep commitment to the procreative values of Western society led him to consider the outcome of psychosexual development in terms of biological necessity. His theory suggests a biologically instinctual drive towards species propagation at the same time as it points to an explanation in terms of the psychological representations of diverse sensual experiences. The structure of Freud's argument encourages neglect of questions of cultural learning and social values and instead focuses attention upon the anatomy of sex differences and hypothesized imperatives of species survival. At the very time that Freud was able to account psychologically for the allegedly natural revulsions and anxieties which the perversions arouse, he himself was trapped by the prevailing scientific and commonsense theories of his day. As we have noted in Chapter 1 and elsewhere (Archer and Lloyd, 1975), the clarity and apparent certainty of biological explanations is powerful and very seductive.

The decision to examine criticism only from within the psychoanalytic movement reflects our recognition of the impact of Freud's thinking on the understanding of sexuality in the twentieth century. In order to give full attention to its complexity, we have ignored many other critics. Those who disagree fundamentally with concepts such as the unconscious and infantile sexuality attack psychoanalytic theory, but they often fail to illumine the nature of this influential theory. Rather than examine sociological critiques of psychoanalytic theories of sexuality, we consider the use of sexuality in defining people's positions in society.

Social Uses of Sexuality

In the beginning of this chapter we approached the issue of the similarities and differences in women's and men's sexual experiences from the viewpoint of an outside observer or of a rational participant observer.

Our examination of psychoanalytic explanations introduced a new level of analysis and the inner world of feelings. We considered theories about the effects of infantile experiences in shaping men's and women's unconscious attitudes – the aims and objects of their sexual pleasure. Here we will examine the impact of sexuality on the definition of roles in society and the impact of social values on sexuality.

'Xaniths' of Oman: A Third Gender Role

We begin by looking at a report on the *Xaniths* of Oman, an Arab sultanate on the eastern side of the Arabian peninsula (Wikan, 1977). Wikan suggests that the Omani gender system can best be understood by thinking of it not in terms of the two gender roles with which we are most familiar, those of male and female, but by viewing the *Xaniths* as a third gender. After examining her ethnographic material, we consider the issue of homosexuality and its relation not only to the definition of roles in society, but also to the worlds of unconscious sexuality and of normative sexual statistics. We begin by describing the behaviour of the *Xaniths* from their own viewpoint and from that of Omani men and women, and only then do we consider their gender identity.

Wikan's analysis is aimed at elucidating sociological aspects of gender identity and so she gives little attention to questions concerning the historical or psychological origins of the *Xaniths*. *Xaniths* are biologically men. They sell themselves in passive homosexual relationships, but these transactions are not their main source of income. They work as skilled domestic servants and are in great demand, earning a good wage. Their dress is distinctive, cut like the long tunic worn by men but made of pastel-coloured cloth. Although they retain men's names, they violate all the restrictions which *purdah*, the system of female seclusion, imposes on men. They may speak intimately with women in the street without bringing the women's reputations into question; they sit with the segregated women at a wedding and may see the bride's unveiled face, but they may not sit or eat with men in public or play the musical instruments reserved for men. *Xaniths'* manners, perfumed bodies and high-pitched voices appeared effeminate to Wikan. She described the *Xaniths* as transsexuals in the sense that their essential sexual identity is that of a woman rather than a man.

Transsexuals are no longer a great rarity in our own society. In her book *Conundrum* Jan Morris (1974) described her own journey from boyhood, through the army, marriage, fatherhood and a successful career in journalism, to her long-sought identity as a woman. In her case and that of many less well-known transsexuals, the path to achieving their desired identity is an arduous one involving hormone treatments, deliberate study of the habits in dress, movement and speech of the desired gender, and finally surgery. In our society the change implies not only learning to behave in the gender-appropriate manner, but in changing one's anatomy in so far as medical skill will allow.

The Omani situation is illuminating because male transsexual passage is a more social phenomenon. There are three quite different possibilities open to *Xaniths*. Should they wish to become men again, they need only marry and prove themselves able to perform heterosexual intercourse with their brides. Some *Xaniths* never choose this path and remain as women until they grow old, when, having given up prostitution and homosexual intercourse, their anatomical sex again places them – though perhaps only tenuously – in the category of men. In addition, Wikan reports that some *Xaniths* become women, then men and then women again. This comparative ease of passage, based as it is on behaviour rather than anatomy, is one of the pieces of evidence which Wikan provides in arguing that Omani *Xaniths* represent a gender role – a third one – intermediate between Omani male and female gender roles. She argues that its function is to maintain the sharply differentiated roles of men and women, which we shall examine more closely. If *Xanith* is indeed a role, this may explain the relative ease with which men pass from the male category into *Xanith* and back again to male. That in old age, when they are no longer sexually active, *Xaniths* are again classed with men suggests that these transitions are of a different order from those which transsexuals in our own society experience. In our own society the passage must be complete and involves something more than just role-appropriate behaviour.

Before accepting Wikan's argument, let us consider the evidence which she offers in asserting that *Xaniths* represent a third and intermediate gender role. In a sense this proposition is difficult to entertain, so contrastive and exhaustive are our concepts of male and female gender roles. Wikan (1978) has defended her claim that the *Xaniths* function as a third gender role from attack by two anthropologists. In answering Brain's (1978) criticisms, she points to the need for precision in labelling behaviour such as dressing like the opposite gender, entering contracts (for instance, marriage) as if one were a member of the opposite gender or engaging in sexual relations with members of one's own gender. The degree of institutionalization too is crucial for her analysis, and she points to the important difference between being able to recognize sexual deviants from their dress or walk and the socially recognized suspension of rules such as those which seclude women from any men except biological men socially categorized as *Xanith*. In Omani society, sexuality is embedded in a precisely specified rule-system to define a socially recognized role.

Shepherd's criticisms (1978) arose in the context of her own fieldwork in Mombasa, a town on the east coast of Africa which has had centuries of contact with Oman. In Mombasa Shepherd found both male and female homosexuals, and this led her to question the completeness of Wikan's gender role analysis which was based on male prostitutes alone. In replying, Wikan stresses the importance of analysing the situation both in terms of the behaviour which can be observed by the anthropologist and in terms of its meaning for the actors. Wikan attacks Shepherd's assertion that Omani men act as *Xaniths* for economic reasons and that these then influence their status in the society. The money received for sexual behaviour is not their main source of income, and *Xaniths* may even offer payment to other men when they become old and less attractive. These same data refute Shepherd's argument that homosexuals are treated as inferiors in the manner of women who in marriage sell their sexual favours for economic security. Economic motives cannot provide an adequate explanation, for, as Wikan points out, no amount of money can guarantee that a *Xanith* will pass the test of manhood on his wedding night.

At this point we might wish to return to the inner world of psychoanalysis for an explanation. The Omani appear willing to accept that people's natures are different and their social stance is one of non-involvement; concern is confined to closest kin. A husband may feel ashamed by his faithless wife, or parents may be saddened and grieved by their son's passive homosexual tendencies, but social concern is strictly limited. Again our own society provides a sharp contrast. A question we can ask is the degree to which social recognition and the drawing of boundaries – for example, in designating people transvestite, transsexual or homosexual – influence our views of them and their own views of themselves. This issue has been posed within a French intellectual tradition and has been raised by Foucault in his history of sexuality (1979). He sees our society as aiming to classify everything, even things which he believes to be essentially unclassifiable. The aim of this classification is to allow differential status to be attached to categories of people. These are concerns of a very general nature indeed.

The problem of classification and the ease with which it can be achieved becomes a useful principle in reconsidering the gender role system in Oman. Omani women wear their hair long, carrying it forward from a central parting, and are clothed in tight-waisted, brightly patterned tunics. Their heads are covered, as are those of men. But men wear loose-fitting white tunics and have short hair. *Xaniths'* hair is medium length, and they never cover their heads; their solid-coloured tunics are close-fitting and they wear make-up. Wikan believes that these distinctions are essential and reflect *Xanith* status not as biological women but as a third gender. She argues that, given Omani patterns of dress, were *Xaniths* to assume the full woman's costume their anatomical status as males would be ambiguous. Dress serves to define three distinct social categories.

The Omani gender role system only comes alive when we look at the roles of men and women and their attitudes towards sexuality. Oman was first opened to the Western world in 1971, so it is not surprising to discover that gender roles are defined in terms of strictest Muslim custom. From the age of three, girls must be covered except for their hands, feet and face. At puberty they don the facial mask which is removed only before closely related men – fathers, husbands, sons and brothers. Fathers arrange their daughters' marriages, and once married a woman may not leave her home without her husband's consent. Yet Wikan warns us not to assume that women are unhappy or subjugated, for in response to this modesty and dignity women are treated by men with honour and respect.

Men are perceived to have a strong sex drive which is difficult to control and requires frequent release. Ideally, satisfaction is sought with a man's wife, though if a man is a migrant labourer or unmarried, problems arise. Strictly speaking, prostitution is illegal, but both male and female prostitutes are available. Besides costing five times as much as a man, going to a female prostitute involves a third party, the husband, while going to a *Xanith* is a transaction between two independent people. Prostitution is condemned, but to understand its place in the gender role system Wikan contends that we must appreciate Omanis' commonsense psychology. Omanis entertain ideals about behaviour but appreciate that the world is imperfect. Since the image of themselves which people seek to construct is one of good manners, of behaving tactfully, politely, morally, and amicably, they observe but do not sanction deviant behaviour in any but the most intimate of relationships. In addition, they view others in their full complexity and restrain from judging on the basis of a single act or an isolated set of acts. So widespread is this tolerance that Wikan found her own coolness towards a promiscuous woman being questioned in her circle of friends. In this setting, male homosexuality is tolerated and serves to perpetuate the view of women as pure and honourable. So well defined is the *Xanith* role that the man who seeks release with him in no sense risks his sexual identity, since the 'man' always performs the act of penetration.

Beyond Heterosexual Gender Roles

The Omani view of deviance also contrasts sharply with that of our own society. Although legal sanctions against sexual relations between men have been removed in the United States and England, the French laws are still repressive. If not viewed as criminal, homosexual pleasure is nevertheless often considered sick. It was only in 1973 that the American Psychiatric Association removed homosexuality from its list of diseases, and, as discussed in Chapter 3, research still aims at cure (Dorner *et al.*, 1975). Unlike the Omani attitude to isolated acts of behaviour, our society takes a different view of homosexual practices. For at least one hundred years we have categorized people who pursue homosexual pleasure as homosexuals, a distinct class of person. In Omani society sexual behaviour is embedded in a broader rule system. A *Xanith* can expect to be treated like a man if he performs sexually with a woman. In our society the designation homosexual carries with it moral implications as well as rules of behaviour.

The vast literature on homosexuality is growing at a great rate with the emergence of the Gay Liberation Movement in the seventies. The thesis which we present below, though not representative, is provocative in that it not only draws heavily on Freud's views on sexuality but is also greatly concerned with the impact of society in moulding sexual desire. The original argument attacking the procreative family, or anti-Oedipus, was presented by Deleuze, a French philosopher, and Guattari, a psychoanalyst and active Marxist (Deleuze and Guattari, 1976). We rely on Hocquenghem's (1978) analysis of these works on the nature of sexual desire because his book has recently become available in English translation and includes the arguments currently being debated in France.

To describe desire as homosexual, Hocquenghem asserts, is to make an arbitrary division along the continuum of desire, a division which he claims is imposed on sexuality by Western society to achieve its capitalist ends. Before we consider these claims, let us examine the assertion that the attempt to classify desire as either heterosexual or homosexual is artificial.

We have just noted that in Oman efforts are made to avoid condemning an individual on the basis of isolated acts of behaviour. In contrast, in our own society we seem ever ready to make new classifications. The term homosexual evolved less than a hundred years ago as a means of denoting a category of person: it was used to denote participation in particular sexual acts (Weeks, 1978). The evidence reviewed in the first section showed that homosexual behaviour occurs on a continuum of frequency; Kinsey's scale from 0 to 6 should make us cautious of simple all-or-nothing classifications. But, Hocquenghem argues, our society's aim is not truth, its categories are repressive. The identification of the sexually deviant legitimizes their repression, and in its turn heterosexual, procreative sexuality is strengthened. The repressed, deviant tendencies of those who identify themselves as heterosexual can be used to persecute and condemn those openly identified as deviant.

This argument reflects Freud's concern with unconscious motives. Recognition of the polymorphously perverse nature of all human sexuality makes even those most interested in repression suspect. The language of the anti-Oedipus discourse is altered in the psychoanalytic argument as presented in the reformulation of Freud offered by Jacques Lacan (1966). The reformulation is an attempt by Lacan to rid psychoanalysis of its biological language and to explore the unconscious in terms which he believes to be more appropriate, those of linguistics and of symbolism. In keeping with this project, instinct becomes desire, the penis gives way to the symbolic phallus, but the Oedipus complex remains at the core. For Lacan, as for Freud, the resolution of the Oedipus complex is the turning-point in the child's development: it marks the child's recognition of authority, and the loss of omnipotence, for the phallus symbolizes the patriarchal order. It is our society's patriarchal order which demands repression and renunciation of polymorphous sexuality. No longer can the child obtain just what it desires; the authority of the father stands between the child and its genital wishes for the mother. It is not the biological father but language and the symbolic order which gain ascendance in the child's mental functioning, in the unconscious. The authority of the social order is centrally symbolized by the phallus.

We concluded the discussion of psychoanalytic explanations of sexuality with Schafer's criticisms of Freud's return to evolutionary biology in his efforts to understand adult genital sexuality – masculinity/femininity, activity/passivity. Lacan describes a similar course of development, but in his account the unconscious bears the imprint of society through the social definition of masculinity and femininity. It is the core definition of sexuality derived through the dynamics of the Oedipal conflict which Hocquenghem and Deleuze and Guattari attack. Hocquenghem's argument is relevant here in that he is concerned with the impact of society on the unconscious mind, but he presents an oversimplified view of society and of mental functioning. One problem lies in trying to examine gender differences: nowhere in Hocquenghem's text is there mention of female homosexuals, so we do not know the extent to which this analysis fits female homosexuality. In addition, social class raises difficulties. We have seen in the Kinsey reports that sexual behaviour varies with social class; specifically, Weeks (1978) reports that men's consciousness of themselves as homosexuals varies with class. In Hocquenghem's analysis the social system is undifferentiated and the economic system – that is, capitalism – is invoked instead.

A more penetrating analysis is provided by Foucault (1979), who argues that, rather than being repressive, the bourgeois society which developed with the rise of capitalism has exploited sexuality. The effects, he suggests, are not undifferentiated but influence at least four aspects of sexual knowledge and power. The objects of this knowledge are the hysterical woman, the masturbating child, the Malthusian (procreative) couple and the perverse adult. More importantly, in suggesting that bourgeois society exploits sexuality, Foucault escapes the problem of repression. As we have noted, Hocquenghem accepts the older Freudian notion but turns it on its head. Rejecting the notion that homosexuals feel persecuted and are sick, he argues that so-called normal people who repress all but the heterosexual aspect of desire become paranoid. It is they who are disturbed and project their anxiety on to others.

In this discussion of some French theoretical approaches to homosexuality, and more generally to the impact of society in determining sexuality, we have come a long way from the description of Omani *Xaniths*. The discussion has allowed us to link the social and the unconscious, but it has lost track of the comparison between women's and men's sexuality. This seems to be the cost of achieving a broad social perspective.

Before concluding this section on social uses of sexuality, we should note the work of Gagnon and Simon (1973). They see sexuality as extremely susceptible to cultural patterning. Sexuality can be defined by the rules which a particular society imposes on social interaction and uses to determine positions in society. Gagnon and Simon stress that individuals can create their sexual identities through a vast potential variety of scripts which the interactive rules allow. This view elaborates and formalizes the comparative tradition of such eminent anthropologists as Margaret Mead, and it poses important questions about the development of sexual identities. The questions which it ignores are those raised by psychoanalytical explanations – why a particular individual chooses one identity rather than another, or why the genitals are the focal point in all societies' constructions of sexuality. Each of the approaches makes a contribution, even though each leaves many questions unanswered. Masters and Johnson's most recent research on homosexuality (1979) still reflects their physiological bias, but by providing information on the sexual behaviour of homosexuals they may help in combating a common prejudice in our society. To begin to understand the nature of men and women's sexuality we need to know more about what they do, why they do it and how it is viewed in the society in which they live.

CHAPTER 5

Aggression, Violence and Power

'Most violence, most crime ... is not committed by human beings in general. It is committed by men.' So wrote Jill Tweedie in her column in the *Guardian* (27 April 1978). Similarly, organized groups who commit violent acts in the name of 'the people', the state or their country – such as the army and the police – consist largely of men. Violence is seen as the masculine way of reacting to the difficulties and frustrations of life. The feminine way, as we shall show in the next chapter, is typically viewed as a more passive response.

Feminist writers such as Ms Tweedie, who claim that violence is a *male* problem rather than a human problem, are undoubtedly correct in the sense that most overt acts of violence towards other adults are now and were in the past committed by men. They do, however, omit to mention that a great deal of female encouragement has fanned the flames of male violence. The idea that toughness and aggression are admired masculine features, the sending of white feathers to those men who rebelled against this masculine stereotype, the direct encouragement given to wrestlers by women from ringside seats, and offers from prostitutes of free sex for US soldiers going to Vietnam are all examples of different ways in which women have played their part in perpetuating male violence. Many others could be mentioned. Germaine Greer went so far as to claim that 'violence has a fascination for most women'. Although this may be an overstatement, it does describe one side of an ambivalent attitude which women have to male aggression.

Whether or not we would want to portray women as inciting men to violence or as discouraging them, it is clear that when it comes to committing overt acts of violence this is generally left to the men (although there has been a recent trend towards female violence, which we shall mention later in this chapter). Are minor acts of violence, losing one's temper and verbal abuse also characteristically male, or are such lesser acts of aggression more equally distributed between the genders? We pose this question since there is the possibility that the two genders have the same degree of motivation to be aggressive, but men are more likely to act out such violent impulses than women. Most people do not believe that this is the case: it is generally thought that on average men *are* more aggressive than women, as well as being more violent. This widespread belief is detected in the reports of social psychologists' descriptions of gender stereotypes, and the notion of masculine aggressiveness has been incorporated into our language in phrases such as 'fiercely masculine'. So people *believe* that men are aggressive, but is this really true? It is, if we take the findings of psychologists who have measured aggression in the two genders as our evidence. In this case, therefore, lay opinion and the psychologist's measures agree that men are more aggressive than women.

When we say that men are more aggressive than women, we could mean that men are more aggressive to one another than women are to other women; alternatively, we could be concerned with aggression between the genders – why men commit more aggressive acts against women than women do against men. Research on these two questions has been pursued along different lines, with different explanations being offered in each case. The respective 'levels' of aggression within each gender have been studied by psychologists – generally in rather artificial conditions – and have been explained in terms of either biology or socialization. Aggression by men towards women has only recently been recognized as a problem and has been studied more by sociologists. There have been some attempts to explain this aggression in terms of the family backgrounds of the violent men.

So far we have employed the terms aggression and violence rather loosely. Violence usually refers to acts involving great physical force and is often used of events in the animate and inanimate world alike. When using the word violence to apply to human actions, emphasis is placed on the physically damaging nature of the act itself, rather than on the person's intentions. Aggression is a more difficult word to define, because it has a number of partially overlapping meanings. It can refer to active ambition or assertion of the self, or forcefulness: used in this sense, it describes a way of acting or a personality characteristic, and is closely related to aspects of the male stereotype described in Chapter 2, such as active, assertive and confident. Aggression can also refer more specifically to the motivation behind acts of violence, and in this sense it can be thought of as consisting of three aspects: the injury inflicted, the intention behind the act and the emotion accompanying it. In practice, aggressive acts tend to contain different combinations of these three aspects. Aggression meaning assertiveness and aggression meaning motivation to commit a violent act can be linked if we regard an assertive person as being more ready to commit violent acts if his intentions are frustrated.

The measures which psychologists use to study aggression take various forms: for children, they consist of either observations of fighting and other aggressive acts in nursery school and school playground settings, or measures of destructiveness and fantasy aggression in play, or ratings of aggressiveness by parents, teachers and peers (Oetzel, 1966; Maccoby and Jacklin, 1974). For adults, a variety of different laboratory methods are used by social psychologists. These include providing opportunities for verbal aggression and criticism, and measuring a person's willingness to administer what are believed to be electric shocks to another individual (Baron, 1977). Various 'hostility scales' involving self-appraisal ratings and questionnaires are also used for measuring aggressiveness as a personality characteristic.

In this chapter we first describe research on gender differences in aggression and violence, addressing the question 'Are men really more aggressive than women?' We then discuss the possible explanations offered by psychologists for gender differences in aggression and violence which we outlined above. Finally, we consider the wider subject of power relations between the genders.

Are Men Really More Aggressive than Women?

The general impression given by many reviews of studies on aggression is that, irrespective of the measure used, men are generally more aggressive than women. In some studies no gender differences have been found, but reports of greater female aggression are rare (Maccoby and Jacklin, 1974). Greater male aggression is generally found from an early age onwards; it occurs during play in children as young as 2 and 3 years of age (Maccoby and Jacklin, 1974).

Let us now take a closer look at some of these studies.

Studies with Children

The majority of reports dealing with young children have used nursery schools as the setting. It is relatively easy for psychologists to gain access to these schools, but the results of such studies will reflect any biases which may exist in the types of children attending them. For example, in the United States, most of the children observed in these studies were middle class. In more than twenty investigations published before 1966, boys were observed to be more aggressive than girls (Oetzel, 1966). More recent reports, which include a greater proportion of studies on English children, are generally in agreement with the earlier results. One study carried out in fifteen different nursery schools, day nurseries and playgroups found that conflicts between boys were more frequent than those between girls or between girls and boys (Smith and Green, 1975). Another study, which compared English children with Kalahari San children, found more aggressive actions and facial expressions in boys than in girls in both samples (Blurton-Jones and Konner, 1973).

Fewer observational studies have been carried out on school-age children. In a combined sample of 3–11-year-olds from six different cultures, observed during free play, there was more physical and verbal aggression by boys than by girls (Whiting and Edwards, 1973). In an English study of boys and girls in the classroom, 11-year-old boys showed more physical aggression than girls of the same age (Archer and Westeman, 1981).

A related gender difference which is often reported in these observational studies is that boys' play involves more 'play-fighting', particularly wrestling and tumbling, than does girls' play (for example, Smith and Connolly, 1972; Blurton-Jones, 1972). This gender difference is also observed in the Kalahari San study of Blurton-Jones and Konner (1973). Play-fighting differs from 'real' fighting in that any aggressive acts such as chasing, wrestling or hitting out are usually accompanied by laughing, making a face or some other sign that 'it is all in play or fun' (Garvey, 1977).

There are very few exceptions to the general pattern of more frequent aggression by boys than by girls in pre-school and school-age children. The occasional study (for example, Blurton-Jones, 1972) may report no gender difference, but there is little sign of any apparent reversal of the usual gender difference. If we are to look for possible cases of such a reversal, a distinction between verbal and physical aggression must be made – an important distinction, particularly in relation to gender differences. Indeed, there is a common belief that girls and women make up for their lack of physical aggression by verbal hostility, often referred to by such terms as cattiness or bitchiness. Some psychologists, notably Bardwick (1971) and Feshbach (1970), also suggest that girls show more verbal and 'prosocial' aggression than boys (prosocial aggression refers to rule enforcement, such as saying,

'You mustn't do that' or 'I'll tell teacher if you don't stop'). Although the evidence for greater male aggressiveness is weaker in the case of verbal aggression (Maccoby and Jacklin, 1974), there are few actual instances of girls being more verbally aggressive than boys as Bardwick and Feshbach suggest. In one study of the level of fantasy play towards a doll, girls were more verbally aggressive than boys (Durrett, 1959); and in another, on the behaviour of 11-year-olds in the classroom, girls were again found to show more verbal aggression (Archer and Westeman, 1981). There are, however, other studies in which boys are found to be both physically and verbally more aggressive than girls (for example, Whiting and Edwards, 1973). Altogether, there is relatively little evidence for the suggested reverse gender difference in verbal aggression.

Studies with Adults

In studies of aggression in adults, rather different measures are used. Laboratory studies typically involve measuring how willing someone is to give an electric shock to another person in a contrived situation. Measures of aggression outside the laboratory include questionnaires about aggressive and hostile feelings, and the analysis of aggressive content in daydreams. Generally these measures indicate either a higher level of aggression in men than women, or no gender difference; only occasionally is the reverse gender difference reported.

Maccoby and Jacklin (1974) review research on gender differences in aggression and confidently conclude that the major fact highlighted by studies of aggression in young adults and in children is that 'males are consistently found to be more aggressive than females'. Do other psychologists agree with Maccoby and Jacklin's conclusion? Baron (1977), for one, does not. He suggests that laboratory studies published in the early 1960s did show a gender difference in aggression, but that this had largely disappeared by the late 1960s and mid 1970s. Two possible explanations are offered to account for this trend. The first involves a procedural difference: studies reporting a large gender difference do not expose the subjects to provocation, whereas those finding no difference often involve provocation. Baron therefore suggests that at low levels of provocation men are more likely to behave aggressively than women, but that when provoked both react in a similar manner. Baron's second explanation is the change in female roles in recent years, including a lessening in passivity. This explanation is more consistent with his emphasis on a relationship between the date of the study and the appearance of a gender difference. It is, however, based on very few studies, and there have been many earlier reports of no gender difference in aggression. Baron's conclusions should therefore await assessment in the light of further evidence.

Another recent review has challenged the generality of a gender difference in aggression. Frodi *et al.* (1977) conclude that in most laboratory studies the occurrence of the expected higher level of male aggression is variable and depends on a number of more specific gender differences. A gender difference is more likely to occur in studies where the subjects are not angered. There is also an indication that women are more likely to shy away from physical aggression (as represented by willingness to administer electric shocks). Frodi *et al.* suggest that women generally experience greater anxiety about aggressive feelings than men, and that this provides a powerful inhibiting factor on their level of aggression. They point out that aggression and anxiety about aggression are inversely related for women but not for men, and that several other studies show that women are more anxious after being aggressive than men. A further factor is that women may generally have more empathy for their victim than men: thus the presence of a justification for aggression may increase female aggression and hence abolish the gender difference. Finally, there is some evidence that certain aggressive cues such as guns or knives might provide a stronger instigation to aggression in men than in women.

In the same review, Frodi *et al.* conclude that studies of self-report measures of 'general hostility', analyses of aggressive content in dreams and daydreams, and interpretation of projective tests all indicate that men are more aggressive than women. But this contrasts with the less consistent pattern found in laboratory studies, apparently because these other measures are based on the subjects' own reports of their behaviour and consequently may reflect the influence of gender stereotypes.

How representative are the studies of aggression which we have described so far? The ages used in these studies reflect the ready availability of children, adolescents and young adults (usually university students) as subjects for psychological research. Maccoby and Jacklin's review of gender differences in aggression contains no studies of subjects over twenty-four years of age! On these grounds alone, any conclusions drawn from psychological literature must be limited. Another major limitation of psychological studies is their reliance on artificial measures of aggression produced in laboratory experiments and on self-report measures. If we look at sources outside social psychological research, such as violent crime statistics and cross-cultural surveys, we can obtain evidence from a wider age range in real-life conditions. Such sources generally show that men commit the vast majority of violent acts. According to statistics for the United States up to 1969, men heavily outnumbered women in committing violent crimes, and five times more men were arrested in connection with murder (Johnson, 1972). Similarly, in the United Kingdom, twelve times more men than women were convicted for violence against other people (*Social Trends*, 1977).

According to these statistics, therefore, violent crime is clearly a male problem. Some commentators suggest that this pronounced gender difference has diminished in recent years, and the subject of female violence has received a fair amount of media publicity, particularly in relation to adolescents and young adults. A number of youth subcultures have encouraged certain forms of violence in both genders, and it is now fairly common for women to be involved in acts of violence reported by the media, although at one time this was almost unknown. For example, a British newspaper report of women muggers quotes an Old Bailey judge as saying that he was 'terrified' by this new aspect of crime – simply because it was carried out by women (*Guardian*, 28 October 1977). Another newspaper report, again from 1977 (*Sunday Times*, 1 May 1977), refers to a 'new strain of violence emerging among our young girls' which had caught the attention of the British National Union of Teachers. However, the violent crime statistics for this age group show only a very small increase during the years 1975–7 when this violence was supposed to have emerged; it is therefore difficult to decide whether these specific cases have been exaggerated. But some studies show an increase among women in typically 'male' crimes, such as robbery, burglary, assault and vandalism, during the last ten to twelve years (for example, Thompson and Lozes, 1976). However, one point to bear in mind in assessing media reports is that female violence is particularly noteworthy, because of its departure from the stereotype of the passive woman. Men in contact with female terrorists view them as more ruthless, more cruel and more calculating than male terrorists, but this opinion is not shared by women commentators (BBC radio programme, *More Deadly than the Male*, 1978).

There are very few observational studies of real-life aggression in adults, as there are for children, since it is much more difficult for a psychologist to witness contexts in which adults are violent to one another. There are, however, some exceptions: a study by Depp (1976) in a mental hospital in Washington D C found that aggressive incidents occurred predominantly among male patients. Cross-cultural comparisons of aggression also show that it is a predominantly male characteristic. For example, a comparison of reactions to bereavement, which often involve feelings of anger and aggressive actions (Parkes, 1975), revealed more instances of violence among men than among women (Rosenblatt *et al.*, 1976). Women, on the other hand, are more inclined to self-injury and attempted self-injury.

Generally speaking, a more clear-cut gender difference is revealed from these studies of real-life violence than from the laboratory studies. This suggests that although overt violence is a predominantly male characteristic, less intense incidences of aggression show a less pronounced gender difference.

Domestic Violence

The research which we have discussed so far is generally about aggression or violence carried out on someone of the same gender. Violence by a member of one gender towards the other, as between a husband and wife, has until recently not been considered a subject for academic research. Nevertheless, violence by men towards their wives has been known for centuries and has usually been condoned by the law. Many men still regard assaulting or physically 'punishing' their wives as a right, and this attitude is supported by Jewish and Christian beliefs about the subservience of women (Davidson, 1977). For example, it is only during the last century that United States law has included any regulations against the severest excesses of wife-beating.

These forms of private violence by men towards women have existed at the same time as a more public disapproval of violence towards and by women. This dual standard persists today and is epitomized by the attitude that it is ungentlemanly for a man to strike a woman unless she is his rebellious wife. Research on violence between men and women reflects the dual standard. On the one hand, laboratory studies of willingness to aggress show that male subjects are more likely to direct a higher intensity of aggression to a male than to a female victim. On the other hand, the few – and comparatively recent – studies of violence within the home indicate that some men show few such restraints about hitting their own wives or lovers in private.

Studies of domestic violence suffer from one obvious drawback: the violent act occurs in private, and in most cases it is not even in the victim's interest to admit that it has occurred. Consequently evidence can most readily be obtained from extreme cases where the violence has ended in murder or where the victim has sought refuge outside the home. A wife's escape from a violent husband is made very difficult through society's reluctance to acknowledge that this form of violence is a social problem. Ninety per cent of a sample of 150 women entering a Women's Aid Centre in New York State (AWAIC) reported that they would have left their violent relationship earlier had the resources been available (Roy, 1977). Two thirds had already sought police help, and 90 per cent of these women reported that the police had avoided making an arrest. Over two thirds of the sample said that the police had been unhelpful. The general impression obtained from these women was that they were unable to obtain help, either officially or privately.

In some cases it is the husband who is the victim of his wife's violence, but this form of violence is almost totally unrecorded, and there is little public recognition that it exists. If a man is a victim of his wife's violence, the stigma and the expected ridicule would provide ample reason for hiding what has happened. It is only from studies of divorce proceedings and from some fairly recent survey studies of domestic violence that evidence has been obtained for this form of violence.

Studies carried out at Women's Aid Centres tell us about the circumstances of those women who have experienced extreme domestic violence and have been able to leave their former home. Roy (1977) obtained figures for the frequency, onset and form of violence, the type of help sought, the involvement of drugs and alcohol, and the reasons for remaining in a violent home. The frequency of violence varied from less than once a month in 20 per cent of cases, to more than once a week in 25 per cent of cases. More frequent violence was associated with the use of a weapon and with sexual abuse. Violence often began early in the relationship. In 90 per cent of cases it was associated with alcohol or drug problems, although it was not necessarily confined to the period of intoxication.

Survey studies normally either concentrate on families for which incidents of violence have been reported to the authorities, or else they try to assess the frequency of unreported incidents of violence within more typical families. Gelles (1972) did both by interviewing two small samples of families in which violence had been reported to a social work agency or to the police, and then by comparing these with neighbouring families. There were 80 families altogether, and in most instances only the wife was interviewed. Over half the respondents reported the occurrence of at least one violent incident, and about a quarter reported regular violence, defined as between once every two months and every day. As expected, families obtained from the police records contained the highest proportion of violent incidents (85 per cent), those from the social work agency rather less (60 per cent) and the neighbours the least (30 per cent).

The frequency of violence by husbands against wives was greater than that by wives against husbands, but the percentage difference was not very great (47 per cent compared to 32 per cent). More repeated violence – defined as over six times a year – was shown by a quarter of the husbands and by 11 per cent of the wives. The methods of violence were different, husbands tending to use forms which require physical strength such as pushing, choking, punching and kicking, and the wives more often using hard objects. Husbands often made violent threats by punching or kicking an object such as a door, or by firing a gun, and implying that this was what they would next do to their wives. Wives more often used a knife or a heavy object, saying that this was 'protective' – to stave off the possibility of more severe violence by the husband.

Gelles's respondents gave a variety of reasons for these acts of violence: some involved the notion of the husband punishing his wife or 'knocking her to her senses'; others involved frustration producing aggressive feelings which were directed to the wife because she was the nearest available target; alternatively, violence may have resulted from conflicts within the family over disciplining children or over sexual relations. Gelles's study has a number of shortcomings, some of which he acknowledges: for instance, the sample size is small, it is not random, and the information is derived from the wife's account of their domestic disputes. One drawback which he overlooks is the lack of any statistical tests carried out on the results: thus one cannot be sure about which differences are chance variations. Gelles's research also provides very little information about the dynamics of the violence – how it fits into other aspects of the relationship between husband and wife – and the extent to which husbands and wives differ in their readiness to use violence as a solution to family problems. By providing only percentage occurrences for various categories of violent acts, it is difficult to tell how many of the acts are responses to previous violence and how many represent the initiation of violence.

A more recent study of domestic violence, carried out by Steinmetz (1977), obtained information from husbands, wives and their children in 57 families and found some incidence of marital violence in 60 per cent of these. This high figure probably results from the author including throwing objects as a form of violence, since this was the most common form of violence reported. The frequency of violence by husbands and by wives was very similar; as in Gelles's study, however, such a simple tallying of numbers of incidences provides only a superficial picture of domestic violence. Steinmetz reports that men generally do more damage as a result of their violent acts, and he regards this as a consequence of their greater size and strength. Occasionally this may be reversed, and he cites an example of an older husband who is beaten by his younger wife.

These studies show that both husbands and wives may commit violent acts against one another in the home, and that these differ in terms of their form and how damaging they are. But little is revealed about possible differences in the context and meaning of violent acts committed by husbands and wives.

Explaining Gender Differences in Aggression

We now turn from considering the nature and extent of gender differences in aggression to the explanations which psychologists have offered for greater male aggression and violence. We consider these under the headings of biological and environmental explanations. The first links men's aggression to their biological make-up, an example of biological reductionism (see Chapter 1). The alternative comes from developmental psychology and emphasizes the learning experiences of boys and girls. It includes the influence of commonsense views, in particular the approval of 'toughness' and aggression for boys.

Biological Explanations

Can male aggression be explained in terms of biological differences between men and women? Research on animals has shown that the male is the more aggressive sex in many species. This aggression is often associated with organs specialized for fighting, such as the antlers of stags and the spurs of cockerels. These weapons and the greater aggressiveness of the male are both dependent on the male hormone testosterone and are greatly reduced in castrated animals, one of several reasons why agricultural animals such as bulls are easier to manage and are less likely to damage one another when they have been castrated. What could be simpler, therefore, than to explain the greater aggressiveness of human males in terms of testosterone action? This is essentially the viewpoint of those psychologists who favour a biological explanation for male aggression (for example, Hutt, 1972a; Maccoby and Jacklin, 1974; Gray, 1971a).

First, we outline the evidence from animal studies for the claim that males are generally the aggressive sex, and briefly mention the role of testosterone in animal aggression. We then discuss research which is aimed at discovering whether there is a link between testosterone and aggression in men. Finally, we briefly discuss the importance of size and strength differences between men and women as factors contributing to greater male violence.

What are the animal sex differences in aggression? In a wide range of animal species, the male is more aggressive than the female – more ready to fight or threaten. But there are many exceptions and qualifications. First, male aggression is seasonal in many species, occurring when the males are in breeding condition. This may be associated with the establishment or holding of particular areas or 'territories'. This is commonly the case in fish and birds. In many mammals seasonal breeding, accompanied by male aggression, occurs without territory formation, for example in the red deer and the elephant. In other mammals, such as rats and mice, the male is more consistently the more aggressive sex.

Females also show a form of 'seasonal' aggression. This is associated with defence of a nesting site, eggs or young, and occurs in a wide variety of species. Unlike male aggression, it has only recently been studied either in a natural setting or in the laboratory. For example, female house mice who are suckling their young become just as aggressive as males. In some mammals the female is as aggressive as the male (or more so) even when she has no young. Examples include European voles (several species of *Microtus*), hamsters and gerbils (Frank, 1957; Payne and Swanson, 1970; Swanson, 1973). Even in species where the female is supposedly 'non-aggressive', such as the house mouse, this description is not quite accurate: laboratory-reared females derived from wild mice will attack another mouse after being housed in isolation for a period of time (Ebert and Hyde, 1976).

The evidence for the male sex being the predominantly violent one amongst animals is, therefore, not as overwhelming as is often suggested. Psychologists who make generalizations from animal to human aggression tend to concentrate their attention on species in which the male is typically more aggressive than the female, such as the rat or mouse, and to ignore those in which both sexes are similarly aggressive, such as the hamster or the gerbil.

What is the role of sex hormones? Experimental studies using rats and mice have shown that testosterone, which is present during early development and after the age of puberty, is necessary at both of these times for the typically higher level of aggression in the male. Some psychologists (for example, Hutt, 1972a; Maccoby and Jacklin, 1974) have relied on such research to provide a model for hormonal influences on human aggression. They suggest that in human beings, as in rats and mice, testosterone causes the male to be more aggressive than the female. We are sceptical about this conclusion, since it ignores the variability and the complexity of the relationship between hormones and behaviour in animals. As we have already pointed out, in some species the male is more aggressive than the female, but in others – such as the gerbil and the hamster – he is not. In the hamster, female hormones are implicated in affecting aggressive behaviour. Why should psychologists choose rodents such as the rat and the mouse for their speculations about human aggression, and ignore these others where the pattern of hormonal control is different? We could also ask why rodents are regarded as relevant to human beings at all. Primates – the group to which the human species belongs – and rodents diverged relatively early in mammalian evolution from a common ancestral stock and have followed different courses of evolution both within and between their respective groups ever since. Much is known about hormones and behaviour in rats and mice simply because of their convenience for laboratory experiments, and because of the tradition of using them for behavioural research. But whether such information is relevant to human beings can only be assessed by actually studying human beings and comparing the findings for the two species. Let us look at research on the possible relationship between testosterone and aggression in men.

There are two stages in the life of a human male when testosterone could exert a direct effect on parts of his brain and hence on his behavioural predispositions: the first is during prenatal development, and the second is at puberty. The major source for the first is the work of Money and Ehrhardt (1972), which we referred to briefly in Chapter 3. Money and Ehrhardt looked at girls who had, for one reason or another, been exposed to testosterone during their prenatal development, and compared their behaviour with that of a group of normal girls, obtaining their information from interviews with parents and with the girls themselves. Although they found evidence of rougher, more energetic play in the hormonally treated girls, there was no indication of an effect on aggression – that is, real fights – during childhood. (There are many problems in interpreting their studies and these are discussed more fully in Chapter 9. Principally, they are the difficulty of separating effects which might have arisen from the action of testosterone on the brain from those which might have arisen as a result of parents' reactions to their girls' genital abnormalities.)

There are several studies seeking to relate aggression to testosterone secreted at puberty or during adult life. The first of these was carried out by Persky *et al.* (1971), who found in a group of young men that the higher the rate of testosterone production, the higher the score on questionnaire measures of aggression and hostility. However, two subsequent studies (Doering *et al.*, 1974; Kreuz and Rose, 1972) failed to confirm this relationship. Meyer-Bahlberg *et al.* (1974) used a slightly different method: they selected 'aggressive' and 'non-aggressive' groups of subjects on the basis of questionnaire scores and compared the rate of testosterone secretion and blood levels of testosterone; but they found no differences between the two groups. Kreuz and Rose made a similar comparison, this time involving prisoners convicted either for physical violence or for non-violent crime: again, no differences in testosterone levels were found, although ten prisoners with a history of more violent and aggressive crimes *in adolescence* did show higher plasma testosterone levels than another eleven prisoners. Kreuz and Rose suggest that testosterone may have played a part in predisposing the individual to be aggressive in adolescence, but that it had a less pronounced effect thereafter. Another positive finding is that of Ehrenkranz *et al.* (1974), who report that twelve prisoners with a history of chronic aggressive behaviour showed higher blood levels of testosterone than a group of non-violent prisoners. A study of a group of sex offenders (rapists and child-molesters) also showed that those who were judged to be the most violent, according to questionnaires, had higher testosterone levels than other sex offenders whose testosterone levels were in the normal range for the general population (Rada *et al.*, 1976).

It is clear from these studies that a link between testosterone and various indications of aggression, past or present, is certainly found, particularly in studies comparing individuals who had shown high and low levels of violence. What exactly does this mean? Does a high testosterone level cause aggression, as would be predicted by those who favour a biological explanation for gender differences in aggression? One of the pitfalls in inferring a causal relationship from this type of evidence is that one cannot rule out the possibility that a person's psychological state may have produced measurable changes in body chemistry (see Chapter 1), that being or feeling aggressive raises testosterone levels. This is certainly known to occur in rhesus monkeys: in a newly formed group there is usually fighting which results in the establishment of a 'dominance hierarchy'. Rose et al. (1972) found that defeated or 'subordinate' males showed an 80 per cent fall in blood levels of testosterone under such circumstances, whereas the dominant monkey showed a progressive rise. A male from an established breeding colony also showed a large increase in testosterone levels (over 200 per cent) twenty-four hours after he had dominated strange males who had been added to his group. Other studies, both on monkeys and on human beings, indicate that testosterone secretion is generally lowered by stressful situations (for example, Mason et al., 1969). There is also some evidence that conditions associated with anger may increase the secretion of the hormone (Archer, 1979). In view of these findings, the higher levels of testosterone in certain violent prisoners (Kreuz and Rose, 1972, Ehrenkranz et al., 1974) or in aggressive young men (Persky et al., 1971) could represent a *consequence* of their aggressive actions.

Furthermore, the view that testosterone could cause aggression in human males represents a narrowly conceived reductionist approach which neglects the complex interaction between hormones, mental state, behaviour and the environment. We have indicated one example of this complexity – the consequences of environmental events and their associated mental states for hormone levels. The question of how testosterone is connected with the aggression of human males must await more sophisticated research designs than the present ones, which are largely based on simple cause-and-effect notions.

The studies which we have reviewed so far have all been concerned with measuring hormone levels in men who differ in their aggressive actions. There is little evidence as to whether the larger increase in testosterone secretion at puberty seen in boys than in girls is associated with a pronounced increase in male aggression or hostility, and whether there is a relation between testosterone secretion and aggression in individual adolescents. Even if a link between aggression and testosterone secretion at puberty could be established, this would not provide a complete explanation for gender differences in aggression. As we have seen, the greater aggressiveness of the human male is first observed at about three years of age – long before the rise in testosterone levels at puberty.

The causes of the gender difference in aggression are likely to be varied and complex. So far we have considered the biological reductionist explanation, that testosterone might have a direct effect on the brain and so increase the likelihood of aggressive behaviour in the male. We are considering here the possibility of a difference in aggressive motivation between the genders. A less direct biological contribution might result from sex differences in size and strength. These are, of course, only average differences, but they are sufficiently marked to affect the likelihood of success in physical violence and to assume particular importance in relation to violence between a man and a woman. For example, in the study of domestic violence by Steinmetz (1977) described in the previous section, similar types and incidences of violence were found to be committed by men and women, but greater damage generally resulted from the men's acts. Steinmetz even suggests that men and women have an equal potential for committing acts of domestic violence and initiate similar acts of violence, but that husbands have the capacity to do more damage. She also suggests that this may occasionally be reversed when the usual size and strength differences are reversed.

Sex differences in size and strength also play an important part in occupations which involve the possibility of violence. Until recent years, size and strength have been regarded as essential for police and the armed forces, and women have been relegated to non-operational roles apparently for this reason. Nevertheless, modern weapons – even hand-held ones such as the gun and the grenade – have proved effective equalizers of size and strength differences, and in recent years women have come to play an increasingly large part in some unofficial military organizations, such as politically motivated terrorist groups. The United States army has also included a larger proportion of women during the last few years and has recently allowed them in combat roles (Davidson, 1978). We shall return to this subject in the final chapter on social change and the future. We now turn to a more traditional pyschological explanation for the gender difference in aggression.

Environmental Explanations

Explanations in terms of the different upbringing of boys and girls are part of a more general explanation which has been applied to a number of other psychological gender differences (see Chapter 1). When applied to aggression, the argument is as follows. Throughout childhood, violence and aggression are strongly disapproved of in girls. They are not expected to respond aggressively even if they are attacked; they receive more sympathy and approval – and ultimately their own way – if they cry and attract the attention of an adult or an older brother than if they hit back. Boys, on the other hand, are encouraged to be tough and to stick up for themselves. This is not usually meant as an open encouragement for them to be violent, but more of a message that violence is all right if not taken to extremes, that it is an appropriate way of 'looking after yourself' and can in many circumstances be a way of improving social status with other boys. Perhaps the most important message that boys learn is that they must at all costs avoid being thought to be afraid to fight. Boys also see members of their own gender engaging in violence, whereas girls generally do not.

This analysis describes the many ways in which stereotypic ideas about men and women in relation to aggression and violence are learnt by boys and girls, and come to influence their actions and feelings. Developmental psychologists have set out to analyse these learning experiences by splitting them up into convenient units. They have mainly concentrated on *how* boys and girls learn rather than on exactly *what* they learn. Examples include how boys and girls are encouraged or discouraged for being aggressive or violent, and how they come to imitate and identify with aggressive and non-aggressive adults and children.

Rewards and punishments for aggressive behaviour are an important aspect of this explanation. In schools and nursery schools they are administered in different ways to boys and girls. For example, teachers reprimand or restrain girls more than boys for their aggressive acts (Serbin *et al.*, 1973). Imitation is another important method of learning aggressive and non-aggressive responses. Psychologists have studied this process by setting up controlled experiments. The following is a well-known study carried out by Bandura *et al.* (1961). Children aged between three and six watched an adult 'playing' either aggressively or peacefully with 'Bobo doll', a large inflatable doll on a solid base.

The children were then taken into another room and given toys to play with, and it was found that they imitated the behaviour of the adult in their own play. The boys imitated aggressive behaviour more than the girls.

The children also remarked on the appropriateness of the adult's aggressive behaviour. When performed by a man, it was generally regarded as being appropriate, whereas aggression was seen as inappropriate for a woman. Some of the children remarked that the woman's aggressive behaviour was 'not the way for ladies to behave' and that she was 'like a man'. Male aggression met with more approval, with comments such as 'He's a good fighter like daddy' and 'I want to sock like Al,' Al being the man's name. The man also influenced the children's behaviour to a greater extent than the woman did, presumably because her behaviour was inappropriate for her gender. Other studies of imitation show that the important feature in determining whether or not a child will imitate an adult is whether the activity is regarded as being appropriate for the gender of the child watching it, regardless of the gender of the adult (Barkley *et al.*, 1977). Thus, if a girl already regards aggression as unfeminine or inappropriate for her gender, she will not imitate a woman who behaves aggressively. In our society, and in many others, female aggression is seen as highly inappropriate and undesirable, so that the misgivings about female aggression expressed by the children in Bandura's study are merely reflections of a more widespread stereotype prevalent in our culture.

We can further illustrate attitudes to female aggression by considering women's boxing. On a BBC radio programme (*Today*, 18 January 1977) the boxer Joe Bugner talked of his refusal to fight on the same bill as women boxers. He said he had seen a women's boxing match and had been appalled by it because it 'seemed like real fighting'. These remarks were made by a man who has had a very successful career in precisely the same activity that he disapproved of for women. Clearly, it was not boxing that had appalled him but rather that female boxers had violated a commonsense view about how women should behave. Women's boxing takes place in the United States, where feminism has been taken more seriously than in the United Kingdom and elsewhere. Even so, it is illegal in many states, and has to be restricted to those such as North Carolina where it is legal. When describing a successful American woman boxer in an article in the British *Sunday Times* (12 March 1978), the reporter went out of his way to emphasize her femininity. Not only did Cathy 'Cat' Davis 'fight like a man', but she was also 'desirable', 'blonde, blue-eyed and 25'. The readers had to be convinced that she really was a woman, since her chosen activity involved a fundamental violation of most people's view of femininity.

Women's boxing illustrates the strength of attitudes against female aggression. Of course this does not represent a universal reaction, since women's boxing does after all take place, indicating that some people are able to accept it. But the usual attitude would be to regard it as a deviant activity, and the majority of adults and children who exhibit aggressive behaviour both in real life and in books, television and films are men. It is not surprising therefore to learn that males tend to respond to television violence more than females, and that boys show more imitation of television and film violence than girls.

The learning, or socialization, view of aggression is generally used in a more specific form to explain why males are more violent to other males than females are to other females. But it has also been applied to violence between men and women. Several studies have reported that husbands who beat their wives often come from homes in which they were beaten or witnessed their fathers beating their mothers (for example, Roy, 1977). Men and women who observe their parents being violent are more likely to be violent to their marriage partner than those who have not (Gelles, 1972). There is also evidence that parental violence influences the type of aggressive act which is favoured. Gelles explains family violence in terms of the experience of coming from a violent domestic background making a person more prone to react violently to later stresses.

We have discussed the various reasons why men show more acts of aggression than women, taking into account the possible influence of hormones, of size and strength, and of the different learning experiences of men and women. These involve influences which reflect attitudes and beliefs about violence derived from the wider society in which the person lives. As such, they represent more than an individual's personal views and preferences. They are ultimately related to the nature of the wider society, and in particular to the power relations between men and women.

Power

In considering gender differences in aggression and violence, our approach has been primarily psychological or personal. Power is usefully examined by expanding our horizon to include sociological and anthropological explanations. Unfortunately, sociologists themselves do not agree about the definition of power. In his analysis of power and authority, Lukes (1975) has suggested several distinctions which can be used to classify the major differences among social theorists. One of the most basic of these is whether power is seen as the result of the collective exercise of a communal and consensual will or whether it reflects an imbalance or asymmetry in relationships. This distinction can be seen in commonsense views of gender roles. The first is represented by 'the natural order' view, which suggests that men and women recognize their differences but also their shared needs; for these reasons both are content, men to pursue their careers and women to look after children. The second is the contemporary argument that women have been denied equal opportunities by men. Legislation arises from a recognition of the inequality and is designed to correct it.

According to Lukes, there are three different ways of looking at power when it is used to refer to asymmetrical relations. Usually these involve conflict and resistance. The first is in terms of compliance: the powerful person or group can impose its decision or will on the less powerful. This definition is commonly used in psychological research. According to biological accounts, the larger size and greater aggressiveness of men explains the subjugation of women. A second view sees power as being exercised through dependence. Power relations which arise from conditions of economic dependence between industrial nations and producers of raw materials are of this type. It can also be applied to the economic dependence of women on men, and to the conditioning of psychological dominance and compliance between men and women. The third view of asymmetric power relations is in terms of inequality. Those in positions of power have greater access to material and social rewards. Feminist anthropologists and sociologists have pointed out numerous ways in which women are kept in low-paid jobs, encounter difficulty in career advancement, are excluded from certain occupational roles and are assigned primary responsibility for child care (Mead, 1935; Polatnick, 1973; Walum, 1977). These all exemplify power inequality.

Even among anthropologists of a feminist persuasion there are different views about the exercise of power by men and women. One group recognizes a universal division of labour and power asymmetry which places women in the domestic sphere with responsibility for child care and food preparation, and which sees men as hunters, fighters, clearers of the land or workers in the public domain. These analysts view authority as male, but do not accept the inevitability of patriarchy. They question the failure of women to struggle and resist. A second group has begun to re-examine the relative power of men and women in particular societies. This allows them to argue that in some Middle Eastern societies women's power in the domestic sphere entails considerable control of material and social rewards through female solidarity groups. In a similar vein it is argued that in certain peasant societies the informal sector of the society may involve important power through the control of information. Rogers (1978) has argued convincingly that much anthropological analysis is not only male-centred but is also biased in terms of our own society's values in that we see the public and formal sectors of society as offering greater rewards. In this way men are seen to occupy positions of power everywhere, and women are viewed as inevitably inferior.

Rogers has presented an innovative model which seeks to explain gender differences and the balance of power. The notion that men and women construe the world differently is central to her model, and she describes it as 'ideological differentiation'. The kinds of differences which we have described in earlier chapters, those in terms of the different roles filled by men and women and the specific actions expected according to gender, are labelled by Rogers as 'behavioural differentiation'. If we bear in mind that in any particular society men and women may or may not be expected to behave differently or to construe the world differently, we can construct a classification of societies in terms of four types of gender differentiation. The two clear cases would be: first, societies in which gender is ignored both behaviourally and ideologically; and second, those in which men and women are clearly differentiated along both dimensions. Reports suggest that in the pioneering days on some *kibbutzim* a total absence of gender differentiation existed (Tiger and Shepher, 1975). It was, however, difficult to maintain. The definitions of male and female gender in Oman, which we described in Chapter 4, provide an example of a society with both behavioural and ideological differentiation.

Of the two mixed types, our own society offers an example of a culture in which behavioural differentiation is expected but in which there is no clear expectation of ideological differentiation. Men and women are expected to act differently but to inhabit the same conceptual world. The other type is difficult to imagine – it describes societies in which men and women are expected to behave in a similar fashion although they are believed to be fundamentally different by nature and to live in different conceptual worlds. It is interesting to ponder the four types of societies, but even more fascinating to consider their meaning for the distribution of power between men and women in our own culture.

We can now ask how Rogers's models of behavioural and ideological differentiation relate to the distribution of power. Rogers construes power according to both the inequality model of asymmetrical relations and the consensual model. If resources can be shown to be distributed equally between men and women, we would conclude that there was no inequality in the distribution of power. Rogers urges that we look at both the domestic/informal and public/formal sectors of society in our analysis of power. Ideological differentiation supports Rogers's view of equality. By recognizing that men and women inhabit different worlds, the public and domestic, and the formal and informal sectors, are each seen as providing comparable rewards.

Omani gender relations provide us with an example of the determining effect of the eye of the beholder. When we apply Western values, Omani men appear to exercise vast power over Omani women. They determine their movement and company. Yet if one accepts an Omani world-view, with gender differentiation both of behaviour and of ideology, this hierarchical relationship between men and women is called into question. Since each inhabits a separate world and has a distinct nature, they are not to be compared – each gender is necessary for the other's survival.

As our discussion has indicated, behavioural differentiation occurs in our own society along a variety of dimensions. But the question of ideological differentiation is more problematic. One alternative is to view men and women as fundamentally different. This is represented by the commonsense notion that differences between men and women reflect the 'natural order', and by the view of those scientists who have tried to explain behavioural (and role) differences by arguing that men and women are fundamentally different. The alternative view is that men and women do live in essentially similar conceptual worlds. This is represented by the commonsense notion that behavioural differentiation results from 'conditioning', and by the parallel scientific view held until quite recently by most psychologists and anthropologists. In anthropology this view has been challenged by the discovery that male and female anthropologists have different models of the world (Ardener, 1972). Our view is that although there is behavioural differentiation between men and women in our society, the conceptual worlds are essentially similar. This similarity becomes apparent if we contrast our society with others which show marked ideological differentiation between men and women, such as the Omani. According to Rogers's analysis, when behavioural differentiation is associated with ideological similarity, this should result in a hierarchical relationship between men and women, and inequality in the distribution of material and social rewards.

Henley (1977) argues that there is ample evidence of the power imbalance between men and women in our society from their individual behaviour. She has studied the non-verbal messages which are exchanged through smiles and frowns, glances and gestures, movements towards and away from others. Some scientists have used them to provide information about friendship, sexuality and emotions generally, but Henley believes that they are indicative of the dominance of men and the submissiveness of women. Examination of the behaviour listed in her table and a moment's thought should confirm her contention that staring, touching, interrupting and pointing – the gestures of dominance – are also those of men.

Table 5.1. Gestures of Dominance and Submission

Dominance	Submission
Stare	Lower eyes, avert gaze, blink
Touch	'Cuddle' to the touch
Interrupt	Stop talking
Crowd another's space	Yield, move away
Frown, look stern	Smile
Point	Move in pointed direction, obey

Based on Henley (1977).

When differences in non-verbal communication are first pointed out, they come as a surprise. Men are usually not aware of their assertiveness or women of their compliance. One of Henley's aims has been to help people to become conscious of the inequality which their gestures indicate. Although men and women could claim that their actions follow only the dictates of convention and common courtesy, their interaction, at an unconscious and unintended level, has been shown to reflect the inequality of power between genders in our society. This is true whether we examine touching, gazing, personal space or the use of time. These power relationships are also expressed in language (Walum, 1977).

The naturalistic study of communication leaves little doubt about the unequal distribution of power in our society and the widespread, though perhaps unconscious, recognition of male authority. Laboratory studies of power provide a less revealing picture of behavioural gender differentiation. Power has been conceptualized primarily in terms of compliance, whether the particular variable is labelled competition, dominance or specifically compliance. Many laboratory studies use a game format in which one player can impose a decision upon another. Children have been studied using a device which breaks apart if both children pull it, but which will yield a marble to the non-contender if one child pulls. Competition leads to joint failure, whereas cooperation produces success for one person. Although Maccoby and Jacklin were sceptical about this game in which competition is clearly maladaptive, they reviewed twelve studies involving children between 3 and 11 years old. There were no highly consistent gender differences, but pairs of boys tended to be more competitive and pairs of girls more cooperative. When boys were partnered by a girl they became more cooperative, though girls paired with boys became more competitive.

The Prisoners' Dilemma is a more abstract and adult game which is also used to measure competition and cooperation. In this game both players are hypothetical prisoners accused of a crime. They may make one of two moves: either confess the crime or deny it. If both refuse to confess, they must both be set free for lack of evidence. The prosecutor (experimenter) bargains and offers to be lenient if both confess, or, if only one confesses, to let him go free and give him a reward while his partner receives a stiff sentence. It is presumed that if a player chooses to confess he is more concerned with his own welfare (competitive motive), whereas if he refuses he is concerned about the welfare of his partner (cooperative motive). The game is usually played a great many times consecutively, and the resulting complexity of the pay-off probabilities has led Nemeth (1973) to question whether the players are aware of the supposed competitive and cooperative consequences of their choices.

In twenty-three studies based on the Prisoners' Dilemma, Maccoby and Jacklin found little evidence of consistent gender differences. Deaux (1976b) has noted differences in strategies, though she recognized the ambiguity which typically surrounds the players' motives. A competitive choice may reflect a desire either to gain a reward or to defeat an opponent. Similarly, in a cooperative choice the motive may be to maximize personal pay-off, to disregard rewards altogether or to strive to appear generous. In an attempt to disentangle these different motives, Wyer and Malinowski (1972) designed a variant of the Prisoners' Dilemma game in which it was possible to distinguish *competitive responses* – winning at a partner's expense – and *individualistic responses* – getting as much for oneself as possible. Although the direct comparison of men's and women's performances revealed no gender differences, the gender of one's opponent was important, as it was in studies of children. Men were more competitive against other men and against highly successful players of both gender, and women were more competitive against low achievers of both gender. While there were no overall differences, men appeared keener to win at the expense of other men and of winners, and women were more motivated to win when faced with a loser. The position of men and women in society at large appears to influence their signal value as challenging or less challenging opponents within the confines of the laboratory game.

Another way in which power has been conceptualized in psychological experiments is in terms of leadership. Power, measured as a psychological trait called dominance, is investigated for gender differences which influence leadership ability. Deaux (1976b) reviewed leadership studies of adults in groups. Two of her questions are of particular interest: 'Do women emerge as leaders as often as men?' and 'Do men and women cope with the role of leader with equal success?' Even the election of Britain's first woman Prime Minister cannot deceive us into believing that women are called or rise to positions of leadership as often as men.

Deaux reported a study by Megargee (1969) in which men and women were assessed for dominance by means of a questionnaire, and then formed into pairs so that each contained one person high and the other low in dominance. The pairs were then asked to choose a leader. When two women or two men were paired, the highly dominant person was chosen as leader 70 per cent of the time. In mixed pairs which contained a highly dominant man, he was chosen 90 per cent of the time; but in mixed pairs containing a highly dominant woman, she was chosen only 20 per cent of the time. It was observed that in the discussion prior to the choice of leader, dominant women usually decided that the man would be their leader. The failure of the dominant woman to become leader is difficult to understand if we consider only the final decision. If we look at the interaction, however, it can be seen that the dominant women were exercising control and power by choosing the man as leader. This study highlights problems of research on dominance, in that there are differences between dominance as measured by a questionnaire and its behavioural manifestation in willingness to assume positions of leadership. In our society authority is expected to reside in men; they are employed as symbols of power, even when the decision is actually taken for them by a woman.

A study of gender differences in the exercise of leadership was also reviewed by Deaux and was shown to be influenced by symbolic power relationships in the wider society (Jacobson and Effertz, 1974). The experimenters set up all-male and all-female groups, groups with two men and a female leader and groups with two women and a male leader. All four types of groups had to complete a difficult problem-solving task and evaluate the performance of their leader and fellow members. The performance of all four differently composed groups was considered equally poor by the experimenters. Despite this view that the groups performed in a similar fashion, the male leaders were rated as poorer by their fellow members than were the female leaders. Leaders themselves, however, rated the performance of women group members below that of the men. Deaux suggests that these results reflect gender stereotypes: men are supposed to be good leaders and women good followers. According to this interpretation, groups which fail must have poor male leaders, while women in groups which fail must be poor followers. Not only are men expected to assume authority, but they are expected to exercise it with skill. Similarly, the submission of women is expected to be well practised and successful.

Despite the ease with which we have fitted studies of competition and cooperation, and of dominance and leadership, into a framework of inequality in power relations between men and women in our society, it should not be assumed that the psychological picture is unambiguous. Maccoby and Jacklin's attempt to compare boys' and girls' dominance was thwarted by the emergence of single-gender playgroups. Another difficulty was a confusion in differentiating toughness, aggressiveness and dominance. Dominance alone posed difficulties in deciding whether to measure it by assessing success in influencing others or by assessing intentions too. These problems occur both in examining psychological power motives and in trying to conceptualize the exercise of power in society.

The obvious solution, defining an act as an exercise of power only if it is a successful attempt to gain compliance, can be seen in laboratory games and in studies of decision-making in situations of conflict in the wider society. Lukes has labelled this the one-dimensional view. It has been criticized by social theorists who argue that power can also be exercised by those in authority to keep conflict out of the decision-making arena. As an example of this, the two-dimensional approach, it could be argued that male interests in keeping the birth rate up prevented open discussion of abortion. In suggesting his own three-dimensional view, Lukes would argue that there was a further exercise of power by men to be seen in their ability not only to keep the issue of abortion out of public debate but also to shape women's consciousness. In this more subtle exercise of power, it is only recently that women have become aware of the real issue – control over their own bodies.

Given the very real complexities attached to the definition of power, it is hardly surprising that psychological studies appear partial and incomplete. As we have already noted in examining other behavioural domains, in the absence of a well-articulated psychological theory it is to be expected that explanations will reflect commonsense notions about the nature of gender differences.

CHAPTER 6

Fear, Anxiety and Mental Health

Aggression, the subject of Chapter 5, and fear, the subject of this one, are closely linked emotional states. The same type of external conditions will often produce one or the other, and the switch from fear to aggression or from aggression to fear can take place rapidly (Archer, 1976b). Fear inhibits aggression and aggression inhibits fear.

If we consider the masculine and feminine stereotypes in our society, it is apparent that men are regarded as responding aggressively in the face of life's frustrations and difficulties. A closely related attribute, and one which more strongly and consistently prescribes male behaviour, is that men are supposed to be brave and not to show fear. Women, on the other hand, can show that they are afraid but are not supposed to behave aggressively. In modern Western society and in many other cultures, boys begin to learn early in life that they should not show fear and that they will be ostracized and ridiculed for doing so. This reluctance to show emotional 'weakness' is maintained and strengthened throughout adult life, although many men will display emotion in the privacy of their homes.

Male 'braveness' is an integral part of many professional sports. Reporting on the reluctance of professional cricketers to wear helmets, John Arlott wrote: 'Batsmen were for long reluctant to take any steps to protect their heads from assault, for fear of being branded "unmanly", or even, as one Test player put it, "afraid"' (*Guardian*, 12 June 1978). In a similar vein, the phrase 'to take your punishment like a man' means to accept it without undue complaint or emotional upset, or bravely. The belief that braveness is a sign of manliness reaches almost masochistic proportions on the rugby football field, where actual injury is common and is of course borne without complaint. Rugby players, it is reported, feel like 'real men' if they have a few injuries after the game (BBC radio programme, *Today*, 18 January 1978).

Braveness is related to the masculine *stereotype*, and as such is an ideal which is difficult to realize. The discrepancy between actual behaviour and stereotypic demands may lead to difficulties. What happens if a man *is* afraid and cannot assume the confident aggressive manner which one of his gender is supposed to achieve? There are ways of making a frightened man feel tough. The use of drugs, in particular alcohol, is one. It is no coincidence that alcoholism has been mainly a male problem, since 'Dutch courage' is needed more by men than women. A song about Scotsmen's drinking habits sums up the change of heart induced by alcohol:

'*Stone cold sober they come in like Mickey Rooney,*
Three pints later they go barging out like big John Wayne'
(Billy Connolly, BBC TV programme *Checkpoint*, 17 August 1978).

How to get over feelings of fear and inadequacy can be seen as a recurrent male problem. Alcohol and drugs may provide one kind of (temporary) answer; presenting a tough aggressive exterior is another. Women, on the other hand, are much freer to express feelings of fear and inadequacy, and such responses usually get sympathy and comfort from others, particularly men. It is socially more acceptable for a woman to be fearful and timid than to be an alcoholic or too aggressive.

A partial explanation of the pattern of gender differences in aggression, fear and mental health in terms of social attitudes is provided later in this chapter. It differs from the approach taken by those who suggest that there are biological differences in the emotional make-up of the two sexes and who argue that our social attitudes merely reflect these differences. Before discussing these and other explanations, we examine evidence for the claim that women are more fearful and anxious than men.

Are Women More Fearful and Anxious than Men?

There are relatively few studies that will help us to answer the question of whether women show a greater degree of fear and anxiety than men. Books on fear usually contain little or no information on the subject: for instance, in Rachman's book (1978) there is no entry for sex or gender differences in the index, and in Sluckin's (1979) their coverage is restricted to about half a page. More attention is paid to gender differences by Gray (1971b); he suggests that women show more pronounced fear and anxiety than men as a result of their hormonal constitution. We shall return to this explanation later.

Broadly speaking, there are three types of study on possible gender differences in fear which we could consider relevant: those carried out on animals, on children and on young adults. We are concerned here with gender differences in adult humans, and therefore studies of animals or children will be relevant only if they show clear parallels with adult differences. Such parallels were apparent in the case of aggression, which we discussed in Chapter 5. But on the subject of fear, Maccoby and Jacklin argue that the parallels with studies of rats and mice are slight and there is little point in considering these studies in relation to human gender differences. Gray (1971a, 1971b) takes a different view, which we shall outline later.

Maccoby and Jacklin (1974) review studies of the development of fear responses in infancy. In some studies, girls first showed a fear of strangers at an earlier age than boys did, but this finding was not a consistent one and it may indicate girls' intellectual maturity. Kagan (1978) reviews several studies carried out subsequent to Maccoby and Jacklin's survey, and argues from these that girls do generally show an earlier onset of fear of strange social situations than boys. Girls' fear response also wanes at an earlier age than that of boys. Kagan regards this particular gender difference as part of the generally earlier maturation of girls than of boys, and he claims that girls come to recognize strange and unfamiliar events and people at an earlier age. Is this early gender difference relevant to adult gender differences in fear? Kagan believes that it is not, and argues that differences in the age of onset of the fear response in infancy are unlikely to have any long-term significance.

Maccoby and Jacklin (1974) also review studies of older children's fears. They conclude that there is some evidence that girls are more fearful than boys, but this is not a consistent finding. The measures in these studies were either direct observation or parents' records. In older children and in adults, the most common measure is a questionnaire inquiring about the person's fears. Interpretations of questionnaire findings often fail to distinguish between how fearful people think they are and how fearful they actually are when confronted by something frightening. Thus most of the evidence on older children and adults has been obtained by asking people to rate how fearful they are rather than by assessments of their behaviour. In the case of aggression, such self-report measures were seen to exaggerate gender differences along stereotypic lines (see Chapter 5). We can expect what people say about their fearfulness to reflect gender stereotypes about fear and courage as well.

Gender differences, when reported in questionnaire studies, tend to show females displaying greater intensity of fear than males (Maccoby and Jacklin, 1974). Since we have no experimental or observational studies to compare with these ratings, we cannot estimate the extent to which they reflect men's unwillingness to admit their fears. Maccoby and Jacklin also pointed out that many of the questions are biased towards items more likely to be related to girls' than to boys' fears: for instance, items include fear of animals and of walking home alone at night, but not fear of failure or appearing cowardly.

A study by Speltz and Bernstein (1976) attempted to differentiate between willingness to admit fears and the actual expression of fears. Male and female undergraduates who had reported either high or low fear of snakes (assessed by a fear questionnaire) were given a behavioural test which involved being asked either to enter a room containing a snake or to pick up a snake. Among people who reported a high degree of fear, men were generally more able to enter the room or go near a snake than women. These results indicate that men who described themselves as highly fearful were more able to overcome their expressed fears when confronted with a real snake than were highly fearful women.

Although we should be cautious about generalizing from a single study of a particular type of fear, it does suggest that even when men and women are matched for equivalent levels of reported fear, women actually show more avoidance of the feared object. There may be a different relationship between stereotype, self-report and actions than we have so far considered. The stereotype may influence men's actions more than verbal reports. Does this mean that it is easier for a man to say 'I'm scared of snakes' than to appear frightened?

This discussion is very speculative, since there is really very little information about gender differences in fearfulness. Another possible source of information is from clinical evidence, but again we have the problem of the discrepancy between what people say and what they do. Women apparently report more phobias – extreme fears which interfere with their everyday living – than do men.

Anxiety is an emotional state similar to fear in many of its physical manifestations; it is not, however, directed to specific objects or people and is usually more prolonged. Self-report questionnaires based on symptoms such as difficulties in sleeping or headaches are available for assessing anxiety states in both children and adults. The consensus from available studies of children is that girls report greater general anxiety than boys. Similarly, clinical anxiety states are found more

frequently in women than men; these are discussed later
in the section on mental health.

How can we explain these findings? We first consider
based viewpoint. In a wide-ranging article Jeffrey Gray
there are biologically based gender differences in both
fear (Gray, 1971a). His argument on aggression is reasonably straightforward: the male is the more aggressive sex in the animal world.
However, animal sex differences in fear have not been so widely studied,
and there is no clear pattern to compare with human gender differences.
Gray bases his particular argument almost entirely on laboratory tests
of fearfulness, or 'emotionality', in rats and mice (Archer, 1973). These
tests mainly involve assessing the extent of an animal's 'emotional'
defecation and its reluctance to move when it is put into an unfamiliar,
brightly lit, enclosed area. On the basis of such tests, Gray suggests
that male rodents are more fearful than females. Although his interpretation of the rodent tests is in dispute (Archer, 1971, 1975), this particular issue is not essential to Gray's theory of human gender differences.
He does not base his argument about human gender differences directly
on evidence from rats and mice; rather, he uses the studies to show
that some animals display sex differences in fearfulness, and that these
are under the control of their sex hormones. He then suggests that
although the human gender difference is in a direction opposite to that
suggested for rats, it nevertheless has a similar biological – hormonal
– basis. Gray cites no direct evidence that sex hormones are involved
in the human gender difference. He does speculate as to whether the
difference he identified between rodents and human beings exists
between primate and rodent groups, or between human beings and
other mammals (Gray and Buffery, 1971). There is very little evidence
on which to evaluate his hypothesis, and until information is available
from a much wider range of animals there is very little that can be
derived from such a forced and speculative comparison of laboratory
rodents and human beings. The argument for a biological basis to
human gender differences in fear is therefore a particularly weak one
(Archer, 1971, 1975).

An alternative, and more convincing, explanation is the one which
we have already outlined: boys and girls receive different messages
from adults and other children about when they can show fear, anxiety
and similar emotions. Early in life, boys come to realize that they must
avoid certain 'feminine' types of behaviour. Among these are too open
an expression of emotional upset, such as crying or whining, or readi-

to display particular fears. Boys and girls show some knowledge
. masculine and feminine stereotypes even at early ages. One of the
characteristics that young children of 2 to 3 years of age attribute to
a 'boy' doll is that he 'never cries' (Kuhn *et al.*, 1978). Children between
5 and 8 years old know many of the adult stereotypic personality
descriptions, including the 'feminine' characteristics of emotional and
weak (Best *et al.*, 1977).

We can only provide broad outlines for a 'socialization' explanation
of gender differences in fear and anxiety. In contrast to aggression,
there has been little or no research into the degree to which boys and
girls imitate emotions shown by people of the same and of the opposite
gender; nor have we found any research documenting the degree to
which the expression of emotional upset and fear is encouraged or
discouraged in boys and girls.

Are Women More Moody than Men?

This question is often asked in relation to the more pronounced and
regular fluctuations in reproductive hormones that occur throughout
a woman's life. Thus the question becomes, 'Do women's hormones
make them more moody than men?' More specifically, women are said
to be particularly prone to emotional outbursts or depression prior to
menstruation, immediately after childbirth and at the menopause, and
changes in hormonal levels at these times are held to be responsible.
What is the evidence for such claims? Let us look first at the menstrual
cycle.

Menstruation

A variety of psychological changes have been reported during the
different phases of the menstrual cycle. The most well-known of these
are negative mood changes, such as anxiety and irritability, reported by
many women just before menstruation (for example, Moos *et al.*, 1969;
Paige, 1973). Similar changes have been shown in laboratory studies
using behavioural measures of frustration (Schonberg *et al.*, 1976) and
physiological measures of emotional arousal (for example, Vila and
Beech, 1978). There are also reports of an increase in antisocial or
'neurotic' activities such as shoplifting, accident proneness and
attempted suicide (Dalton, 1969, 1979).

In medical literature, such behavioural changes are commonly linked with physical changes; these are referred to as the 'premenstrual syndrome', a term first used in the early 1930s (Janiger *et al.*, 1972). Various physical explanations have been offered for the premenstrual mood changes: for instance, Dalton (1969) believed them to be a consequence of the change in mineral salt balance, and others have suggested that they result from lowered progesterone levels (for example, Hamburg and Lunde, 1967).

A number of methodological criticisms have been made of studies claiming to demonstrate psychological deficiencies during the premenstrual phase (for example, Parlee, 1973; Sommer, 1973; Tavris and Offir, 1977). There are also criticisms of the physical explanations of premenstrual mood changes, which point out that it is not possible to exclude psychological influences from studies of the menstrual cycle. There are unmistakable physical signs that menstruation is on the way, and the possibility that a negative mood change before a period represents the learnt anticipation of an embarrassing, unpleasant and inconvenient event cannot be ruled out. Neither can we regard reports that premenstrual mood changes are lessened in women taking oral contraceptives as evidence for a direct hormonal cause of the mood change (for example, Bardwick, 1971). The synthetic hormones in the pill may remove the physical signal that triggers a learnt response to the forthcoming period. If this type of explanation sounds implausible, consider the following study. Paige (1973) investigated premenstrual symptoms in a sample of women, half of whom were using a contraceptive pill. In general, she found that premenstrual anxiety – assessed by analysing the content of a story – was lessened in those women taking the pill. But the reduction in anxiety depended on the woman's menstrual flow lessening, and not solely on hormonal levels. If the woman still had a heavy menstrual flow while on the pill, she would be more likely to show signs of premenstrual anxiety. These results suggest that mood changes before a period result from a psychological reaction to the more obvious physical symptoms of menstruation, rather than being the direct consequence of a change in hormone levels.

Paige also carried out a larger-scale study to investigate the extent to which premenstrual and menstrual distress was related to measures of general health, reactions to psychological stress, and attitudes to motherhood, sexuality and menstruation. She found that women who had more symptoms during menstruation also had the same types of symptoms at other times, suggesting that they were more prone to psychosomatic symptoms.

Paige discovered too that the severity of menstrual symptoms was related to cultural attitudes and reflected different religious beliefs. Amongst Jewish women, adherence to menstrual taboos prescribed by their faith was most likely to be strongly related to severe physical and emotional symptoms. For Catholic women, traditional views about a woman's role – that a woman's place is in the home – were more likely to be related to severe menstrual symptoms. Since it is unlikely that the severity of physical symptoms could have caused these particular social and religious beliefs, and since religion provides the main source of negative attitudes about menstruation and sexuality in our culture, Paige's study provides further evidence for the importance of negative attitudes to menstruation in determining menstrual distress.

Several other researchers (for example, Parlee, 1973; Sommer, 1973) also argue that widespread negative attitudes about menstruation in our culture, as documented by Clarke and Ruble (1978) and by Birke and Best (1980) for example, may be sufficient to explain many pre-menstrual symptoms. It is important to note that this type of explanation is not intended to imply that menstrual distress is simply imaginary or a sign of neurosis or hypochondria (Paige, 1973; Birke and Best, 1980).

Postnatal Depression

Emotional changes are often reported after childbirth. These include depression, fearfulness and irritability, sometimes referred to as the 'baby blues' or 'postnatal depression' if they are particularly severe. Various surveys in the United States have found that some emotional upset occurs in as many as 30 to 60 per cent of women (Sherman, 1971). Again it is suggested that physical factors such as a sudden fall in progesterone levels cause the mood changes (for example, Hamburg and Lunde, 1967), and a link is suggested between susceptibility to premenstrual and postpartum symptoms (for example, Dalton, 1971). Although the subject has not been as well researched as premenstrual changes, alternative culturally based explanations can also be offered to account for these emotional changes. Paige (1973) suggests that a woman has good reason to react emotionally to all major reproductive events, since they represent her main avenue of achievement and self-expression. Thus, reacting to the reality and the responsibility of looking after a baby after the excitement and anticipation of pregnancy, and to the realization that freedom, mobility and social contacts are curtailed, could well cause depression. These suggestions are speculative, since very little research has been carried out on this subject. One exception is a study by Breen (1975), who sought to understand the meaning of a woman's first pregnancy and childbirth. Good adjustment was related to factors evident during pregnancy and after the birth. Successful mothers saw themselves as active both before and after the child was born. If women are deprived of a feeling of control by obstetric practices, this may place them at risk at a time when their hormones are changing dramatically.

Menopause

Anxiety, irritability and depression may also accompany the menopause (for example, Sherman 1971; Tavris and Offir, 1977), but they appear to be less pronounced and more of a reaction to the physical changes rather than a direct effect of hormonal changes. A well-known study found that depression in a sample of middle-aged women was related to the loss of the maternal role which often occurred at about the same time as the menopause (Bart, 1971).

Mood Changes and Hormones

From this brief survey, what can we conclude about the theory that a woman's hormones are directly responsible for mood changes before menstruation, after childbirth and at the menopause? Firstly, we can conclude that the evidence is not as convincing as it might have appeared at first sight. Secondly, there are plausible alternative explanations in terms of the attitudes, beliefs and expectations surrounding significant changes in a woman's reproductive life. A more comprehensive explanation of the mood changes would have to include consideration of both the physical changes and their significance for the women concerned.

Although it has been common to ask whether a woman's emotions are linked to her reproductive hormones, the same question has seldom been asked for men. It is of course easier to tell when a woman's hormones are changing, owing to their more regular fluctuations and external manifestations. Men undergo quite large fluctuations in testosterone levels, but these are neither accompanied by obvious external signs, nor do they follow an identifiable and regular pattern. One study (Doering *et al.*, 1974) investigated the possible relationship between what men said about their emotions and testosterone levels. A sample of twenty young men was used, and the measures were obtained every other day for two months. A relationship between the two was found for some individuals but not for others. The precise relationship between emotional state and hormone levels also varied between different individuals. The strongest overall relationship of testosterone and mood was with depression, but again there was a great deal of individual variation.

Are There Gender Differences in Mental Health?

The adjective 'emotional' is part of the female stereotype. In this chapter we have examined studies of fear and anxiety which may be components of emotionality. We have considered the impact of stereotypes on reports of fear and anxiety and on the behaviour of men and women. When we look at more extreme states of fear and anxiety which interfere with normal living and are viewed as mental illness, gender stereotypes are just as likely to be important. As we saw in Chapter 5, crime statistics reinforce our notions of the aggressive male. Similarly, when we look at reports on mental health or psychological disorders, the stereotypic description of women as more emotional than men is echoed by the greater number of women in many categories of mental illness.

A classic study of gender stereotypes in mental health is that of Broverman and her colleagues (1970). They asked professional clinicians to describe healthy men and women. The verbal portraits of a healthy man and a healthy person were very similar; a healthy woman, however, was seen as more conceited, excitable in a minor crisis, submissive, emotional, less adventurous, aggressive, competitive, independent and objective. Many writers, including Williams (1977), have remarked on these findings that the description of a healthy woman, different as it is from that of a healthy man or person, seems scarcely a picture of health.

Despite the problems involved in making a comparison between mental health in the two genders, we can compare the extent to which various types of disorders appear in men and women. We begin by looking at statistical reports and then consider possible explanations for differences in mental health. As with many other comparisons of men and women, different types of explanations have been used to account for the same findings. Theories may stress biological differences; they may seek to explain vulnerability by looking at the world of inner experience; or they may indicate sources of stress in the daily lives of adults in our society.

Two approaches have traditionally been used in diagnosing mental illness. The first asks whether an individual's feelings and behaviour deviate from the norm; the second treats mental disturbance as yet another clinical entity – an illness. Viewing psychological disturbances in a normative manner leads us to ask what is normal and to treat behaviour which differs from the average as deviant. It is difficult enough to answer the question of normality without the added complication of gender stereotypes. Behaviour acceptable for a man – for example, aggression – may be less seemly for a woman. Similarly, emotional outbursts attract greater censure in men than in women. Thus gender stereotypes influence the diagnosis of disturbed behaviour and are implicated in the forms of treatment offered and the explanations proposed.

The illness model, on the other hand, while emphasizing the distress and suffering that psychopathology causes, makes assumptions of a biological nature about diagnosis, explanation and cure. Both of these approaches have been attacked by proponents of anti-psychiatry: the normative approach for its victimizing the deviant (Laing, 1967); and the medical model for its biological emphasis, since it is asserted that society manufactures madness (Szasz, 1970). That existing knowledge does not allow immediate identification of precipitating physiological factors is taken as evidence of the failure of the medical approach. We shall avoid taking a stand on this controversy and use the terms mental illness, psychopathology and psychological disorder almost interchangeably because we are not committed to a single explanation. Diagnosis, as we shall see, is a treacherous issue, but not one to be solved by adopting one model or another. The types of behaviour which we consider are characterized by fear, anxiety or depression, and are a source of distress to the person involved and frequently to those around them as well. They can also be considered as more pronounced or extreme forms of emotional states experienced by almost everyone.

In this section, which deals primarily with official statistics, the classification of psychological disorders follows established psychiatric practices. In the data for English mental hospital admissions, the *Manual of the International Statistical Classification of Diseases, Injuries and Causes of Death* (1967) is used. In the American studies, a system developed by the American Psychiatric Association (1968) is often employed. These systems rely on the appearance of criterial symptoms or constellations of symptoms for the identification of particular disorders.

A few definitions may be kept in mind while examining these statistics. Full definitions which involve a theory about mental illness are beyond our brief. It is generally agreed that the most severe disorders are the various psychoses which involve loss of contact with reality, self or other people. Those behavioural disturbances with a recognized biological component, such as alcohol poisoning or severe infection, are grouped together and described as organic psychoses. The many psychoses with no known pathology of the central nervous system are usually labelled the functional psychoses. This category includes the

Table 6.1. First Admissions to Mental Illness Hospitals and Units in England, 1975

	Men	Women	Total
Schizophrenia, schizo-affective disorders and paranoia	2,476 47%	2,741 53%	5,217
Depressive psychosis and involutional melancholia	1,739 35%	3,223 65%	4,962
Alcoholic psychosis	338 70%	144 30%	482
Senile and presenile psychosis	1,576 31%	3,559 69%	5,135
Other psychoses	2,341 37%	4,019 63%	6,360
Psychoneuroses	3,244 36%	5,879 64%	9,123
Alcoholism	2,247 75%	756 25%	3,003
Drug dependence	383 70%	162 30%	545
Personality and behavioural disorders	2,857 52%	2,682 48%	5,539
Other psychiatric conditions	1,007 42%	1,406 58%	2,413
Undiagnosed	5,373 37%	9,043 63%	14,416
All diagnoses	23,581 41%	33,614 59%	57,195

Based upon DHSS, *Health and Personal Social Services Statistics for England, 1977.*

schizophrenias with widely known bizarre behaviour, certain paranoid states and severe affective disorders such as manic-depressive psychosis, with its alternating moods of intense elation and despair.

The psychoneuroses, which include anxiety attacks, irrational fears such as agoraphobia, hysteria and various obsessions and compulsions, are considered milder disorders. This does not mean that individuals necessarily experience less distress; but they may be able to function at work and in the family, and some may never seek treatment. Clearly it is difficult to estimate the number of psychotics and neurotics who never seek treatment, though community surveys provide some indication of the number of people who are ill but have not sought treatment.

With these general distinctions in mind we can examine some statistics. We begin by considering first admissions to all mental hospitals and units in English in 1975. Table 6.1 shows the actual number of first admissions according to standard diagnostic categories, and also the proportions of men and women in the various categories.

The only categories in which men predominate are alcoholic psychosis, alcoholism, drug dependence, and personality and behavioural disorders. The category with most women – senile and presenile psychoses – is likely to be related to women's greater life span. The overall picture to emerge from these statistics is one of more frequent first admissions of women (59 per cent), particularly in the categories of the functional psychoses and psychoneuroses.

Similar figures have been reported in the United States (Gove and Tudor 1972). The figures closest to those for the United Kingdom indicate that 52 per cent of first admissions diagnosed as suffering from functional psychoses are women, while 59 per cent of those described as psychoneurotic are women. These percentages rise for people discharged from out-patient psychiatric clinics and reach their peak in general hospital treatment, where women comprise 59 per cent of those treated for functional psychoses and 65 per cent of those treated for psychoneuroses.

Studies of communities and analyses of treatment by general practitioners produce similar statistics (Gove and Tudor, 1972). A study of doctors in New York found that women were more frequently diagnosed as suffering from psychological disorders (Locke and Gardner, 1969). The figures were analysed by age as well as by sex and showed that the period from 35 to 44 years of age was that of the greatest vulnerability for women: 25 per cent of their problems were diagnosed as being of a psychiatric nature. The peak decade for men was between 45 and 54 years, but even then only 16 per cent of their symptoms were considered evidence of psychopathology.

An English study of general practitioners publishes related, though not strictly comparable, findings. All visits to a group of London doctors were monitored for a year. For every 1,000 women registered, 175 visits during the year were diagnosed as involving a psychiatric illness, while only 98 visits per 1,000 registered male patients were similarly diagnosed (Shepherd *et al.*, 1966). Within these groups, women were more likely to be described as suffering from some form of psycho-neuroses – 67 per cent as compared with only 57 per cent of men so diagnosed.

So far we have focused on functional psychoses and psychoneuroses generally, but other disorders may furnish clues to experiences of unusual fear and anxiety – namely, phobias and physical illnesses with an origin in psychological distress. Few surveys report phobic reactions alone. Frazier and Carr (1967) used statistics based upon reports from out-patient clinics in the United States. Looking at Table 6.2, we see a familiar pattern. Not only were there more women among all patients

Table 6.2. Patients Leaving Treatment in 933 Out-patients Clinics in the United States, 1961

	Men over 18	Women over 18	Total
Total patients	33,046	44,966	78,012
Psychoneurotic disorders	6,543	14,302	20,845
Phobic Reactions	169	452	621
as % of total	0·5	1·0	
as % of psychoneurotic disorders	2·6	3·2	

Based on Frazier and Carr (1967).

leaving clinic treatment in 1961, but there were also more women in the psychoneurotic and phobic reaction sub-categories. Looking at the figures another way, we can also see that phobic reactions are somewhat more common among the psychoneurotic disorders of women than of men, even after we have taken account of the differential incidence in the gender groups.

Illnesses such as stomach ulcers and backache are believed to reflect an emotional conflict, though their symptomatology is somatic. Men and women show different patterns here: men are more likely to develop peptic and duodenal ulcers and skin disorders, while migraine, high blood pressure and insomnia are more common in women (Garai, 1970). It has been suggested that women react to emotional conflict by developing a psychological disorder, whereas men display physical symptoms; but Gove and Tudor (1972), using hospital statistics, community surveys and studies of general practitioners, report a higher incidence of psychosomatic disorders among women. Although we cannot provide a definitive conclusion, it appears most unlikely that the psychosomatic illnesses, taken as a group, are more common among men; in fact there is some evidence that more women report suffering from these complaints (Mayo, 1976).

Suicide is included in this discussion of mental health, even though the meaning of each act is not clear. We assume that people who succeed have been deeply distressed; and even if we interpret unsuccessful suicide attempts as cries for help, some fear, anxiety or depression is undoubtedly present. The statistics are unequivocal: more men than women commit suicide, using more violent methods (Stengel, 1964). However, the reverse is true of attempts at suicide: four women make unsuccessful attempts for every man who fails (Garai, 1970). (These figures were published a decade ago and may no longer describe the situation accurately.) Rates of suicide among women have been rising, and the once prevalent notion that male suicide was related to employment difficulties while female suicides reflected interpersonal problems has been overtaken by recent studies. Loneliness and isolation, usually factors in the suicide attempts of women, have been implicated in the suicides of elderly men in a British study (Whitlock, 1973), while the suicide rate for women who are medical doctors and psychologists has been found to be almost three times as high as that of other American women (Schaar, 1974). In the latter study it appears that employment difficulties may be producing intolerable strain on women.

The picture which we have drawn is necessarily incomplete given the space available, but before we interpret these limited findings it is important to consider the impact of marriage on the mental health of men and women. Returning to suicide, we note a study by Gove (1972) which showed that marriage seemed to protect men from suicide even though across all categories – never married, divorced, widowed and married – men committed suicide more often than women did. At an extreme, divorced men committed suicide four times as often as divorced women.

Marriage has a different effect for women. Returning to the statistics for mental illness, it is the single, divorced and widowed women who are comparatively free of psychological disorders. Married women seem to make up the surplus of women among the mentally ill (Williams, 1977). Only among men are we likely to find that the seriously ill, the schizophrenics, remain single. Psychotic men may find difficulty in establishing and maintaining a stable relationship and in providing a home. Speculation about the effects of marriage and its relation to mental health leads readily to a discussion of the demands of gender roles and their impact on psychological wellbeing. But before we examine this or any other explanation, we need to consider the reliability of the data which we have presented.

Are Gender Differences in Mental Health Reliable?

We have already hinted at problems in both the diagnosis and the reporting of mental illness in men and women. These are complex issues and we can do little more than raise some of the important questions.

A feminist perspective on mental health statistics gives rise to a reluctance to view them as mere 'facts'; rather, the position of women – and men – in society is viewed as inseparable from their psychological condition. Chesler (1972) asserts that mental illness is a condition into which women are pushed and that hospitalization may provide a haven when role pressures become too demanding. Lipshitz (1978) contends that the problems of diagnosis are magnified by the fact that the overwhelming majority of hospital doctors are men who may well expect women to be over-emotional. The willingness of physicians to ascribe psychological disturbances to women is indirectly verified by the large numbers of American women who are prescribed psychoactive drugs – tranquillizers, sedatives and stimulants (The National Commission on Marihuana and Drug Abuse, 1973). This controlled and legitimized form of addiction among women has been compared with men's use of alcohol and illicit drugs (Stoll, 1978).

Adding to the tendency of male physicians to see women as psychiatric patients may be women's own tendencies to seek help. Studies have shown that women more frequently seek help with emotional problems (Phillips and Segal, 1969). In addition, once individuals come to psychiatric clinics, doctors are reluctant to admit that treatment is not required; they tend to diagnose and prescribe for those seeking help (Ingham and Miller, 1976).

Though it is difficult to measure distress or the need for treatment directly, we can look at research on men's and women's willingness to reveal intimate details about themselves. More than fifteen years ago American studies suggested that women were more willing to reveal intimate details of their lives to close friends (Jourard, 1964). Since then, there has been a general shift towards greater interest in psychological phenomena. One of our undergraduate students compared letters to *Jackie*, an English magazine for teenage girls, and found that the problems posed in 1978 were more intimate, sexual and interpersonal than they had been in 1968. A greater concern with the world of emotion and inner experience may also be occurring in men, and it may be reflected in a greater willingness of men to reveal intimate details.

Willingness to reveal personal experience and emotional problems is probably not the whole explanation for the higher incidence of mental illness among women. In a study which systematically explored bias in reporting, it was concluded that women did experience more symptoms (Clancy and Gove, 1974). Despite the numerous methodological problems in this field, the evidence suggests that there is something other than women's willingness to seek help influencing the incidence of mental illness in men and women. We have noted already that surveys of mental health in the community at large avoid the help-seeking bias, and even these surveys suggest greater mental illness among women.

How are These Differences Explained?

Our discussion of mental illness in men and women has repeatedly tended to link gender roles and stereotypes to more frequent diagnoses of mental illness in women. Let us look more closely at this view and then move on to psychological and biological explanations.

Our statistics for mental illness in the United States are derived from the research of Gove and Tudor (1973). They approach the issue of gender differences in mental health from a sociological perspective and attempt to link the greater frequency of mental illness in women to gender roles. In particular they examine the role of the housewife in order to show the risks inherent in it. Although their statistics are presented only as incidences of illness in men and women, their explanation hinges upon the role of the full-time housewife. This gives it a middle-class bias, since working-class women are often forced by economic circumstances to work as well as keep house. Gove and Tudor summarize the sources of stress in being a housewife under five headings. They are:

(1) Restriction of possibilities of gratification to home and family to the exclusion of work satisfaction.

(2) Frustration of needs for competent performance and achievement in so far as child-minding and housework appear to require little skill and command little prestige.

(3) Lack of demands or structure, allowing time to brood over troubles.

(4) Limited satisfaction for working wives who view their careers as secondary, who experience discrimination in opportunity for advancement and who carry a double load, working as well as keeping house.

(5) Lack of specificity of demands in so far as women are required to adjust to their husband's and children's needs and neither to formulate nor to afford priority to their aspirations.

Besides marshalling evidence for the different effects of marriage on men and women, Gove and Tudor consider historical and cultural comparisons. They point out different rates of mental illness in different communities, and relate cohesiveness of traditional communities to an overall lower incidence of mental illness with even lower rates for women. Economic stress and unemployment are found in communities in which there is more mental illness, and in these men outnumber women in the ranks of the distressed. The limits of sociological explanations become clear when we attempt to account for social change. Not only have women's roles changed in recent years but so too have men's roles, and these changing gender roles undoubtedly influence each other.

Sociological explanations are often combined with psychological explanations to account for gender differences. This has been the case in efforts to explain the consistent reports of a higher incidence of depression among women. Some investigators have suggested that the greater frequency of diagnosed depression in women – 65 per cent in Table 6.1 – is illusive and that depression in men is masked by physical symptoms (Beck and Greenberg, 1974). In an exhaustive review of the literature, the possibility that alcoholism and crime may mask depression in men was considered, but the authors concluded that the greater incidence of depression among women is a reliable phenomenon and not a methodological artefact. Psychoanalytic theory and learning theory have each been combined with a sociological perspective to explain the higher incidence of depression among women.

Psychoanalytic theories of the causes of particular neuroses or psychoses do not elaborate the theme of gender differences. Rather, this issue is considered in the developmental theory of infantile sexuality and is most clearly specified in terms of the Oedipal complex. In Chapter 4 we noted that this aspect of the theory has come under considerable attack because of its view that women, as a result of their resolution of the Oedipal complex, are typically more narcissistic, lower in self-esteem and more dependent than men. We saw that the critics, including psychoanalysts, have sought to emphasize the influence of society on the development of women.

A recent psychoanalytic account considers societal influences on mental health and examines the increased incidence of phobias in successful women after marriage (Symonds, 1971). The author argues that marriage and the implications which it carries for dependency may act as a trigger when internal conflicts are already present and unresolved.

Chesler (1972) followed a different strategy and related societal factors to Freud's classic work on depression, *Mourning and Melancholia*. In it Freud differentiated realistic loss and its resolution through the mourning process from melancholia, in which the failure to come to terms with real or imagined loss leads instead to feelings of lower self-esteem and self-worth. In normal mourning the loving and aggressive feelings towards the lost object are integrated, whereas in melancholia the aggressive feelings are turned towards the self. Chesler argues that the dynamic mechanism applies to depression in women, but that the loss – that of status as potent, mature members of society – is real. Women, she suggests, are socialized to accept loss, not to seek a strong ideal-self. To ward off the anger which this frustration induces, they turn it inwards with resulting depression. Quoting a study by Bart (1971) of depression in middle-aged women whose children had recently left home, and noting the greater incidence of depression in women with a large number of children, Chesler maintains that continuing satisfaction is denied even to women who accept the feminine role. This occurs because the role becomes redundant when the children grow up and leave home, and because a satisfactory performance is usually prevented when the family is large.

Another line of theorizing which has distant roots in psychoanalytic explanations of psychopathology is that which views depression in terms of the feelings of helplessness which characterize it (Bibring, 1953). This approach has been developed by Seligman (1975) within a learning theory model. He has shown, both with human beings and with other animals, that individuals who repeatedly find themselves in situations in which their behaviour cannot control unpleasant stimulation do not attempt later to gain control in manageable circumstances. The effect is heightened when people in experiments are told that their problem-solving outcomes are determined by chance and when individuals who believe that luck determines their fate are involved. Seligman argues that depression is characterized by helplessness specific to beliefs about one's own ability to influence events, and he demonstrates this in comparisons of depressed and non-depressed people. In one study he showed the different effects of success and failure on the performance of these two groups in tests involving both skill and chance. The manipulation affected non-depressed individuals' expectations of success in tests of skill, but depressed individuals' expectations of performance on tests both of skill and of chance were affected.

We can only touch upon the thought-provoking results which Seligman's approach has yielded. The overall picture which emerges from laboratory studies of learned helplessness leads to the characterization of depression in terms of passivity, lack of observable aggression and reduced effectiveness in solving problems. It has been suggested that the gender role socialization of women leads to a similar outcome and that the adult role of women is one in which there is little opportunity for effective control (Litman, 1978). From similarities between the experimental induction of learned helplessness and an analysis of female life-histories, Litman constructs a plausible account of the greater incidence of clinical depression among women.

Explanations of mental illness which draw heavily upon biological differences between men and women are very diverse, though they share a common starting-point. The psychoanalyst Helene Deutsch (1945) saw the passive and masochistic tendencies of women as an adaptation to their reproductive functions in menstruation and childbirth. In this chapter we have already mentioned Gray's suggested hormonal explanation for the greater numbers of women showing fears and anxiety states. We have considered the proposition that women show more marked mood fluctuation than men as a result of the hormonal changes associated with their reproductive lives. Some psychiatrists have focused on the use of oral contraceptives, childbirth and the menopause, and have tried to relate these events to gender differences in psycho-pathology.

Evidence concerning the influence of hormonal factors on depression was examined in a scholarly review (Weissman and Klerman, 1977). At a number of points the existing research was incomplete, and the authors concluded by suggesting closer collaboration between endo-crinologists and psychiatrists in order to document the effects of particular hormones on depression. Evidence for the impact of mood variations during the menstrual cycle or of oral contraceptives on raising the level of female depression was inconclusive; premenstrual tension could contribute slightly to the numbers of women among depressives, but particular physiological explanations could not be offered and no specific hormones have been implicated. The search for an under-standing of the impact of oral contraceptives has been impeded by serious methodological problems. It would not be ethically possible, in an effort to disentangle psychological effects of the pill, to employ control groups who would receive inert placebos offering no hormonal protection from conception. Although the evidence of an increase in depression following childbirth is clear, a precise biological explanation is not forthcoming. We noted that the notion that women are at risk because of the extreme hormonal changes experienced is called into question by the lower-than-average rate of mental illness during pregnancy.

Perhaps most surprising is the conclusion that the menopause is not characterized by an increase in mental illness generally or in depression in particular. Life events, such as the 'empty nest' syndrome described by Bart (1971), were seen to be of at least as great importance in account-ing for continuing risks of mental illness as any hormonal changes triggered by the end of menstruation.

We have drawn upon only some of the biological explanations which were examined by Weissman and Klerman. The review considered psychosocial accounts in an equally thorough fashion and concluded that it was most unlikely that any one of the explanations they had examined would provide an adequate explanation of the various illnesses described as depression.

The explanations which we have considered, be they sociological, psychological or biological, do not attempt to predict individual incidences of mental illness. The approaches which we examined all addressed the question of why there are more women, as a group, treated for depression and other disorders.

Even though it is not yet possible to offer an adequate explanation for the greater incidence of depression, psychoneurosis and functional psychoses in women, we close this discussion by considering some research which is a step towards a more complex and inclusive type of explanation. It also suggests why particular women may be at risk. It is a methodologically sophisticated and sensitive study reported in a volume as long as this book (Brown and Harris, 1978). We can only outline the theory presented to account for clinical and subclinical depression among women in Camberwell, London.

The Brown and Harris study is not a treatise on gender differences *per se*. They only investigated depression in women and sought to explain the higher incidence among working-class women in Camberwell. They were able to show that the difference occurred only during particular life stages, either when working-class women had a child younger than six years of age at home or when they had three or more children at home under fourteen years of age. Furthermore, they were able to account for class differences in depression in the face of equally stress-provoking life events involving long-term loss or disappointment, such as the death of a parent, grown children moving far away, the discovery of a husband's infidelity or severe illness in a close personal friend. Although stressful life events were more common among working-class women with children, even when they were compared with middle-class women who experienced the same degree of stress within their lives, the rate of clinical depression was four times greater for the working-class women.

Role identities, interpersonal and intrapsychic elements are each given a place in Brown and Harris's account of depression. The important intrapsychic elements are the absence of feelings of self-esteem and mastery. These echo Seligman's notions of learned helplessness. Inner feelings of self-worth are shown to be protected or exposed by role identities. Women able to maintain a positive outlook despite a distressing life event would have employment outside the home, an intimate relationship with their husbands or boyfriends, and fewer than three children at home under the age of fourteen. No outside employment, lack of intimacy and three children under fourteen are vulnerability factors associated with general feelings of hopelessness and clinical depression. A fourth vulnerability factor, the loss of the woman's own mother before she was eleven years old, while related causally to the interpersonal factors, would appear to have an important impact on the world of inner experience, on feelings of self-esteem and mastery. It is the greater likelihood of there being one or more of these vulnerability factors in the background of working-class women which Brown and Harris invoke to explain the class difference in depression. We have chosen to conclude with their study because it points the way towards a meaningful integration of some of the factors which could be involved in future accounts of the differential occurrence of depression and other mental illness among men and women.

CHAPTER 7

The Family

In the next two chapters we consider the worlds of home and work, the domestic and public spheres of social life. It is generally believed that a woman's place is in the family and a man's in the wider world. In Chapter 5 we considered the argument of some feminist sociologists and anthropologists that it is male power which keeps women in their place – the home. Even when women are engaged in full-time employment, they are expected to clean, cook and shop – to keep house for their families. So pervasive is this view among single employed Americans that the time women reported spending on household tasks was twice as much as that reported by men (Robinson and Converse, 1966).

Examination of the family and the world of work offers evidence of the usual behaviour of men and women, their gender-appropriate roles and psychological dispositions. We challenge accepted beliefs by asking whether men can keep house and provide satisfactory care for young children, and whether women have the abilities and motivation to fill skilled jobs and meet professional demands.

We begin our discussion of the family by picking up a major theme from the comparison of mental health in men and women – the impact of marriage on each gender. This emphasis on the family should not be interpreted to mean that we believe the only legitimate unit within which to raise children is a family formed by a man and woman in a legally sanctioned relationship. Still, marriage is a major institution in our society; 93 per cent of people are married at some time in their lives. With the rising numbers of divorces, marriage at later ages and widowhood, a significant part of adult life may also be spent living on one's own or in relationships outside legally sanctioned marriage.

The demographic data which we examined in Chapter 2 reviewed alternative household types besides those of married people with children and those of single adults. We saw that 12 per cent of households in England were composed of only one adult and some children. As men remarry more quickly after divorce, and children usually live with their mothers, the majority of one-parent families are headed by women. Despite the growing number of one-parent households, we begin our examination of the family by considering the impact of marriage on the two genders and by examining the role of the housewife. Until quite recently sociologists focused on adult work roles, and that of the housewife was largely ignored. Female sociologists have sought to correct this omission (Gavron, 1966; Oakley, 1974). Again in a sexist manner, the contribution of mothers to child care has been carefully scrutinized by psychologists, while that of fathers has largely been ignored. After examining the structure of the family, the roles in it and its social function, we consider in detail one particular function, that of child-rearing. We first consider early attachment and the mother's function. After questioning women's unique contribution to early development, we compare the roles of mother and father in socialization.

Marriage and the Family

In our society, when a woman becomes a wife she usually expects – or is expected – to change her name, her residence and sometimes her job. Women also change more psychologically as a result of marriage. A review of longitudinal studies reported that wives were likely to modify their personalities and their values in line with their husband's expectations (Barry, 1970). This study also noted that marital happiness was related to the husband's success both economically and at an interpersonal level. We have already seen that the loss of self-esteem and control in marriage has costs for women which are reflected in the greater incidence of mental illness, particularly depression. Being at work protects women from the full impact of marriage. Single women fare better than single men, for in our society men thrive with the care they receive in marriage, whereas women are healthier living on their own.

In theory at least, marriage brings changes for both sexes: a woman becomes a wife and usually a mother, while a man becomes a husband and usually a father. Indeed, it has been very unusual for a man to assume the role of father outside of marriage. In the summary table adapted from one originally presented by Stoll (1978), we can see that the demands of marriage throughout the adult years are different for men and women. Only as a man reaches retirement do his primary concerns shift from work to the family. In Stoll's five stages of female development, the primary focus for a woman is other people – her husband, her children, her grandchildren and finally, in divorce or widowhood,

Table 7.1. Roles of Men and Women in a Family Household

Stage of Development	Men	Women
I. Entry	Becoming a husband or mate:	Becoming a housewife:
Marriage or living together	Change to responsibility status	Change to depending status
		Acquire domestic skills
	Redefine self as 'full adult'	Redefine self as 'mature'
II. Expanding Circle Childbirth	Becoming a father:	Becoming a mother:
	Increased support responsibilities	Acquire child-care skills
	Change in self-definition	Restrictions on many activities
	Readjustments in spouse role	Major self-redefinition
		Change in spouse role
III. Full-house Plateau Completed family	Self-resignation:	Self-development:
	Major redefinition of self to work	Increased community involvement
	Acquire fathering skills	Return to work part-time
		Acquire child-rearing skills
IV. Shrinking Circle Departure of children	Self-change:	Search for new roles:
	Change in self-regarding, sexuality and masculinity	Becoming a grandmother
	Disengagement from work	Return to work or education full-time
	Acquire leisure pursuits	Reorient to spouse
		Change in self-regarding, sexuality and femininity
V. Disengagement	Widowed, divorced:	Widowed, divorced:
	Becoming a potential spouse	Becoming a potential spouse
	Change to independent status	Change to independent status
	Acquiring domestic skills	Increased economic responsibility
(Remarriage)	Becoming a husband, stepfather	Becoming a wife, stepmother
	Change to responsibility status	Change to dependency status

Adapted from Stoll (1978).

another partner. As Nancy Chodorow (1978) notes, the modern family, stripped of almost all other functions, has become 'a quintessentially relational and personal institution, *the* personal sphere of society'

In summarizing a topic as vast as the family in a few hundred words, it is easy to overlook differences of culture, class and historical era. Sociological accounts, intent upon showing that family roles are socially constructed, take care to point out the time-boundedness of views of family roles and functions based upon the modern middle-class family (for example, Walum, 1977). The complete separation of production and reproduction, the economy and child-rearing, as we know it, is only a few centuries old. Before the rise of our modern industrial society, the family was often a social and commercial centre. In rural areas women might work the land, look after livestock and poultry, make clothes, process and store food, as well as bear children and rear them. In cities the homes of the mercantile class were centres of trade and production. Passing merchants along with apprentices were housed and fed; children were trained; food, clothing and household articles were made in the home. In the poorest families, female labour extending beyond child care was necessary for survival. The onset of the industrial revolution found women and even young children in mills and mines. It is often forgotten that the professions have also undergone great changes. Two and three centuries ago women were active medical practitioners, functioning not only as midwives and nurses but generally providing care in the community (Mitchell and Oakley, 1976).

Urbanization and the concentration of production in factories relocated production; the rise of formal education weakened the apprentice system and education in the home; the manufacture of food and improved storage methods contributed in reducing dramatically the functions of married women. Baking bread and cultivating a garden have come to represent a nostalgic quest for meaning and purpose in the life of married middle-class women, alongside the remaining functions of child birth and rearing (French, 1978). We have already noted in Chapter 2 the growing numbers of married women working outside the home. The middle- and upper-class Victorian ideal of women restricted to the home has recently been eroded; however, it was never possible for working-class girls, who went to work before they reached puberty.

Once the family has been stripped of most functions other than reproduction, it becomes seductively easy to seek explanations for its continued existence in biology. So powerful is this lure that an avowedly feminist sociologist, Alice Rossi (1977), has recently espoused such a position. Her assertion of biological necessity is noteworthy in that she had previously argued for sexual equality in the same journal,

Daedalus. Rossi's affirmation of a biosocial approach to the family can be dismissed as part of a general retrenchment which the women's movement has experienced in the late 1970s, but this ignores the seriousness of Rossi's contribution to our understanding of the family. Instead, we consider her current position at length and also two critiques of it.

In her original paper Rossi (1964) adopted the view that women became mothers as the result of their socialization. Taking this social learning position, she proposed an undifferentiated education for boys and girls – a stance which many enlightened parents adopt but have difficulty in maintaining when it is undermined by the gender-stereotyped gifts of well-meaning friends and relations or the gender-differentiated world of formal education. From her current biosocial perspective, Rossi questions the wisdom of striving for equal participation by men and women in the public sector and in the home; in particular, she questions the quality of child care which can be provided by men and even by women whose lives are committed equally to their families and to their work outside the home. This is certainly a radical change. Let us examine the argument which Rossi puts forward to support her current position.

Rossi's fundamental assertion is that sociological theories which ignore 'the central biological fact that the core function of any family system is human continuity through reproduction and child-rearing' are bound to be inadequate. Though she holds no brief for the older view of the isolated nuclear family as the sole normal institution for reproduction and child care, neither is she sympathetic to the egalitarian approach, which she sees as an attempt to deny or obliterate all differences between the genders. In terms of Rogers's model, which we examined in Chapter 5, the egalitarian position implies no behavioural or ideological differentiation between the genders – a view which Rossi now questions but which is, in fact, close to her own earlier position in which she included not only equal participation by men and women in the worlds of work and home, but the transfer of parental obligations to institutional care. She traces her present unease to her awareness of a deep separation between parenting and sexuality and also to the impact of institutional life on young children. Her strongest statement is that 'communally reared children, far from being liberated, are often neglected, joyless creatures'. These observations and much self-examination led Rossi to seek answers in our evolutionary history. She is in fact arguing for gender differentiation at a behavioural level and trying to provide ideological justification for this differentiation by asserting that the very nature of men's and women's sexuality is different, as are their respective commitments to parenting. To do this she draws upon evolutionary and hormonal accounts of differences between the sexes.

Theories drawing on human evolutionary history in hunting and gathering societies, already familiar from Chapter 3, are elaborated by Rossi in a new direction. So far we have encountered arguments which seek the origins of men's greater size or aggressiveness in hunting. The assertion that women's manual dexterity, persistence, and physical and emotional endurance reflect the reproductive success of those females capable of combining the production and care of their young with gathering and small-game hunting is a new one. Rossi is careful to disclaim strict genetic determinism, but argues instead that men and women learn different skills with differential ease. She asserts that men would require greater training to be as good parents as women, since their interests in reproduction are primarily sexual and lacking in a relational bond to the young. Similarly, she claims that female cosmonauts and soldiers require special training to compensate for the absence of male musculature. Rossi sees fathering as being socially learned, while successful mothering, she believes, evolved over millions of years.

But a genetic heritage is not enough. Rossi also considers the importance of foetal hormones in organizing the brain to respond in a gender-appropriate fashion. Here she reviews the arguments which we summarized in Chapter 3 about the interaction of hormones and behaviour, but again she emphasizes potentials for gender-appropriate behaviour. From the genetic code which organizes male and female physiology to hormones which regulate behaviour, the message is that for each sex it is easier to acquire behaviour appropriate to its own gender.

Rossi is open to criticism, but we must not underestimate her scholarship and sophistication. In spelling out the consequences of considering biological factors in role learning, she is careful to distinguish rare from common roles. For example, to become a neurosurgeon requires delicate manual dexterity, and this is more common in women. Rossi notes that very few people become neurosurgeons, and although social pressure has barred women – those most likely to have the requisite aptitudes – a few men with sufficient manual dexterity are available. When large numbers of manually dextrous workers are required, as in the electronic industry, women predominate. So too with parenting. Here Rossi believes that nature gives women the edge. She characterizes men as

essentially less interested in the young and efforts to train male nurturing as unlikely to be successful. The unisex pattern, she claims, is a
masculine pattern through which children are neglected due to reduced
interest and commitment to nurturing.

Despite her plea for contemporary sociological theory to incorporate
knowledge from biology, Rossi is not sanctioning the rearing of children
by women in isolated nuclear families. She is aware of the hazards which
this poses for women, and she also stresses the costs of such isolation
for children in terms of sibling rivalry. This awareness leads her to
suggest the establishment of growth centres where children can learn
how to interact with age mates and be trained by experts in development. The emphasis is on the child's social development rather than
on providing alternative supervision aimed at giving mothers the freedom to pursue careers or find jobs. Given the costs of such programmes,
Rossi sees growth centres evolving as self-help groups, providing a
sense of community for parents and children alike.

Rossi was aware that her views would draw fire from feminists – and
they have. Cerullo *et al.* (1977–8) assess Rossi's paper in the context
of an entrenchment which they define as the return to favour of the
isolated nuclear family. Appreciative of Rossi's feminist contribution
to studies of the family, they nevertheless disagree with her about which
strategy to employ in the face of the apparent failure of egalitarian
socialization to counter existing gender differences. One strategy is to
re-examine and refine socialization theory; the other that of looking to
biology to explain the failure of educational efforts, is the one adopted
by Rossi. Her critics cite a number of points at which alternative explanations are possible. Rather than arguing that the long period of physical
dependence of the human infant has led to an inbuilt need for the infant
to bond to its mother, they contend that it points only to a need for
prolonged infant care. Thus, while feminist scholars have sought explanations for the virtually universal division of labour by gender in
economic and political conditions as well as in socialization, Rossi has
played down these efforts and sought an account of existing gender roles
in our evolutionary history. The counter-argument is that Rossi is
assuming the necessity of social organization as we know it (Cerullo
et al., 1977–8). Rossi's new position also places women firmly in nature,
makes society natural in its existing institutions, and is, in fact, a form
of biological determinism. Her critics assert that the very model which
Rossi sought to pursue, that of interaction, is lost as soon as she attempts
to determine from current conditions absolute estimates of the relative

contributions of biology and social learning to women's gender roles and women's parenting abilities.

Nancy Chodorow (1978) has attacked Rossi's biosocial model not only on biological grounds but also in the context of her own account of mothering. Rather than ascribing women's mothering to genes, hormones or socialization, Chodorow claims that the question 'Why do women mother?' remains to be answered. Along with Rossi she finds a simple socialization explanation inadequate and she looks to modern psychoanalytic accounts, particularly those known as object relations theory, to explain the role of the mother in men's and women's inner worlds.

Chodorow's arguments take us back to the psychoanalytic concept of the Oedipal conflict, which we first considered in Chapter 4. Post-Freudian theorists have examined the child's earliest years and have outlined differences in the development of adult sexual aims and object choices based on pre-Oedipal relationships. The very different demands of male and female development become clearer when the importance for an individual of the first year of life and the relationship to the primary mothering agent is considered. A boy need not relinquish his feelings for mothers, though he must renounce his desires for his own mother; but a girl must turn away from her mother only to compete with her or other women for the love and attention of her father and men more generally. Boys can carry over into heterosexuality the qualities of their first love; but heterosexuality for girls involves loss of the mother to some extent, and feelings of jealousy and competition with the mother as well as love in relation to the father. Chodorow sees these early experiences as crucial, since in heterosexual relations men and women live in very different inner worlds, significantly determined by their different experiences of primary love in the pre-Oedipal period. These differences influence not only adult relationships between men and women, but also mothers' responses to their male and female infants.

The complete account which Chodorow presents is considerably more complicated, since she provides an explanation of each gender's struggle for freedom from primary love and dependence as well as their fantasies about its recapture. The struggle is different for men and women. It may result in male hostility towards women, while for the female it can lead to an idealization of the male. At the risk of over-simplification, we can say that men potentially regain the mother through heterosexuality, while for women the consequences of post-

Oedipal heterosexuality, tempered as it is by pre-Oedipal wishes, are that the mother can be regained only by becoming mothers themselves. Thus, according to Chodorow, men and women have very different needs and feelings about bearing and looking after children.

In this discussion of gender differences as they are realized in the family, our attention has centred primarily on adults. We presented Chodorow's psychodynamic theory not as an account of development, but as an explanation of the willingness of men and women to accept the traditional roles of husband and wife, father and mother. In the section which follows, our primary focus is the growth and wellbeing of the infant and child *per se*. In looking at psychologists' descriptions of the optimal conditions for development, we seek guidelines for the optimal distribution of child-care responsibilities. Rossi has taken a firm stand on the issue. She believes that the evolutionary history of the human race has predisposed women to be more able caretakers than men. In the section which follows we examine psychological theories which seek to explain how the needs of children in their early years are best met.

Mothering and Attachment

In entitling this section 'Mothering and Attachment', we are not only following the conventions of the psychological literature but are also seeking to draw attention to the pervasive stereotype of women as mothers. Many people believe that it is natural for women to mother. We will explore the extent to which psychological theory and research supports this view.

Developmental psychology has undergone dramatic changes in the past twenty-five years. These changes reflect general shifts in the theoretical outlook of psychologists and are not confined exclusively to theories of child development. Along with a general attack on behaviourism, the view that the infant is a passive lump of clay to be modelled according to the needs of society has gradually been abandoned. Changes in psychological accounts of development also reflect shifts in public attitudes about family roles.

One of the scholars most influential in changing the public's view of the nature of infant development was John Bowlby. An expert in adolescent and child psychiatry, he was asked shortly after World War II to undertake for the United Nations a study of the problems of homeless children. His report, which has been the focus of much research and controversy, contains the widely quoted conclusion that 'mother-love in infancy and childhood is as important for mental health as are vitamins and proteins for physical health'. Absence of mother-love was referred to as maternal deprivation. The report had an immediate impact: major improvements in the institutional care of children were introduced, and women examined their mothering function much more critically. Critics have accused Bowlby's ideas of speeding the return of women to the home after demobilization (*Sunday Times*, 9 July 1976) and of encouraging the social seclusion of women with young children (Morgan, 1975).

By the time a second summary edition of Bowlby's conclusions was published, a good deal of new research had been undertaken. In her contribution to the revised edition (1965), Mary Ainsworth, a colleague of Bowlby, identified eight major issues. We list them all to give the flavour of the controversies, although obviously some are beyond the scope of our discussion. Stated in the form of questions, the issues which Ainsworth noted are:

(1) How is maternal deprivation to be defined?

(2) Can mothering be provided in an optimal manner by more than one person?

(3) Are the effects of maternal deprivation the same in all children?

(4) Does maternal deprivation impair all aspects of a child's development?

(5) Can different developmental impairments all be traced to maternal deprivation?

(6) Are the impairments permanent or can they readily be put right?

(7) Is maternal deprivation implicated in juvenile delinquency?

(8) Are the results of deprivation seen in children raised in institutions a particular reflection of their lack of mothering, or are they a consequence of the general impoverishment of their environment?

Bowlby's original report identified a problem, that of pysychological and developmental impairment in children, and sought an explanation for it in the mother–child relationship. The research which followed, including much of Bowlby's own, aimed at understanding this relationship, especially the processes of attachment and separation. Though trained in psychoanalysis, Bowlby was dissatisfied with psychoanalytic accounts of the growth of mother-love. Freud held that the choice of the mother as the baby's first love object developed from the feeding relationship, from the breast which initially satisfied a physical need. Academic psychologists of a learning theory persuasion offered an account which was similar in its emphasis on physical needs. They believed that the mother acquired incentive value and came to be a secondary reinforcer for the infant through her temporal and spatial contiguity with primary drive, physical need and satisfaction.

A serious challenge to these cupboard-love theories came from Harry Harlow's (1958) experiments with infant rhesus monkeys. He substituted inanimate objects for mothers and observed the development of baby monkeys. Harlow devised two sorts of surrogate mothers, each with a face and each able to provide milk. One was simply a wire frame, the other was covered with terry-cloth. Offered the choice of the two, which provided milk, infant monkeys preferred the terry-cloth mother. When offered the wire mother with milk and the terry-cloth surrogate without, the monkey fed from the wire mother but spent much time clinging to the terry-cloth surrogate. The experience of feeding had not enhanced the attractiveness of the wire mother.

In a major work published in 1969 Bowlby presented a comprehensive theory of attachment, drawing heavily on ethological studies of animals in natural surroundings as well as on the experimental work of Harlow. We summarize his theory briefly as follows:

(1) The human infant is essentially social and predisposed by a number of instinctual response systems, which are primarily non-oral, to form an affective tie to its primary caretaker.

(2) The affective tie develops in a regular manner and is usually well established in the second half of the first year.

(3) In the normal course of development the mother is both the primary caretaker and the attachment figure to whom the infant is bonded.

(4) Once the affective tie or attachment bond is well established, separation from the mother results in anxiety and protest.

(5) Prolonged separation results in an orderly sequence of protest, despair and finally apparent detachment from the mother, so that upon her return the child may show no enthusiasm or interest.

(6) Total loss of the mother in the early years has a variety of long-lasting detrimental consequences.

Bowlby replaced psychoanalytic and learning theory explanations with an evolutionary account. The various instinctual responses which lead to attachment – crying, gazing, grasping and smiling, for example – are considered to enhance the infant's chances of survival by increasing closeness to the mother and protection from predators.

Although Bowlby's theoretical formulations have been seriously challenged, recognition of the importance of mother–infant attachment has led to important innovations in the care of infants (Klaus and Kennell, 1976). Hospital deliveries in Europe and the United States increasingly include a period just after birth during which mothers and fathers are encouraged to look at their babies and begin to get to know them. The care of premature and ill babies has been modified; mothers are invited to stay in hospital and take part in nursing their own children.

Developmental psychologists have undertaken a great deal of research to investigate the sequence and objects in the development of attachment, to explore the consequences of individual differences in the strength of the attachment bond for other aspects of the infant's and young child's behaviour, and to assess the consequences of brief separation and the introduction of strangers, as well as to determine the long-term consequences of maternal deprivation. We have had to select a few questions which are relevant when considering the impact of gender differentiation in the provision of care for the young. The general question most relevant to our concerns is that of monotropism – a term which is used to indicate that attachment occurs to only one person at a time and ideally to the infant's natural mother. Monotropism can be considered in terms of both the infant's attachment to one or more caretakers and the caretaker's ability to form a deep relationship to one or more infants. Klaus and Kennell (1976) reviewed evidence from an infant care centre in Greece which suggested that nurses developed special relationships with particular infants, and that they experienced loss and mourning when their babies left the institution to be placed in adoptive homes.

The issue of a single object of attachment is often confounded with that of the biological mother as the privileged object of attachment. In a sense we are back to the original question – the deleterious effects of the failure to receive sufficient mother love, or maternal deprivation. The process of attachment and the objects of this attachment were investigated by Schaffer and Emerson (1964) in a pioneering longitudinal study of sixty infants observed each month in their first year. In general their results support Bowlby, but they showed that the development of specific attachment need not be exclusive to a single person. In the very first month in which specific attachment was identified, 29 per cent of their babies developed such a tie with more than one other person; indeed, 10 per cent had ties with five or more other people. Even when the attachment object was a single person, the bond was not restricted to the infant's mother. For a few infants their sole bond was formed with a father or grandparent.

The *kibbutzim* of Israel, which have often been cited in arguments about child care in our own society, also provide data on the issue of attachment. In a *kibbutz* the care of infants is shared between parents and *metaplot* (singular: *metapelet*), trained caretakers who live with the children in special infant houses. In a recent study the reactions of infants to separation and reunion – measures of the strength of attachment – with their mothers and their *metaplot* were made (Fox, 1977). In the seven *kibbutzim* in which Fox worked, primary care of the infant usually passed to a *metapelet* when the infant was three to four months old, and by the time the child was one and a half years old the parents visited once a day for three hours in the afternoon. Fox argued that as attachment figures mothers and *metaplot* were interchangeable, and that each provided the infant with a secure base – one function of the attachment figure. The only measures which did discriminate between mother and *metapelet* were those based upon reunion, but the results were heavily influenced by the greater anxiety of first-born children on being separated from their mothers. In the *kibbutzim* study, infants were shown to form attachments to more than one person at a time, but both of them were women. In the work of Schaffer and Emerson we noted that in addition to forming multiple attachments a small proportion of infants became primarily attached to their fathers. It is reasonable to conclude that the object of initial attachment need not be female or the natural mother.

We see in Fox's study that attachments may differ in subtle ways. Psychoanalytic writers have suggested that it may be more difficult both for an adopted child and for its new mother to form a secure bond (Reeves, 1971). The greater incidence of psychiatric disturbance in adopted children has been related to domestic background conditions as well as to breaks in the continuity of care (Hersov, 1977). When we examine fathers' participation in child care in the next section, we shall consider possible differences in the nature of attachment to mothers and fathers.

Even in this discussion of attachment we appear to be focusing on the adults in the family and neglecting to consider any differences in the ways in which boy and girl infants establish an affective tie with their primary caretakers. Information on this topic is scant. Fear of strangers, a phenomenon which has been observed after the attachment bond is established, has been considered in relation to intellectual development (Decarie *et al.*, 1974). This work has shown a precise difference, the more frequent negative reaction of female infants to being touched by a stranger. Studies employing other measures of fear of strangers have found a trend in this direction, but they have not yielded reliable results (Morgan and Ricciuti, 1969; Schaffer and Emerson, 1964; Tennes and Lampl, 1964). Decarie and her students suggest that the gender difference in fear reflects a difference in the understanding of the situation rather than the kinds of differences in fear discussed in Chapter 6. Comparing infants of the same age and using the results of tests of intellectual development, object permanence and the understanding of causality, they suggest that the negative response to being touched by strangers reflects girls' intellectual precocity. They noted that infants a few months older generally show a negative reaction to being touched by strangers. Before considering further gender differences in the consequences of early experiences of mothering or in dependence and anxiety towards strangers, we shall look briefly at one further aspect of infant care – the optimal number of caretakers necessary to ensure satisfactory development.

Our discussion relies upon two reviews in which Peter Smith (1980) has re-examined Bowlby's original material and surveyed a great number of research reports. Smith supports the general conclusion that there is little evidence that infants require an exclusive, warm, continuous relationship with a single person to develop emotional security (Rutter, 1972). At the same time, Smith considers the possibility of an upper limit on the number of caretakers that a child might encounter and still develop satisfactorily. He concludes that while there may be no disastrous consequences when children are looked after by a few caretakers, perhaps as many as five, it is difficult to predict the result when fifty or more people look after a single child in the early years. In support of his claim Smith cites a study of children who lived in residential nurseries in London for at least four years from the age of four months (Tizard and Hodges, 1978). Tizard and Hodges considered anyone who had worked in the nurseries for at least a week a caretaker and estimated that children encountered about fifty different caretakers in their four years' residence. When assessed at eight years of age, whether they had been returned to their natural parents, or had been fostered, adopted or had remained in care, the majority of these children posed problems at school. Although their intellectual development appeared normal, teachers described them as antisocial, attention-seeking and restless. We can conclude with Smith that there probably is an upper limit on the number of caretakers that children should ideally encounter in their early years.

Given the general conclusion that a great number of caretakers may be detrimental to optimal development, it is worth noting that it may not be the absolute number of caretakers which influences emotional development but the nature of the interaction which occurs between the infant and the changing caretaker. Smith suggests that the casual caretaker experiences difficulty in understanding and predicting the behaviour of the infant, and hence fails to achieve a synchronous and mutually rewarding relationship. This failure would in turn influence the caretaker's already fragile commitment to the infant. In this way there may inevitably be a negative relationship between the number of caretakers and the quality of the care which the infant receives. As we have just observed, these failures are often associated with observable difficulties later in childhood.

In the remaining part of this section we consider differences between girls and boys which may reflect their experiences of mothering and attachment. Rutter (1979) notes in a recent authoritative review that there has been little effort directed towards assessing the different effects of deprivation on girls and boys. In his own research on the Isle of Wight he has shown that short-term deprivation as the result of maternal illness or confinement is related to greater behavioural disturbance in boys than in girls (Wolkind and Rutter, 1973). However, when children are in care for a long time as the result of prolonged maternal difficulties, there is as much behavioural disturbance among girls as among boys. Rutter concludes his review by asserting that there is evidence of differences in mother–infant interaction and in boys' and girls' reactions to stress, but that we cannot yet explain the nature of these differences and their long-term consequences.

It is a short step from the consequences of maternal deprivation to consideration of gender differences in the incidence of mental illness in childhood. Although the diagnosis of psychopathology in children is even more problematic than in adults, mental illness in childhood raises a number of important questions (Eme, 1979). Given the drawback that reports of incidence are based on treated cases rather than on community surveys, available evidence indicates that boys experience more problems of adjustment than girls, more learning difficulties, more psychosexual disorders, and greater severity of antisocial behaviour, as well as more neurosis and psychosis in childhood. These results are puzzling in the light of the adult incidences which we considered in Chapter 6. There we saw that, with the exception of alcoholic psychosis, alcoholism, drug dependence, and personality and behavioural disorders, there was a higher incidence of women in all categories on first admission to mental hospitals and a generally higher incidence of mental illness among women. The discontinuity between childhood psychopathology and adult mental illness is striking.

It would be difficult to dispute the importance of gender role pressures in explaining the higher incidence of mental illness in adult women. An analysis of the strains of the boy's gender role, growing up both in the family and in early formal education in an essentially female world, but one with emphases on masculinity and achievements, is not sufficient to account for the preponderance of boys in these categories of disturbance. There is a need to examine biological factors as well as social mediators of stress reaction in boys. It is tempting to imagine that by pointing to the greater vulnerability of the male from conception, his developmental immaturity, and to a host of other biological differences, we have explained the differential male reaction to psychological stress and deprivation. Our argument by analogy does not so much explain as highlight the need, already pointed out by Rutter, to provide explanations for the differential consequences of deprivation in girls and boys. It appears that our scientific evidence echoes the old wives' tale that boys are more difficult to raise, though we are not much closer than they to understanding why this should be so.

The consequences of mothering and attachment which we have just considered are of a pathological nature. It is reasonable to ask whether in the normal course of development boys and girls acquire similar needs for other people, and whether the strength of their attachment and dependence is generally the same. Psychologists have struggled to find satisfactory definitions and measures of dependence with which to approach the study of individual differences. Maccoby and Jacklin (1974) considered dependence by grouping together reports of behaviour oriented towards the maintenance of closeness – proximity-seeking, touching and resistance to separation – and behaviour oriented towards eliciting social contact – attention-seeking, social skills and social responsiveness. Maintenance and elicitation, directed both at adults and at other children, were each examined.

The general picture which emerged was one of little differentiation by gender. No clear differences were seen in studies of the maintenance of closeness with parent or with other adults. Although studies in which one or the other parent left the infant did show more male disturbance,

Maccoby and Jacklin generally subscribe to an ethological view and share Bowlby's notion of the adaptiveness of attachment. The greater disturbance of male infants following parental separation may be viewed as another aspect of their differential response to stress. Thus when normal circumstances hold, male and female infants respond in a similar fashion, but fear or stress may differentially affect them.

The susceptibility of psychological research on dependence to the influence of prevailing stereotypes was noted by Maccoby and Jacklin. In observational studies of proximity-seeking no clear differences between boys and girls appeared; but when rated by their nursery-school teachers, girls were reported as being more likely to seek social contact. Given the evidence available, we conclude that in normal situations, when undue stress or fear are not aroused, girls and boys are similar in their needs for, and in their efforts to maintain, contact with other people.

Mothering and attachment in the normal course of development appear to result in no major differences in girls' and boys' capacities for social responsiveness or dependence. The greater male vulnerability to stress may mean that boys find some situations more damaging than girls do, but knowledge about the caretaking process does not yet allow us to identify these situations with great precision. At best, we conclude that most infants develop satisfactorily when cared for by a few concerned people. The adults need not be female but they must be sensitive to, and responsive to, the infant's needs.

Fathers and Mothers

In this section we consider the contribution of men to the care of children. This topic has been approached in a number of different ways. At one time psychologists examined the effects of father absence, believing that by comparing the intellectual, emotional and social development of children growing up with and without fathers they would learn about the influence of fathers (Lamb, 1976; Biller, 1976).

If the two-parent family is viewed as a functioning unit, it is difficult to understand what might be learned about the effects of the father in child care from an examination of families where the father is absent. Even if we believe such an enterprise to be profitable, trying to define father absence raises questions similar to those we encountered when discussing maternal deprivation. For example, is the father who leaves home before breakfast and who returns from work after the children are in bed to be considered an absent father? Are families in which grandfathers or older male children fulfil the role of a father to be classified as fatherless? Given an adequate definition of absence, it is also important to identify the age of the child and the length of the absence.

Rather than focusing on fatherless families, we first consider the general impact on children of growing up in one-parent families. These are a frequent alternative to two-parent families in modern Britain and many other Western countries. Secondly, we consider men's contributions to child care as described by their wives. Thirdly, we compare the behaviour of fathers and mothers, having already noted that infants form attachments to fathers as well as to mothers. We begin our comparison by examining the nature of the infant's bond with its father and mother and then look briefly at each parent's share in play and in routine infant care. Finally, we examine the effects of fathers' personality on the development of their children.

We begin by considering the effects on children of growing up in a one-parent family. As we noted in Chapter 2, the majority of single parents are women, although there are more older children living in motherless homes. The National Child Development Study, which was based upon all children born in England in a given week in March 1958, showed that at the age of seven there were six and a half times more children living with only their mother than with only their father (Ferri, 1976). By eleven years of age the proportion had changed: there were four and a half times more children living with only their mother than with only their father. Motherless families are usually the result of either death or marital disruption, as it is rare for a father to raise an illegitimate child. Fatherless families arise through the death of a spouse, marital breakdown or illegitimacy.

Children who grow up in one-parent families show lower average performance and progress on educational tests, and poorer school adjustment. These findings could reflect either the psychological effects of growing up in a one-parent family or general social differences between one- and two-parent families. The National Child Development Study showed that differences in the reading levels of seven- and eleven-year-olds from one- and two-parent families were greatly reduced when socio-economic factors were taken into consideration. However, arithmetic ability still remained low among children from fatherless families; this particular effect has also been reported in a number of other studies of father absence (Lamb, 1976).

Teachers rate children from one-parent families as less well-adjusted

(Mack, 1976). Mothers who raise children on their own report that they have more problems with their children, especially with their daughters. These findings based upon adult ratings of children's behaviour may be influenced by teachers' and mothers' negative stereotypes about growing up in one-parent families or 'broken homes' (Mack, 1976), and should be treated with caution.

We cannot ignore the financial hardships experienced in one-parent families. Although two-parent families show important differences related to the father's occupation or social class, these are further accentuated in one-parent families (Ferri, 1976). Among manual workers 6 per cent of two-parent families receive government aid (supplementary benefits) to bring their incomes up to a minimal level. In motherless families in which the father is a manual worker this figure rises to 18 per cent and in fatherless families it reaches 52 per cent. Even in families in which the father is a non-manual worker there are great differences: 31 per cent of mothers on their own receive supplementary benefits in contrast to only 2 per cent of intact families. Income is generally a problem in one-parent families, but the economic deprivation experienced by children who live alone with their mothers is greater.

There are difficulties other than those directly related to finance, but these differ little according to the gender of the single parent. For example, 2 per cent of children in two-parent families spend some time in the care of the state; yet when divorced or separated men and women raise children on their own, the proportion rises to 12 per cent. The difficult life conditions of the one-parent family are further reflected in the greater number of schools which these children attend. Both care and schooling are also influenced indirectly by economic factors.

In mothers' reports of their husbands' contribution to child care we again see the influence of financial factors, even in two-parent families. The National Child Development Study provided information about fathers' contributions to child-rearing. When the children were seven years old, and again when they were eleven, their mothers were asked to estimate the amount of help they received from their husbands in looking after the children. The mothers described more than half the fathers as taking an equal or a large share of responsibility for their children's care (Lambert and Hart, 1976); 10 per cent were described as leaving everything to the mother – these men tended to be the fathers of younger children in larger families or to have experienced financial difficulties in the year preceding the data collection.

Since these findings are based on wives' accounts of their husbands' behaviour, we may be tempted to dismiss them as subjective and biased. It is therefore important to find other evidence of the impact of fathers on their children's development. The National Child Development Study provided further data linking parental interest and performance at school (Lambert and Hart, 1976). When both parents visited school to discuss their child's progress with the teachers, performance on both reading and arithmetic tests was seven months ahead of children whose mothers alone visit the school. When neither parent took an interest in schooling, children were on average thirteen months behind on both tests. Parental interest is thus important, and fathers can make a sizeable contribution to their children's school performance. From the viewpoint of a child, this study suggests that it is best to be one of a few siblings or an older child in a family without financial problems in which the father takes an active interest in his children's development.

There can be little doubt from the evidence which comes from the National Child Development Study that an actively involved father benefits his children. Our next question concerns the nature of his contribution – more specifically, whether the affection offered and evoked by fathers, their play and care of their children, are very different from that offered by mothers.

In our discussion of attachment theory we concluded that there is abundant evidence that an emotional bond is established between the infant and one or more adults in the second half of the first year. Although research initially focused on the mother-infant bond, Milton Kotelchuck and Michael Lamb have each carried out a series of studies to investigate the father's place in infant social development (Kotelchuck, 1976; Lamb, 1976, 1977a, 1977b).

Kotelchuck's early research explored infant behaviour in a laboratory playroom in which a mother, father and an adult stranger appeared and departed according to a fixed schedule. The activities which he observed and measured can be divided into two classes: those related to attachment, such as crying, touching, remaining close; and those related to affiliation, such as looking and vocalizing. This distinction is similar to that which we have already considered in discussing dependence, between maintaining contact and eliciting it.

Kotelchuck observed that between the ages of nine and twenty-four months infants directed different attachment and affiliative responses to their parents and to the stranger. In addition, there was no easily interpretable difference in the pattern of responses offered to father or mother. These results have been replicated in cross-cultural studies in Guatemala and in infants' own homes in the United States (Kotelchuck, 1976). Although the overall conclusion that infants react differently towards their parents and towards a strange adult may stand, it is still possible that there are differences in the type of emotional bond which the infant establishes with each parent, and that there are differences in the interactions with the father and the mother.

Studies of infants' preferences for fathers or mothers when confronted with a stranger may furnish clues to qualitative differences in the emotional bond established with each parent. They have produced conflicting results. Different research settings yield different preferences (Lamb, 1977a). In conditions of stress when both parents are available, a preference for the mother may appear; but in less difficult circumstances no consistent preference is observed. The attachment and affiliative activities of infants were studied in their own homes in two longitudinal studies (Lamb, 1977a, 1977b). Infants aged between seven and thirteen months showed no preference towards either parent in their attachment behaviour, but over this six-month period they developed a stronger preference for their parents compared to the stranger. Lamb suggests that this heightened attachment to both parents when faced with a stranger may be part of a focusing process which is also seen as a preference for the mother in conditions of stress. This process occurs at the end of the first year.

Lamb's study of infants in their second year provides a number of intriguing results. At home, attachment behaviour can indicate preference for the father, although both parents are still preferred to a stranger. However, when the amount of activity of each of the three adults – father, mother and stanger – is statistically equated, more affiliative behaviour is found to be directed towards the stranger than to either of the parents. These results, and the general decline in attachment and affiliative behaviour over the second year, highlight the importance of age in any discussion of the relationships of children with their parents. As the infant develops in the first two years, the bond with the father and mother grows and changes.

Just as there are preferences expressed by the infant, so too there are differences in the ways in which fathers and mothers interact with their infants. We begin by looking at differences in parental behaviour generally, and we then consider differences specific to the gender of the infant.

Until recently, few differences had been recorded in parental play patterns in the first six months of life. The use of videotape recording in the past few years has allowed a much closer examination of the ways in which infants and adults interact, and studies have reported detailed analysis of the sequences of behaviour (Parke, 1979). This finer analysis suggest that there may be stylistic differences in fathers' and mothers' speech and touch. In the second half of the first year and in the second year many differences in parental play have been observed (Lamb, 1977a, 1977b). Mothers engage the young infant in conventional games such as peek-a-boo and pat-a-cake, and fathers tend to indulge in more rough-and-tumble play. In the second year fathers often play the games that their infants instigate and engage in physical play, whereas mothers read more to their infants. Even when the child is two and a half years old, fathers still play in a physical fashion, whereas the play of mothers is of a more instructional and verbal nature (Clarke-Stewart, 1977). Parental play differs not only in quality but also in quantity, with fathers playing with their children more as the children get older.

We think of routine infant care as the special province of mothers, knowing that many fathers have never changed their soiled infants. Fathers may be particularly important in a different way – in play. As early as the first year infants respond more positively to play with their fathers than with their mothers (Parke, 1979). By the second year they respond more often to playful overtures from their fathers, and in a contrived laboratory setting two thirds of children aged two and a half chose their fathers first as playmates. Parke concludes that each parent makes a different contribution to their child's development, the father by providing exciting physical play and the mother with physical care and verbal interaction. Although these comparisons have been made in two-parent families, they may provide hints about which behaviour could be in short supply in one-parent families.

So far in our discussion of parental behaviour we have not indicated whether the infant or child was a boy or a girl. In fact the infant's gender is important in determining the behaviour of adults. In a laboratory study six-month-old babies were each dressed as a boy and as a girl. Mothers who themselves had a six-month-old infant were invited to play with them, and were either told that the baby was a boy or a girl (Smith and Lloyd, 1978). The gender of the baby influenced the mothers so that they not only said different things but the same physical action of the baby evoked different responses. When the baby was presented as a boy, mothers responded with further physical action; but they offered comfort and soothing if the baby was presented as a girl. In this laboratory setting, mothers responded to an unfamiliar baby in terms of their own gender stereotypes.

In daily life, stereotypes and parental preferences also guide fathers' and mothers' responses to their children. Both fathers and mothers have been observed to look more at infants of their own gender and to provide them with more stimulation in play (Parke and Sawin, 1977). Fathers' preferences for male children has been shown in their greater involvement – talking more and playing more with male infants (Rebelsky and Hanks, 1971; Rendina and Dickerscheid, 1976). Fathers' desires for a male child can scarcely be doubted when we observe that fathers talk more to a first-born baby shortly after birth if it is a boy. Later-born males and all female infants are spoken to less often (Parke, 1979). From the theories and evidence which we have examined, there can be little doubt that fathers and mothers bring different expectations to child care and behave in subtly different ways towards their offspring.

The final issue that we consider in this brief examination of men's and women's behaviour as parents relates primarily to fathers. We look at the impact on children of personality differences among fathers. We begin by looking at the masculinity of fathers and its influence on the development of boys. Two of the most influential theories of psychological development, psychoanalytic and social learning theory, both agree that the model of masculine behaviour which the father provides is important.

The methodological problems that we encountered in the measurement of masculinity and femininity in Chapter 2 reappear when studying the impact of the father on his children's development. If boys are first measured on a scale of masculinity and then asked to describe their own fathers, it is hardly surprising to find a similarity, because one person is making both ratings. One way around this problem has been to construct an artificial situation from which fathers' and mothers' behaviour can be rated for dominance, an important component in masculinity and femininity. The assumption is made that in everyday family life the parents will display similar amounts of dominance. This technique has been used in studies in which parental dominance was related to pre-school and school-age children's gender role preference (Hetherington, 1965). The child's gender role preference is measured using a stick figure called I T which is gender-neutral. The child is asked to choose from masculine and feminine objects those they think I T would like. Sons of dominant fathers tend to choose masculine objects.

Although the picture which at first emerges seems straightforward, later research has shown the process to be more complex (Biller, 1976). Boys' own perceptions of their fathers' dominance have proved to be better predictors of their own gender preference and orientation than psychological assessment of parental dominance. In addition, when fathers who are rated high in dominance on the basis of their inter- actions with their wives behave in a restrictive and controlling fashion towards their sons, the boys tend to be less masculine. Furthermore, unless the father is dominant and active in the family, his masculine behaviour in the world of leisure has little impact on his sons. Speaking again from the child's viewpoint, for a strong masculine identity to emerge in boys it is important to have a father who is actively in- volved in the home and takes a major role in family decision-making. Fathers who seek achievement primarily in the world of work and who leave the home to their wives may find their sons do not share their masculine preferences.

The point of our discussion is that paternal participation is im- portant for masculine development in boys. The importance of the father has also been noted for feminine gender identity in girls (Biller, 1976). Biller views femininity positively: women are seen to be both in- dependent and assertive as well as nurturant and sensitive. A masculine father is believed to facilitate his daughter's feminine development. Indeed, some psychologists have argued that fathers have a more important part than mothers to play in their children's gender dif- ferentiation (Biller, 1976; Heilbrun, 1965).

Our picture of masculine fathers dominating family decision-making and thereby ensuring that their children are clearly differentiated as men and women cannot be left without noting a few reservations. First of all, a father may have views which are considered narrow and restrict- ing by his family. His sons may show artistic tendencies and his daughter may pursue dangerous and demanding sports of which he disapproves. In such cases a father's efforts to impose his notions of gender-appropriate behaviour could produce considerable family dis- cord. On the other hand, a father who sought to realize his own mas- culine ambitions through one of his daughters could meet with opposition. We cannot overlook the limits which a child's own nature imposes on parental influence. Fathers make an important contribution to gender differentiation, within the limits of their children's disposi- tions and their own natures and positions in the wider society.

CHAPTER 8

Work, Intelligence and Achievement

In Chapter 7 we discussed the family, traditionally regarded as a woman's sphere of influence and responsibility, and we considered why it is that women look after children. Here we examine the world of work, a man's sphere of influence, and ask why it is that men occupy the most prestigious and highly valued positions in it.

The first explanation which we consider suggests that men and women possess different abilities and skills, and that these suit them for the worlds of family or work or for different occupations within the world of work; furthermore, it is often claimed that gender differences in ability result from biological sex differences. After examining the possibility that different abilities may underlie gender differences in work and achievement, we consider other explanations and discuss a number of related influences – stereotypes about women and work, opportunities, education and training, and aspiration and motives for occupational success.

We begin by examining some statistics on men and women in different occupations. Before discussing reasons for differences in occupational patterns, we must consider whether it is true that men achieve greater prestige and status in the world of work.

Do Men Get Better Jobs and Earn More Money than Women?

In Chapter 2 we examined some British statistics on men's and women's occupations and found a number of differences related to the world of work. For example, among school leavers who do not go on to higher or further education but embark instead on an apprenticeship training, boys outnumber girls seven to one. Among those continuing their education, boys more often enter degree courses although girls train as teachers and nurses. Girls are six times more likely than boys to enter a clerical occupation. These figures can be summarized by saying that more men enter higher-status and potentially better-paid occupations than women, they receive more occupational training and are more likely to be found in jobs with good promotion prospects.

Another way to look at gender differences in the world of work is to compare the incomes of men and women with similar educational backgrounds. Some recent American statistics are shown in Table 8.1. Education increases income, and both men and women with four or more years of college (including university) education earn more than twice as much as their same-gender peers who have less than eight years of education; yet the income of the most highly educated group of women scarcely exceeds that of men with only eight years of elementary schooling.

Table 8.1. Income of Full-time Workers by Education and Gender in the United States, 1977

		(Dollars)	
		Male	*Female*
Elementary			
	less than 8 years	9,419	6,074
	8 years	12,083	6,564
High School			
	1–3 years	13,120	7,387
	4 years	15,434	8,894
College			
	1–3 years	16,235	10,157
	4 or more	20,625	12,656

Based on Table 752, *Statistical Abstracts of the USA* (1978).

Participation in different occupations explains the differential income of men and women (cf. Table 681, *Statistical Abstracts of the USA*, 1978). Women account for 97 per cent of private household workers, 78·9 per cent of clerical and kindred workers and 58·3 per cent of service workers (90·4 per cent of 'waiters' – a sub-category of service workers). These are all low-paid occupations.

The overall participation of women in professional, technical and related spheres, where incomes are usually higher, is 42·6 per cent, but this figure masks wide variation across specific occupations. Women account for 98·7 per cent of pre-school and kindergarten teachers, 96·7 per cent of registered nurses, 84·2 per cent of primary school teachers, 79·8 per cent of librarians, archivists and curators and 71·4 per cent of health technologists and technicians. All these professions are generally lower-paid. Among the higher-income professions, women account for only 2·7 per cent of engineers, 2·9 per cent of dentists, 9·5 per cent of lawyers and judges, 11·2 per cent of physicians, 27·5 per cent of accountants and 31·7 per cent of college and university teachers.

Figures for women's participation in the professions vary slightly for Britain (Mackie and Pattullo, 1977). Fewer than 5 per cent of architects, engineers, scientists and solicitors are women. About 10 per cent of university teachers and 27 per cent of physicians are female, but within each of these professions a smaller proportion of women are found in higher-status positions. Only 1·7 per cent of university professors and only 12 per cent of medical consultants are women.

In other occupations we find a similar pattern. Fewer woman occupy high-status positions than would be expected from their numbers in the work force as a whole. This is the case even in occupations where women are in a numerical majority, such as nursing and food retailing: here a disproportionate number of the male minority gain promotion to the top grades. In food retailing, over two thirds of the labour force consist of women, and yet they occupy only 4 per cent of management posts.

If there is a disproportionate number of men in higher-status occupations, where are most women workers to be found? The answer is that they typically carry out dull, repetitive, badly paid jobs which offer them few prospects for advancement. These jobs are concentrated in a relatively small number of industries, so that they are often identifiable as 'women's work' and are considered less productive and important than other types of work. Women's work is found in service industries, in certain manufacturing industries such as food, drink, clothing, textiles and footwear, and in shops and hairdressing. Women are also employed for cooking, cleaning and serving food. Many women work part-time, and the hours which they work often bear a close relation to the age and number of their dependent children. Lowest-paid of all women workers are those who work at home, again because of their dependent children; these include childminders and homeworkers for industry.

In Chapter 2 we observed that, on average, men earn more than women and that this could not be explained by the numbers of hours that each gender worked. A clear picture of the higher status, pay and achievement of men emerges from our brief overview of work. In the remaining sections of this chapter we consider explanations for these findings. The first is the possibility that men and women possess different skills and abilities which suit them for particular occupations that just happen to differ in status and pay. Although this may appear an unlikely explanation to the politically and socially aware reader, nevertheless it is one which has been advocated at various times to explain partially or totally the occupational position of women. In our discussion we consider the more general issue of psychological differences in intellectual abilities between men and women, and how these might be explained.

Gender Differences in Intellectual Abilities

The idea that women somehow think differently from men is a common one. For example, a woman listener to a BBC phone-in programme (12 July 1977) commented: 'My husband says I've got a butterfly mind. He can only concentrate on one thing at a time.' She then asked whether this represented a possible gender difference in thinking. Her particular question was concerned with styles of thinking rather than with any possible difference in intellectual abilities between the genders. It is rather less acceptable to ask whether the genders differ in intelligence, because the notion of intelligence is so value-laden. To say that people are unintelligent is a major assault on their own self-esteem and their value in the eyes of others.

Modern psychologists have made few serious claims that women are less intelligent than men, although it has been claimed that there are more men than women found at both extremes of intellectual ability. In Chapter 1 we referred in passing to nineteenth-century biologists' explanations of men's allegedly greater intelligence. Although psychologists do not now regard men as intellectually superior to women, many men in contemporary Western society behave as though they believed that women are less intelligent or at least less rational and logical. IQ tests were developed to show that on average men and women are similar, but it is often claimed that there is a difference in the overall distribution of IQ scores, with more men at both the higher and lower ends, and more women in the middle. Occasionally this has been referred to as the mediocrity of women hypothesis, and it has sometimes been used as an explanation for the greater scientific, artistic and occupational attainments of men (Heim, 1970). We need to consider this claim as a possible reason for gender differences in occupational attainment.

In Chapter 2 we described various IQ tests and scales designed specifically to measure skills such as verbal ability, numerical reasoning, spatial ability and memory. As consistent gender differences have been reported on some of these sub-tests, some psychologists have suggested that these specific ability differences might suit men and women for different occupations and explain – at least partially – gender differences in occupational choice. Spatial ability is the specific ability most often regarded as crucial for explaining male pre-eminence in the world of science and mathematics. In recent years biological explanations of gender differences in spatial ability have aroused considerable interest. Several types of theory have been suggested; these involve genetic differences, brain lateralization or hormones. Such theories suggest a direct link between the biological and the social, and are used to argue that men are naturally *suited* to certain occupations, just as Rossi and others have argued that women are naturally suited to child care.

Are There More Men with High Intellectual Ability?

A number of psychologists, beginning with Havelock Ellis in 1904, have suggested that the range of mental ability is wider among men than women. In this way it is possible, even in the absence of an average difference in intelligence, to argue that intellectual ability could explain the greater scientific, artistic and occupational achievements of men. Such views have persisted to the present day, and have recently included speculations that gender differences in the range of I Qs can be attributed to genetic factors. Thus Lehrke (1978) has written: 'It is highly probable that basic genetic factors rather than male chauvinism account for at least some of the difference in the number of males and females occupying positions requiring the highest levels of intellectual ability.'

First we consider evidence for the claim that there are differences in the range of intellectual ability between men and women; then we examine some of the recent genetic explanations.

Statistics showing male pre-eminence in achievement over a wide variety of intellectual endeavours are used to argue the case at the upper end of the intelligence distribution. Surveys of mental subnormality institutions, which show a male majority in several different sets of national statistics, are used to document the predominance of men at the lower end.

Critics of the variability theory question this evidence and offer other reasons for these findings. It has been suggested that sampling biases may account for the differences reported, with a higher proportion of male subnormals being cared for in institutions and female subnormals by their families at home (Anastasi, 1958). Critics of the variability theory also propose that in a classic study of gifted children by Terman, which identified more boys than girls at the top range of intelligence, there was differential selection by teachers (Maccoby and Jacklin, 1974).

In studies of children's IQ scores there is no consistent tendency for boys to show a wider range of abilities than girls (Anastasi, 1958; Maccoby and Jacklin, 1974). When the upper and lower 1 per cent of scores from various tests were examined in a recent large-scale investigation of mental abilities, little support was found for the variability hypothesis (Wilson and Vandenberg, 1978).

On inspection, the evidence for the variability hypothesis turns out to be very weak; it rests on a few studies which may be biased in their sample selection. Despite the lack of sound evidence, however, there is no shortage of explanations for the alleged variability difference. Because males show greater physical vulnerability to developmental defects and illnesses, it has been suggested that brain development in males may be less buffered from the environment than in females (Glucksmann, 1974; Maccoby and Jacklin, 1974). A similar theory of brain development has been used to account for the allegedly greater male variability in intelligence, and also to suggest that male intellectual development is more affected by the environment while female development is more affected by genetic factors. This relationship was explored by Bayley and Schaefer (1964) using data from a longitudinal study. They linked IQ scores of children and various measures of maternal behaviour. A recent re-examination of Bayley and Schaefer's study has questioned whether a gender difference, and hence the need for an explanation, exists (Kamin, 1978).

Corinne Hutt (1972a) related the supposedly greater male intellectual variability to a wider pattern of more advantageous and disadvantageous physical characteristics in men than in women. She also linked this general variability to the 'Y chromosome theory' of Ounsted and Taylor (1972). They suggested that the Y chromosome of the male produces a slower rate of development, and in doing so enables the environment to exert more influence on male development. A consequence of this greater environmental influence would be wider variability in male and female characteristics. As we have already shown, the evidence for a wider variability in male IQ scores and for a greater environmental influence on male intellectual development is questionable. The Y chromosome theory is more usually invoked to explain the greater number of disadvantageous physical features which occur in male than in female animals – for example, their greater susceptibility to disease and their greater mortality rates. In the case of greater male mortality, an explanation in terms of a shorter (Y) chromosome producing slower development cannot apply generally, since the female possesses a shorter sex chromosome in many animal species in which male mortality is nevertheless greater (Trivers, 1972).

Another genetic explanation for greater male variability in intelligence suggests that there are genes affecting intelligence on the X chromosomes (Lehrke, 1978). In females, extreme forms of these genes are likely to be countered by effects from other cells, since the female body is a mosaic of cells with maternal and paternal X chromosomes; males possess only one type of X chromosome, that from the mother, so that the same gene will be active in every cell – resulting in more extreme forms of the genes being more readily expressed. The theory rests on the assumption that there are genes influencing intellectual development on the X chromosomes, but the evidence for these, taken from family relatedness of I Q, is very indirect and inconclusive. This, together with the lack of evidence for the original intellectual variability hypothesis, makes the X chromosome theory very unlikely. Despite the lack of firm evidence or convincing explanations, however, the notion that males are both cleverer and more stupid than females lingers on.

Do Specific Abilities Suit Men and Women for Different Occupations?

In Chapter 2 we considered the psychometric approach and described gender differences in specific mental abilities. On average, men perform better than women on tests of spatial and mathematical ability, although women may perform better than men on tests of verbal ability (Maccoby and Jacklin, 1974). These and other results from psychometric tests are often used to explain and justify occupational gender differences. It is usually implied that the psychological ability is stable through time and is biologically based. Thus occupational recruitment patterns are explained by differences in psychological traits, and these traits are in turn explained by biological differences between men and women.

Explanations of this type have been offered for the predominance of women in clerical occupations and of men in scientific and technological occupations. The characteristics of perceptual speed and verbal fluency are said to suit women better for secretarial work (Broverman *et al.*,

1968; Garai and Scheinfeld, 1968). It is also suggested that boys' greater scholastic achievement in scientific subjects might be attributed to an inherent sex difference (Heim, 1970), and that men are better suited for scientific and technological professions as a result of their greater spatial and mathematical abilities (for example, Garai and Scheinfeld, 1968). We shall restrict our detailed discussion of gender differences in mental abilities and their explanations to spatial ability. Differences in spatial ability have been used as an explanation for certain occupations being predominantly male ones; in addition, several biological explanations have been suggested to account for the spatial ability difference.

Spatial ability – or more correctly, visual-spatial ability – generally refers to success in solving problems which involve visualizing a spatial arrangement and carrying out mental operations on it. Related to the spatial ability tests are 'field independence' tests, used by Witkin and his colleagues (for example, Witkin *et al.*, 1962; Witkin, 1967). One of these tests, the Embedded Figures Test, involves the identification of a simple reference figure which is embedded or hidden in a more complex figure, thus providing a distracting background (see Figure 2.1 on page 35). A second test, the Rod and Frame Test, involves matching a rod to the true vertical or horizontal in the face of a distracting background. Witkin and his others (for example, Coates, 1974) argue that the ability to perceive the simple figure or the rod as separate from the background or field – termed 'field independence' – represents the perceptual component of a wider personality characteristic. It is claimed that field independent people can separate the simple figure of the rod because they approach the world as if it were composed of discrete entities. They possess what Witkin calls an articulated cognitive style. On the other hand, field dependent people, who have greater difficulty separating the figure or rod from the field, approach the world in a more global, less segmented manner. A major difficulty with Witkin's interpretation of performance on these tests lies in the close association between field independence scores and the ability to solve other spatial tasks. Later in this section we describe the conflicting interpretations of Witkin and of other psychologists who emphasize the spatial ability component of field independence tests. These interpretations have different implications for explaining gender differences in performance on field independence tests.

Before doing so, we consider the range of explanations which have been offered to account for the better performance of men than women on tests of spatial ability. There is again a choice of environmental and biological explanations, and the latter involve heredity, brain function and sex hormones.

A genetic explanation for spatial ability was first suggested by O'Connor in 1943 (Defries *et al.*, 1979), but it only stimulated research interest when elaborated by Stafford in 1961. He suggests that a gene producing high spatial ability can occur on X chromosomes and that this gene is 'recessive' – that is, it can be overruled by a different gene on the other sex chromosome. If the gene occurs in a male it will always be expressed, because the Y chromosome carries little or no genetic material and hence cannot overrule genes on the X chromosome. In a female, a recessive gene on an X chromosome will only be expressed if the same recessive gene also occurs on the other X chromosome. This pattern of inheritance is known as 'sex-linked', and it is the accepted explanation of why conditions such as colour blindness and haemophilia are more common in men than in women.

The relationship between the spatial ability scores of parents and their children have been examined to see whether these fit the predicted pattern for sex-linked characteristics. In the first study of this kind, correlations were found in the expected direction, and hence it was suggested that gender differences in spatial ability might be attributable to a sex-linked recessive gene (Stafford, 1961). Later studies have produced more variable results: a review of six studies of family relationships concludes that the sex-linkage hypothesis is not supported, and other more rigorous statistical tests of sex-linkage are consistent with this conclusion (Defries *et al.*, 1979).

A second type of biological explanation involves differences in the degree to which mental abilities are controlled by the right or left halves, or hemispheres, of the cerebral cortex in men and women. This type of explanation is applied to spatial and linguistic abilities (for example, Buffery and Gray, 1972; Flor-Henry, 1974; McGee, 1979). The basic idea is that the left and right cerebral hemispheres of the human brain are each specialized for different functions, the left or dominant hemisphere being the one in which language is processed, and the right or minor hemisphere being the one in which spatial processing occurs. Departures from this arrangement are supposed to alter the efficiency of spatial (and possibly verbal) processing by the brain, but there is disagreement about the nature of the alteration. One suggestion is that a distribution of spatial functioning in both hemispheres is associated with better spatial ability (Buffery and Gray, 1972), but another theory suggests that this would lead to poorer spatial functioning (Levy,

1969). Levy's view is more widely accepted, but there is little or no direct evidence to test the possible link between hemispheric specialization and spatial ability (Siann, 1977).

Men and women have been found to show different patterns of hemispheric localization of functioning. Again, viewpoints are conflicting, but the consensus is that boys show earlier right hemispheric specialization than girls for some spatially related tasks, and in young adulthood men show more hemispheric specialization for spatial tasks (for example, Witelson, 1976; Tucker, 1976). It is suggested that these differences result in higher male spatial ability (for example, McGlone and Davidson, 1973; Witelson, 1976). Since there is a disagreement over the precise link between hemispheric differences and specific mental abilities, this conclusion is open to question. There are other difficulties with this explanation too. Gender differences in hemispheric specialization appear at an earlier age than the spatial ability difference (Witelson, 1976; Fairweather, 1976). Boys may well show earlier lateralization of some cognitive functions than girls, but this could be unrelated to adult gender differences in spatial ability.

A third type of biological theory suggests that sex hormones may act on the brain to produce differences between men and women in spatial and other abilities (for example, Dawson, 1972; Broverman *et al.*, 1968). The evidence for these theories is very poor and the reader is referred to Archer (1976a) for a criticism of them.

Theories about environmental influences are posed as alternatives to biological accounts. Although Witkin (1967) was careful not to exclude possible biological explanations, he explained gender differences as part of his general theory of 'field independence' as follows: children whose upbringing involved less parental control and more emphasis on self-reliance and achievement – male attributes in most cultures – would become more field independent, as shown by tests such as the Embedded Figures and Rod and Frame Tests. The adequacy of his explanation of gender differences depends on the adequacy of his theory of field independence. This has been questioned by several psychologists, who have explained the tests either in terms of spatial ability (for example, Sherman, 1967) or in terms of general intelligence (Vernon, 1969). Thus, evidence linking child-rearing influences and scores on field independence tests could alternatively be interpreted in terms of a link between child-rearing practices and spatial ability or a general intellectual characteristic.

A recent study of the development of gender differences in spatial ability examined environmental influences (Siann, 1977). Children of 7 to 16 years of age completed various spatial tests: these included field independence tests, spatial tests of the type used in psychometric testing, and a number of specially designed tests, such as one that involved visualization and another that involved location of place and compass points. Gender differences were inconsistent in the younger children, but the 12- to 16-year-old boys showed higher spatial scores than the girls of this age group. In general, gender differences increased with age, a finding largely attributable to the failure of girls' scores to increase with age.

Higher performance on spatial tests was associated with experience of certain activities, such as chess-playing among the older children, and drawing and painting out of doors among the younger age group. In older children there was a clear relationship between higher spatial performance and experience of three-dimensional forms, for example in woodwork, model-making, or toys such as Lego and Meccano. Surprisingly, no relationship was found between map-reading experience and performance on the place location test, but experience of cycling was associated with higher scores on this test.

One finding of particular interest in relation to occupational and child-care roles was that girls who viewed their future in terms of a career rather than primarily as a wife and mother showed higher spatial scores. In particular, girls who indicated that they wished to pursue careers in areas where understanding of spatial relationships might be helpful did well on spatial tests.

In view of these results, Siann offered the following explanation for the gender difference in spatial ability. Boys and girls engage in typically masculine or feminine activities, and boys' experiences are more relevant to spatial tasks, while girls view spatial tasks as inappropriate for their gender. These gender differences in the practice of, and orientation towards, spatial tasks entail a very different perspective from that of biological theories. Instead of a biological sex difference producing an ability difference which then influences occupational suitability, the occupational gender difference is viewed as part of a stereotype about which intellectual and occupational activities are appropriate for the two genders. Gender stereotypes are viewed as influencing the upbringing of boys and girls to give them different experiences of, and interests in, spatially related tasks.

Although Siann provided a plausible alternative to the biological explanations, there is a weakness in the evidence on which her view is based. Most of it consists of associations or correlations between various experiences and performance on spatial tasks. Logically, this could mean either that gender-related experiences influence spatial performance, as Siann suggests, or alternatively that spatial ability differences influence the child's experiences. Children with high spatial ability might choose to play chess since they perform well at it. But in other cases, where an experience is likely to be common to one gender rather than being chosen by a few individuals – for instance, woodwork and construction toys for boys – this alternative explanation is less likely to account for differences in experience which relate to spatial ability.

What are the Other Explanations for Men's Occupational Achievements?

Returning now to the main question of why men achieve more than women in the world of work, there are several influences which are more likely contenders than ability differences. The first is gender stereotyping about women and work. Stereotypes reinforce the idea that there is men's work and women's work, thereby influencing gender differences in occupational training, opportunity and levels of aspiration. Rather than showing a simple cause-and-effect relationship, stereotypes, opportunity and aspiration all form part of an interrelated system. We have just considered the possibility that gender stereotypes influence the play activities, opportunities and interests of schoolchildren, and provide a foundation for gender differences in abilities and in occupational training. Different training opportunities, which are reflected in apprenticeships, professional training and higher education, serve further to perpetuate gender stereotypes about work.

Stereotypes may exert a direct influence on women's occupational achievements by barring or strongly discouraging them from entering a particular occupation, and they may strongly affect the aspirations and motives of men and women in relation to the world of work.

We begin our discussion by considering how gender stereotypes in relation to work might prevent or discourage women from achieving in high-status occupations; we then discuss their influences on education and occupational training. Firstly, we consider men's and women's aspirations and motivation for achievement in the world of work.

Gender Stereotypes and Work

When we described gender differences in mental abilities, we noted how frequently stereotypic beliefs derived from the world of work influenced descriptions of male and female abilities. For example, women were seen as being particularly suited for the rapid repetitive tasks of the assembly-line (Broverman *et al.*, 1968) or for clerical occupations (Garai and Scheinfeld, 1968).

Stereotypes also exert a wider influence on beliefs about the suitability of men and women for certain occupations. Some of the stereotypic adjectives which we examined in Chapter 2 may be used to justify male and female work patterns. For example, masculine adjectives such as self-confident, forceful, enterprising, assertive, confident, rational and tough are those which are typically viewed as suitable for success in many high-status occupations. Feminine adjectives such as soft-hearted, sentimental, talkative, gentle, fussy, dreamy and emotional are generally regarded as unsuitable for high occupational achievement. Such stereotypic beliefs form part of the attitudes held by many men who fill positions of power in the world of work. One North American study of managers' attitudes to women workers revealed that they regarded women as less dependable than men. In another study, of male attitudes towards women executives, almost half the men interviewed reported feeling that women were temperamentally unfit for management (O'Leary, 1974).

Lists of adjectives typically used in describing men and women provide insights into beliefs about occupational suitability. There are also gender stereotypes specifically related to work. Broadly speaking, these beliefs reflect commonsense views of men and women as different and of men as superior. Men's work is generally valued more highly than women's, and occupations which shift from being male to female preserves generally lose status (Kipnis, 1976). For example, bank clerk was once a fairly high-status male occupation in the United States, but it has since become a woman's occupation and has declined in status. If we take a broad look at occupations and their status in different countries, it becomes apparent that the higher status of men's occupations is much more consistent than the types of work carried out by men and women (Kipnis, 1976). In the United States medicine is a predominantly male occupation and is highly valued, while in the Soviet Union it is mostly a woman's occupation and has a lower status; but even in the Soviet Union senior consultants tend to be male. School-teaching is mainly a woman's profession in the United States, where it is less highly valued than in countries where it is a predominantly male profession.

These broad comparisons suggest that occupational status varies according to whether the work force is male or female. Touhey (1974), a social psychologist, has demonstrated in a laboratory study the effect of female participation in lowering occupational prestige. He asked one group of male and female students to rate the prestige and desirability of five high-status professions such as law and medicine, after they had been told that each one would show a substantial increase in the proportion of women over the next twenty-five to thirty years. A second group of students rated the occupations, but received no information about the expected numbers of women. The students in the first group rated the occupations lower in status and desirability than did students of the second group. These findings are consistent with the view that the status of a particular occupation is higher when there are more men in the work force. In addition, they demonstrate that when large numbers of women enter an occupation, its status declines.

So far we have considered the status of occupations which are perceived as men's or women's work. We turn now to the evaluation of men's and women's work performance. Again, sterotypic beliefs about women are essentially negative. We already noted that many men consider women to be unsuitable for positions of power and responsibility. Studies report that male managers in the United States often regard women as making poorer supervisors than men, and they claim that workers feel uncomfortable with a woman supervisor (O'Leary, 1974; Hartnett, 1978). Surveys of male personnel managers also reveal a disapproval of women occupying senior posts, as well as a more general negative evaluation of women applicants (Hartnett, 1978).

Associated with negative judgements about women and their work performance is the notion that women are less motivated or interested in their work. It is claimed that women are less concerned with getting ahead in the world of work, that they are more content with intellectually undemanding jobs and that they are more interested in the social ties they establish with other workers than with their work. Studies of the occupational aspirations of men and women suggest that they are much closer to one another than such stereotypic views indicate (Cowley *et al.*, 1973).

'Attribution' is a term used by social psychologists to describe people's interpretation of the behaviour of others – for example, the reasons they put forward to explain another person's performance on a problem-solving task. Several attribution studies have been concerned with the reasons that people give for successful and unsuccessful task performance by men and women. These studies are of interest to us in relation to stereotypes about men's and women's work performance. In one study the task consisted of matching labels to objects which were stereotypically either masculine, such as a screwdriver, or feminine, such as a whisk or a colander. Observers were informed about the quality of individual performances relative to a hypothetical average. On the masculine objects, a good performance by a man was more often attributed to ability than was a good performance by a woman. Several other studies of this type have found that ability is more often used to explain male achievements, and causes such as effort or luck are more often attributed to women's success (Deaux, 1976a). Failure is also judged differently according to gender: in women, it is more likely to be attributed to lack of ability.

Kay Deaux suggests that gender stereotypes affect people's expectations about performance. In particular, the idea that men are competent and that women are not is brought to bear in attributing success or failure. Thus a successful man confirms most people's expectations, and the cause of his success can be attributed to a stable characteristic, namely ability. A successful woman contradicts most people's expectations, and a temporary reason for success is more likely to be sought – for instance, that the woman has made greater effort. Similarly, failure is more often expected for a woman and hence is more likely to be attributed to a stable characteristic, particularly lack of ability.

In this way, stereotypes about the competence of men and women affect expectations about their performance and influence attempts to explain it. Although this research is carried out in an academic setting far removed from the world of work, it demonstrates that the same level of performance can be judged to have different meaning when achieved by a man or a woman. Other studies have shown that the same piece of work may be rated more highly when attributed to a man than to a woman (for example, Goldberg, 1968). If judgements such as these are widespread in the world of work – and there is no obvious reason why they should not be – they suggest a further important way in which stereotypic beliefs contribute to the higher occupational achievements of men. A woman may perform as well as a man and still have her achievement regarded as being less valuable.

So far we have examined the influence of gender stereotypes on occupational status and on evaluations of the work performance of men and women. Perhaps the most pervasive stereotype is the belief that a man's main responsibility is to go out to work and a woman's is to look after her family. One consequence of this belief is that a working man is seen as the breadwinner and a woman as merely working for 'pin money'. This view may also be used as a reason for undervaluing the contribution of women workers, for justifying lower pay for women and for regarding men's careers as being of greater importance than women's. Despite this belief, many women workers are the chief economic supporters of households (Hartnett, 1978).

The view that the man must necessarily be the breadwinner is a widespread one, and some indication of its influence can be obtained from the reactions of men with families to unemployment. A study of unemployment in London and Merseyside in the 1970s found that men carried out feminine activities in the home, such as doing the housework and taking the children to school (Hill, 1978). This change of role was one of necessity rather than choice, and it was typically accompanied by a feeling of lowered status. Many men said that they felt degraded because they believed that they should be the breadwinner and were not.

In this section we have been concerned mainly with the influence of stereotypes on the value and status of men's and women's work, and have shown a variety of influences that can contribute to the lower status of women's occupations and to the lower evaluations of women's work performance. Rather than list again which occupations are viewed as male or female preserves, we consider instead how ideas about occupational suitability have influenced the opportunities and vocational training open to boys and girls.

Opportunity and Training

Since the Sex Discrimination Act of 1975, there are few occupations in the United Kingdom which are completely barred to women or to men. Nevertheless, stereotypic beliefs about men and women, and the work suitable for them, still effectively prevent the entry of women into certain occupations and retard their promotion and advancement in many others. Structural constraints also prevent many women from pursuing the uninterrupted careers often necessary for achievement in the world of work. Career development is usually geared to the typical male life-plan, so that there is little provision for the flexibility which would be required if a successful career is to be combined with childbirth and child care. In the United Kingdom a third of the female labour force is responsible for dependent children, and yet there are few childcare facilities; indeed in the twenty years after 1945 there was a decline in day nurseries and nursery schools. This was partly attributable to doubts expressed by some child-care experts about the wisdom of women with young children going out to work. As a result, the majority of employed mothers have to make their own arrangements for the care of their children (Mackie and Pattullo, 1977).

Their generally lower level of further education and training is another constraint on the work opportunities open to women. Again, stereotypic ideas about women and work play an important part. The belief that a woman's place is in the home may guide many girls' aspirations primarily towards marriage rather than towards occupational attainment. In addition, the limited range of occupations regarded as suitable for women may exert a restricting influence on the occupational aspirations, education and training of girls. In many schools, girls and boys are still taught different subjects from an early age, and some school subjects such as physics and woodwork, are perceived as masculine, while others, such as biology and home

Table 8.2 Candidates in 13 A-Level Subjects (Summer 1977)

Subject	Male entries (in thousands)	Percentage of total	Female entries (in thousands)	Percentage of total
Art	10·92	41·9	15·17	58·1
Biology	18·40	49·4	18·84	50·6
British Constitution	11·89	64·6	6·51	35·4
Chemistry	27·48	70·6	11·47	29·4
Economics	28·57	72·9	10·60	27·1
English	22·56	33·5	44·74	66·5
French	8·09	32·1	17·09	67·9
General Studies	15·95	57·3	11·89	42·7
Geography	23·26	64·7	12·67	35·3
History	19·25	49·1	19·92	50·9
Physics	37·07	82·2	8·02	17·8
Pure and Applied Maths.	37·01	77·4	10·78	22·6
Sociology	5·04	31·9	10·76	68·1

From Murphy (1980).

economics, are seen as feminine (Mackie and Pattullo, 1977). This difference in curriculum is reflected in A-Level studies and is shown in Table 8.2.

Career guidance offered to school children is often strongly influenced by gender stereotypes about women and work, and contributes directly to the perpetuation of these stereotypes. According to a careers master at a south London school, nursing and clerical work are the two careers suitable for girls (Mackie and Pattullo, 1977). Other studies show that both men and women careers counsellors are more approving of occupational choices which conform to the gender stereotypes than of those which do not. Publications which provide careers information usually show men and women in traditional stereotyped occupations. Measures of vocational interest, interview methods and test techniques used by careers counsellors also clearly reflect gender stereotypes (Hartnett, 1978).

Earlier we described gender differences in further education and occupational training. Not only do more boys than girls take degree courses, but they are more likely to choose traditional male subjects such as technology, engineering, architecture and science. Girls are more likely to choose subjects such as languages, literature and social administration or business courses.

Aspirations and Achievement Motivation

Having examined the external constraints and influences on women's work opportunities, we now consider achievement aspirations. Given the wide-ranging stereotype that women's work is of lesser value and status, it would hardly be surprising to find that women's aspirations were more limited than those of men.

Earlier we considered attribution research and discussed the judgements that people make about the performance of others. We can also examine the judgements that people make about their own behaviour. It is generally found that women have lower expectations about their own performance than men; women are more likely to view their own successful performance in terms of luck and to view failure as a sign of lack of ability. On the other hand, men are more likely to view success in terms of their ability, and failure as due to the difficulty of the task (Deaux, 1976a). Women's lower expectations have been explained as a further consequence of the gender stereotype of lower competence (Deaux, 1976a).

Gender differences in expectations of success begin early in life, and psychologists have tried to explain their origins. Since there is no obvious difference in boys' and girls' success or failure rate in intellectual tasks, the origin of women's lower expectations must be sought in different attitudes to success and failure by boys and girls, or in different responses to boys' and girls' success by others. Gender stereotypes again appear to be important; girls appear to incorporate a lower belief in their own competence in the self-concept early in life, and this influences their attitudes to their own performance (Parsons *et al.*, 1976). Given that women have lower expectations about their performance than men and attribute outcomes to different causes, how does this influence the way they perform tasks at work and their general level of aspiration?

There is limited evidence that expectation of success on a task increases the level of performance and the length of time that a person perseveres at it (Parsons *et al.*, 1976). But the general level of occupational aspiration may be more related to the perceived possibilities for advancement in a particular occupation rather than to expectations about success in specific work tasks. In a study of employees from a large corporation in the United States, it was found that women in management positions had achievement aspirations similar to those of their male counterparts. But in the corporation as a whole, men were generally more eager for advancement than women. Nevertheless, those men who viewed their achievement opportunities as being blocked showed attitudes to work and advancement similar to the majority of female employees (Tavris and Offir, 1977).

So far we have considered people's attributions of their own ability, and their aspirations for advancement. These are both related to achievement motivation, an aspect of personality which has been researched by psychologists for many years. McClelland and his colleagues first investigated it in the 1940s and 1950s using a test called the Thematic Apperception Test (TAT), in which people were asked to make up stories in response to a series of ambiguous pictures. The stories were scored for themes related to achievement.

Only a few of the earlier studies of achievement motivation included women as well as men. The effects of deliberately stimulating people's interest in achievement was assessed by asking people to carry out a task after being told that good performance on the task indicated intelligence and the ability to organize material and to evaluate conditions quickly and accurately. For men, these sessions led to an increase in the number of achievement-related themes in their TAT stories, but this was not the case for women (Maccoby and Jacklin, 1974). Originally these results were taken as indicating that women showed less achievement motivation than men, although women had displayed more achievement fantasy prior to stimulation. Later findings show that by altering the nature of the session designed to stimulate achievement from one involving competence to social approval, women's TAT scores can be induced to rise more than those of men (Maccoby and Jacklin, 1974).

The conclusions that we might draw from this research are tempered by the use of male characters in the TAT pictures. Even when female characters are used for women and girls, there are problems. It has been found that both genders show fewer achievement-related responses to stories with female characters. The use of pictures of a specific gender leads to confusion of achievement motivation and ideas shared by both genders about appropriate behaviour for men and women.

We cannot conclude from research on achievement motivation that women show lower levels of achievement motivation than men. Not very much research on women and achievement motivation has been carried out since the work of McClelland and his colleagues. An offshoot of McClelland's work is research on 'fear of success', originally carried out by Martina Horner. She asked samples of undergraduates at the University of Michigan to write stories in response to cue storylines. For example, 'After first-term finals, Anne finds herself top of the Medical School class' was the cue used for women, but for men the name John replaced Anne. Horner devised a scoring system for what she described as fear-of-success imagery. This consisted of three main themes: first, social rejection – for example, that success would be linked with losing friends or with sexual unattractiveness; secondly, more general guilt and anxiety about success – for example, that the person would be unhappy or feel unfeminine; thirdly, bizarre or exaggeratedly hostile themes, or denial of the cue altogether. Horner's main and widely reported finding was that 62 per cent of the women but only 10 per cent of the men wrote stories containing at least one fear-of-success image (Tresemer, 1977).

Horner also tested students on a timed task which consisted of unravelling mixed-up letters, and she compared performance when tested in a group or alone. Women who wrote stories with much fear-of-success imagery also tended to show a lower performance when tested in a group than when tested alone. As a result of her findings, Horner suggested that women have a motive to avoid success, and that this explains the inconsistent and unpredictable behaviour of women found in many of the earlier studies of achievement motivation (O'Leary, 1974).

Horner's study was widely publicized. Many psychologists and journalists believed that it provided an explanation for women's low occupational achievement. It seemed to indicate to them that while men are motivated to achieve without too many conflicting motives, women's achievement motivation conflicts with a feminine self-image, resulting in an overall motive to avoid success. The idea of fear of success became so much accepted for a time that there was even a symposium entitled 'Fear of success: is it curable?'

However, there have been many criticisms of the adequacy of Horner's original experiment, of the concept of fear of success, and of its ability to account for gender differences in occupational attainment (for example, Tresemer, 1977; Levine and Crumrine, 1975). Many follow-up studies have been carried out and a variety of results obtained in terms of the proportion of men and women who write stories with fear-of-success themes (Tavris and Offir, 1977; Tresemer, 1977). In a re-analysis of the combined results of nine published studies similar to Horner's original one, carried out between 1971 and 1973, no difference was found between the fear-of-success imagery of men and women. In one fairly precise replication of Horner's study, undertaken in 1975, 70 per cent of the stories written by women and by men contained at least one fear-of-success image. The stories of both genders also contained about the same proportion of sentences with negative remarks about success (Levine and Crumrine, 1975).

It has been suggested that Horner's findings reflect people's understanding of the meaning of achievement for a man and for a woman rather than, as Horner suggested, a deep-rooted personal motive (Tavris and Offir, 1977). Horner followed the earlier achievement motivation studies in asking men to write about a successful man, and women to write about a successful woman. Subsequent studies find that men comment adversely about female success when asked to write about a successful woman. Responses do not necessarily reflect personal motives, but may be related to wider beliefs and attitudes about female success. In other words, the stories may often have been realistic assessments of what it would be like to be top of the class in the circumstances described in the cue-line. Since medicine is a male-dominated subject, it is not surprising that a woman who achieves pre-eminence should arouse ambivalent feelings in others (Tresemer, 1977).

The general idea that success is a mixed blessing, and consequently arouses ambivalent motives, is a widespread and old one. It can be found in Eastern philosophy, in Christian teachings and in psychoanalytical theory. Jung put forward the idea that achievements are often constructed at the expense of other aspects of a person's personality. Most of these ideas are primarily concerned with male success, since it is usually men who are successful.

Although ambivalent feelings and motives towards success may be widespread in men and women, the gender difference found by Horner has not been clearly or repeatedly established, and supportive results are not very numerous or consistent (Tresemer, 1977). Even if Horner's original results had been replicated, the effect obtained was of insufficient size to explain the much larger gender difference in occupational achievement. We conclude that women's lower occupational achievement and status are not explained by a motive to avoid success, but rather that they are the result of a combination of the other influences. Widespread stereotypic beliefs form the basis for undervaluing female occupations and achievement. Stereotypes also prescribe the restricted and lower-status occupations which are regarded as suitable for women. These beliefs both influence, and are derived from, differences in educational and vocational training which are available to men and women. They may also affect men's and women's aspirations and ideas about their own abilities, as indicated by self-attribution studies, but they do not seem to affect the motive to achieve or the avoidance of achievement, at least according to the measures used by social psychologists.

CHAPTER 9

Growing Up Male or Female

Differences in Development: Nature or Nurture?

In Chapter 1 we considered a variety of explanations which have been
offered to explain gender differences by ordinary people and by social
scientists. The simplest of these is to focus on either the biological
properties of the individuals or their social environment. More complex
approaches seek to explain how a person interacts with the environment
and to include the way in which people make sense of or structure their
external world and biological characteristics. Some of the explanations
which we considered were concerned with changes that occur during
development, while others examined adult accounts of their social
world. In this chapter we return to a discussion of explanations, but
focus on the development of gender differences.

When a baby comes into the world, the first question people ask is,
'Is it a boy or a girl?' The infant's genitals provide the answer. This
sex assignment at birth has far-reaching consequences for the child's
life: it entails a prediction that he or she will follow one of two very
different developmental pathways.

How can such a minor anatomical feature as genital appearance indicate so much about a person's future life? It could be that genital differences are related to other biological features which are different in
boys and girls and which control aspects of psychological and behavioural development. Alternatively, the genitals may simply provide
signals which are elaborately interpreted in the social world. These two
alternatives represent respectively the biological and environmental
explanations of the development of gender differences. The argument
between exponents of the two approaches – often referred to as the
nature–nurture controversy – is of widespread significance, recurring
in commonsense arguments and in psychology (see Chapter 1).

Nature: Biological Explanations

Exponents of the biological viewpoint argue that although we use only one anatomical characteristic, genital appearance, to determine the gender of the newborn infant, this is related to other biological differences that will affect the course of psychological development.

Gender differences which are found early in life are often attributed to a biological cause, since it is assumed that cultural influences only begin to operate later. This idea, together with the associated notion that later gender differences can be traced to these early differences, has been put forward in several articles and books about gender differences (for example, Garai and Scheinfeld, 1968; Bardwick, 1971; McGuinness, 1976).

There are a number of criticisms which can be levelled at these arguments. First, the evidence for gender differences in newborn infants is inconsistent and unreliable from one study to another (Maccoby and Jacklin, 1974; Lewis, 1975; Birns, 1976). It has been suggested that a greater number of differences are reported in North American than in European studies because newborn American boys are much more likely to have been circumcised shortly after birth than their European counterparts (Richards *et al.*, 1976). However, a later analysis failed to support this hypothesis, finding few consistent gender differences whether the male infants were circumcised or not (Brackbill and Schroder, 1980). A second criticism is that even if early gender differences did occur regularly and consistently, this would not necessarily indicate that they were of biological origin. Adults differentiate between baby boys and girls from birth onwards, so that we cannot tell whether a particular gender difference observed during infancy is produced by different parental reactions or by different biological maturation in boys and girls (Lewis, 1975; Birns, 1976). One can also criticize the assumption that later masculine and feminine characteristics can be traced to early gender differences on the grounds that there is a lack of evidence for such continuity in psychological development (Maccoby and Jacklin, 1974; Birns, 1976). In view of these criticisms, the claim that gender differences found early in life are necessarily biological in origin is unsound.

More specific biological explanations have been offered to account for psychological gender differences. These may take one of several forms – for example, the action of sex hormones on the developing brain before birth, or the influence of sex hormones during adult life, or differences in brain maturation between boys and girls. Since the last two explanations have already been considered in earlier chapters, we shall consider instead an explanation which we have not so far covered. This is the view, widely known through the work of John Money and his colleagues, that sex hormones affect the brain during prenatal development so as to produce later behavioural and psychological differences between men and women.

In rodents, such as rats and mice, testosterone secreted early in development affects not only the development of the reproductive organs, as it does in human beings (see Chapter 3), but also later behaviour: it influences play in the young animal, and mating patterns, aggressiveness, fear behaviour, eating and activity levels in the adult (Archer, 1975; Quadagno *et al.*, 1977; Olioff and Stewart, 1978). By analogy, some of these findings have been applied to human gender differences – for example, in play and maternal interests. It is well known that boys' play involves more vigorous activities, such as wrestling and tumbling – 'rough-and-tumble' play – than girls' play, and this difference is observed in cultures very different from our own, such as the Kalahari San (Blurton-Jones and Konner, 1973). It is also observed in several mammals, such as rats and rhesus monkeys, where it has been shown that treatment of females with testosterone during prenatal development leads to increased rough-and-tumble play (Olioff and Stewart, 1978; Goy, 1968; Phoenix, 1974). Money and Ehrhardt (1972) reported that girls who were exposed before birth to substances similar to testosterone also play more energetically than normal girls. The hormone-treated girls were more interested in athletic skills and sports, and preferred playing with boys. They were known to themselves and their mothers as 'tomboys'. The girls also showed diminished maternal interests, which were indicated by their lack of interest in dolls and infant caretaking, and by their infrequent daydreams about pregnancy and motherhood. Money and Ehrhardt explain both of these findings by suggesting that the hormone has had a masculinizing effect on the girls' developing brains. In explaining rough-and-tumble play and the lack of maternal interest, studies of early testosterone exposure and later behaviour in rodents are cited to support the argument, although no clear connection has been established between parental behaviour and early testosterone treatment in rodents (Reinisch, 1976; Quadagno *et al.*, 1977). Money and Ehrhardt suggest that, in the case of human beings, the hormone affects parts of the brain which control play and maternal interests.

Money and Ehrhardt's studies have become well known, but their explanation is controversial. Alternatives have been suggested – in particular, that the girls' parents may have treated them differently. The general belief that these children had in some way been 'masculinized' before birth could have altered their parents' social perception and treatment of them. Ehrhardt and Baker (1974) conclude, on the basis of interviews with the parents, that although these possibilities cannot be ruled out, they do not seem to provide an obvious explanation. An alternative interpretation is that although the influences are not obvious, they operate in a subtle way. Mothers of six-month-olds report few differences in handling their own babies; however, they react differently in a laboratory setting to the same baby, depending on whether it is presented as a boy or a girl (Smith and Lloyd, 1978). Quadagno *et al.* (1977) specifically criticize Money and Ehrhardt's conclusions: they point out that a high proportion of the girls received late surgical correction for genital abnormalities – in other words, they had male-like genitals for some time after birth. Secondly, since Money and Ehrhardt derive their evidence from interviews and questionnaires given to the girls and their mothers rather than from observations of play, this shows only that the girls are *perceived* as 'tomboys' and lacking in maternal interests. The label 'tomboy' may have preceded the behaviour and may be based on parental expectations or on the appearance of the male-like genitals.

There is a more general difficulty in using the label 'tomboy'. A study of autobiographies written by women undergraduate psychology students found that a majority of them described themselves as having been tomboys during childhood; another study of adolescent girls found that 63 per cent reported that they were tomboys; and a large majority of yet another sample also reported being tomboys in childhood (Hyde *et al.*, 1977).

In view of these findings, more direct observations of girls exposed to testosterone prenatally are necessary before we can conclude that differences are attributable to hormone exposure before birth rather than to parental expectations. Even if genuine behavioural differences were found, we should still not rule out the influence of parental reactions. We have covered this particular biological explanation in some detail, since it is widely known and relies mainly on human rather than animal research. The various difficulties and methodological criticisms which we considered illustrate the pitfalls in trying to establish conclusively the existence of a biologically produced gender difference which is relatively independent of environmental influences.

Nurture: Environmental Explanations

'Socialization' is a term which originated in the 1930s and has been used in psychology, sociology and anthropology to describe the acquisition of culturally appropriate values, attitudes and behavioural activities as well as day-to-day aspects of child care. It is usually seen as a process whereby the important influences on development reside in the social environment; the individual is portrayed as responding to these rather than showing spontaneous maturation of behavioural features from within, as is the case for the biological explanations.

Psychologists approach the study of socialization in several different ways. One common approach in the 1950s and 1960s was to investigate the childhood origins of general personality characteristics; in particular, of aggression and dependence (Mischel, 1970). These two attributes were chosen to represent respectively the undersocialized and the over-socialized individual (Danziger, 1971). In relation to the learning of gender roles, aggression and dependence are of interest because they are believed to represent typically masculine and feminine character-istics (Mischel, 1966). Indeed, there is evidence that measures of de-pendence and passivity show a degree of developmental continuity for girls but not for boys, whereas the reverse is the case for measures of aggression (Kagan and Moss, 1962). Overall, however, approaches to the study of socialization based on general personality characteristics have revealed few identifiable childhood antecedents of adult be-haviour. Kagan and Moss chose for their study behaviour which formed important components of the male or the female role, and the extent of the continuity which they found was a reflection of the continuity of gender-appropriate behaviour in boys and girls.

A major difficulty with this approach lies in the use of global concepts such as aggression and dependence. We noted in Chapter 1 that their use reflects commonsense preoccupations. It is assumed that they are single stable personality traits, but this assumption has not been borne out by research. Evidence indicates that different measures of aggres-sion and of dependence show only a low relationship to one another. Much of the more recent socialization research has originated from a behaviourist tradition in North American psychology, directly con-cerned with investigating the general laws of learning in animals. The principles of classical conditioning – learning through association of events in time – and operant conditioning – learning through doing something and then receiving a reward for it – have been widely applied to human learning, including the learning of gender-appropriate responses (Mischel, 1966, 1970). An important principle that has been added to these explanations in their transition from animal to human behaviour is that of imitation, or learning through observing the responses of another individual. Although it occurs in animals (for example, Davis, 1973), imitation was generally neglected by the earlier behaviourists. Imitation is clearly such an important feature in human socialization that it cannot be neglected in the study of gender learning.

The social learning explanation of gender role acquisition maintains that gender differences are acquired as a result of a large number of specific learning experiences, involving principles such as rewards and punishments for appropriate acts of behaviour, selective exposure to different types of 'models', and different imitation of the same models by boys and girls. Children receive parental approval for behaviour which is appropriate for their own gender and disapproval for inappropriate behaviour (for example, Fling and Manosevitz, 1972; Fagot, 1977). These parental reactions can be observed very early in life: for instance, touching is discouraged in infant boys, whereas girls are freer to touch other children (Lewis, 1975). Throughout childhood, parents continue to reward and punish different activities in boys and girls: for instance, mothers may complain when their daughters become dirty, but tolerate dirtiness in boys (Newson and Newson, 1968). Boys may be rewarded with parental approval for being rough: 'I like the way he's rough. He's a proper lad,' remarked one mother about her 4-year-old son (Newson and Newson, 1968).

Boys and girls also receive different rewards and punishments from other children for different activities. Again this begins fairly early in life. For example, Fagot (1977) found that 3–4-year-old children would criticize other children whose play involved opposite-gender activities, and initiate less play with such children. Similarly, a 3-year-old boy who said that he wanted to cook the dinner was told by his girl playmate that 'daddies don't cook' (Garvey, 1977).

Teachers provide another source of rewards and punishments. Nursery-school teachers criticized girls for engaging in 'masculine' activities such as playing with blocks, and boys for engaging in 'feminine' activities such as playing with dolls (Fagot, 1977). Other studies also show that nursery-school teachers encourage and discourage different activities in boys and girls (for example, Serbin *et al.*, 1973).

There are several ways in which gender-typed responses may arise as a result of imitation. Boys and girls may simply be exposed to different 'role models', or they may attend selectively to their own-gender model when those for both genders are available, or alternatively they may learn activities appropriate for both genders but only perform those associated with their own gender. All three strategies are likely to play a part in learning one's own-gender role. Boys and girls may be exposed to different 'models', such as when they play with a parent of their own gender or when they watch different television programmes or read different comics. The two genders tend to play more with their own than with the opposite gender, and hence they will be exposed to different models during play.

Parents typically provide boys and girls with different toys, and this begins early in life. In a study of the contents of 1–6-year-old children's rooms in a number of upper-middle-class homes, Rheingold and Cook (1975) found clear gender differences in the toys which were provided. Boys' rooms contained more objects, toy animals, vehicles and live animals, whereas girls' rooms contained more dolls, dolls' houses, floral wallpaper, fabrics and lace. At eighteen months, provision of these different toys at home did not coincide with the children's play references as observed in the laboratory, where girls spent as much time as boys in a 'masculine' pursuit, playing with a large plastic truck.

Girls generally have greater access to a person of the same gender early in their lives, since their mothers or female caretakers will usually be present for much of the day. The father is usually only present intermittently, so that a boy will have to rely on older boys and on the media in order to imitate people of his own gender. There is some evidence that children attend selectively to people of their own gender (Mischel, 1970); in one study they showed more eye movements to same-gender lead characters in a film. (A more recent study found that boys and girls attend to an equal extent to people of the same and opposite genders portrayed on slides, but the measure of attention used in this study was rather idiosyncratic [Bryan and Luria, 1978]). In his accounts of gender role development from a social learning view, Mischel (1966, 1970) emphasizes the distinction between learning and performance. He suggests that children learn the behaviour of their own and of the opposite gender, but that they differ in the degree to which they perform the two types of behaviour (1966). But lack of performance will impede the learning of many forms of behaviour, so that this particular distinction may be hard to maintain in practice. This applies especially to intellectual performance, but also to the skills involved in social activities such as fighting; by engaging in activities appropriate for their own gender, boys and girls acquire the skills involved in performing these activities.

Some studies suggest that girls and boys can show a similar knowledge of many gender-appropriate responses, but still differ in their willingness to perform these responses. For example, Hargreaves (1976, 1977) analysed the content of children's drawings made in response to the instruction to complete circles by drawing objects: boys and girls showed different responses, boys showing more mechanical and scientific themes and girls showing more domestic themes. When the child was given a parallel form of the same test but asked to fill it out as the opposite gender would, the responses of the two genders were reversed. This study demonstrates a gender difference in response styles and suggests that information about activities of the opposite gender is known but not used.

Another question is whether boys and girls imitate activities simply because they are performed by a member of their own gender. Imitation is often thought to take place in this way, with boys and girls 'identifying' with people of their own gender. However, one experimental study shows that the important feature is whether the observed activity is considered gender-appropriate, rather than which gender is performing it (Barkley et al., 1977). Thus girls imitate behaviour which is seen as feminine, regardless of the gender of the person displaying it. A large number of other studies tend to support the argument that it is not necessarily the gender of the person performing an activity that decides whether it is to be imitated.

There are, therefore, several ways in which boys and girls acquire different forms of behaviour, ranging from the more obvious encouragement and discouragement by rewards and punishment, to the imitation of people performing gender-appropriate activities. The social learning view provides an alternative explanation for differences for which biological explanations have also been offered, such as rough-and-tumble play, fighting, playing with dolls and other 'maternal' activities.

An Interactionist Approach: Cognitive Developmental Theory

The social learning view concentrates on the environment and how this influences the child. A major alternative explanation, the cognitive developmental view, seeks to describe the interaction between the child and the environment, and in particular how the child comes to understand the social world (Kohlberg, 1966). Whereas social learning theorists see the child as essentially passive, Kohlberg's view is that the child is an active agent seeking to make sense of the world outside. He regards internal mental processes, such as attitudes and beliefs about gender roles, as being of primary importance for guiding the child's interaction with the environment.

In many ways the contrast between the social learning and the cognitive developmental approaches is one of different starting points and different emphasis: the former looks at the child from the viewpoint of an outside observer, whereas the latter views the child from within. If we take the example of a boy viewing a football match on television and immediately afterwards going out to play football, the social learning view would explain his behaviour in terms of the (externally) available model, whereas the cognitive developmental view would emphasize the child's ability to understand that he is a boy and to select for viewing, and engaging in, 'boy' activities such as football rather than 'girl' activities such as sewing.

The difference of emphasis means that cognitive developmental theory is stated in a language different from that of social learning theory. Kohlberg uses the concept of 'gender identity', which refers to the child's ability to categorize him or herself as a boy or a girl: gender identity appears, according to Kohlberg (1966) and Money *et al.* (1957), between 2 and 3 years of age, but recent research places it even earlier, between $1\frac{1}{2}$ and 2 years of age (Lewis, 1975). At this time most children begin to make some sort of verbal distinction between words such as 'boy' and 'girl' or 'mummy' and 'daddy'.

A 2- or 3-year-old child has already learnt that there are two categories of person, and that he or she belongs to one of these. Kohlberg regarded this realization as a necessary prerequisite for further learning about gender roles. This suggestion receives empirical support from a later study which found that 2–3-year-old children were positive in their beliefs about their own gender and negative in their beliefs about the opposite one: as children come to regard themselves as boys or girls, they tend to value positively gender-appropriate aspects of themselves and devalue aspects of the other gender (Kuhn *et al.*, 1978). The two features of preference for, and identification with, one's own gender are seen as guiding the processes of imitation and reinforcement, which assume such crucial importance in social learning theory. The two theories differ in that cognitive developmental theory views imitation and reinforcement as being guided by the child's understanding of the meaning and significance of these events, while social learning theory sees meaning and significance as arising from the imitation and reinforcement of gender-appropriate behaviour.

In the earliest years of life, a child knows relatively little about what distinguishes male and female, and does not realize that gender remains constant throughout life. A child of 3 or 4 years of age may think that a girl can be changed into a boy by cutting her hair short; in fact, at least one little boy – who has since grown up into a psychologist – has attempted to change the sex of a girl playmate in this way! Gradually, between 2 to 6 years of age, gender labels are applied more accurately, and the child learns that gender remains constant. This coincides with the stabilization of other concepts – for instance, the child comes to realize that cats are always cats and cannot change into dogs (Kohlberg, 1966; DeVries, 1969). Children also come to realize that girls always remain girls, irrespective of whether they have long or short hair, or how they are dressed or their choice of toys (DeVries, 1969).

Although the child only gradually comes to understand gender constancy, knowledge about the appropriate characteristics of each gender appears almost as early as the realization that there are two genders. Kuhn *et al.* (1978) presented 2–3-year-olds with two paper dolls, one called Michael and the other called Lisa, and asked them in the form of a game a number of questions about activities, characteristics and adult roles. They found that even at this age the children possessed quite an extensive knowledge about which activities were appropriate for boys and girls, and about adult gender roles. At 2 years of age both boys and girls believed that girls would clean the house when they were grown-up, and that boys would be the boss and would mow the lawn.

Kohlberg (1966) suggested that the reasons which children give for males and females performing different activities undergo a series of changes which coincide with the child's general level of understanding about the physical and social world. Ullian (1976) investigated Kohlberg's suggestions by interviewing 6–18-year-olds about their beliefs concerning men and women. She asked a range of questions relating to nurturing, competence, activity level and power. Examples of questions relating to power are 'Who should be the boss in the family?' followed by 'Why?' Ullian claims that the answers to her questions indicate that there are six stages in the development of beliefs about masculinity and femininity: at the earliest age (6 years), gender differences are viewed as being primarily the result of fixed biological attributes – that men work outside the home is seen as a consequence of their greater size and strength. By the third stage (10 years), gender differences are explained in terms of fixed social conventions, but this idea is soon replaced by more flexible notions of historical and social forces. At around 14 to 16 years, gender roles are viewed more as a matter of inner feelings, and masculinity and femininity are seen as part of everyone's psychological make-up.

Essentially Ullian's classification supports Kohlberg's theory, but it includes very little information which would enable an independent judgement of her classification to be made. It is possible that her findings could be described in terms of a series of more gradual changes during development rather than as discrete stages. Ullian's two later stages occur after puberty, but she does not mention puberty as a possible source of change in the gender role concepts: yet it is likely that reactions to physical maturation and adult gender role requirements produce a marked change in the way a person thinks about masculinity and femininity.

We can conclude that while cognitive developmental theory is reasonably convincing in explaining the development of the understanding of gender role concepts at earlier ages, it becomes less so when concerned with later childhood and adolescence. Many aspects of Kohlberg's theory, such as the relationship between beliefs about gender roles and gender-related activities, are not clear. It is, however, a useful theory in that it provides a way of looking at gender role development which takes into account the mental processes of the child and how the child understands the environment – complexities which are neglected by social learning theory.

Nature, Nurture and Models of Development

So far we have described biological, environmental and cognitive approaches to the development of gender differences. The first two attach different degrees of importance to two sources of influence in development: the biological organism – 'nature' – or the social environment –

'nurture'. Most psychologists would now agree that we cannot understand development without considering both these influences, and the cognitive developmental view is one attempt to do so. All too often, though, the intention to consider both nature and nurture takes the form of first recognizing the importance of both, but then forgetting one and concentrating on the other (for example, Bardwick, 1971; Hutt, 1972b). To consider both influences at once is a complex undertaking which finds no support in commonsense notions: it is therefore easier to say that both nature and nurture contribute to development but that one is more important, and to concentrate on the important one.

In order to progress any further in understanding the contribution of nature and nurture in development, it is useful to adopt less of a commonsense view by constructing 'models' of development. In our discussion the term 'model' refers to a precise but simplified representation which seeks to capture important principles underlying the original system. In constructing a general model of development, we have to ask where the controlling influence lies. Both the biological and the socialization views answer this question in relatively simple terms: either the biological or environmental source of influence is regarded as being so much more important than the other that for practical purposes the lesser influence can be neglected (or regarded as having only a weak modifying influence). This type of model is therefore called the 'main effect' model. Mischel (1966), the social learning theorist, would regard different types of reinforcement, modelling opportunities and suchlike as overriding any biological differences between boys and girls. On the other hand, Gray (1971a) or Hutt (1972a), biological theorists, would regard biological differences as being more important, so that environmental influences would only be capable of slightly amplifying or reducing the extent of such differences.

There are several ways of incorporating a control mechanism in a model of development. The most obvious of these is that there is some external or internal standard against which the performance of the individual is matched. This is easier to understand in the case of an external influence: for example, if it is decided that every child must learn a particular skill irrespective of his or her initial ability, performance will be monitored in relation to an 'ideal' imposed from outside until it matches this. A similar but more continuous process could occur with gender role learning, a boy or girl's behaviour being continually matched according to sets of standards shared by parents, teachers and other children.

An internal controlling influence could operate through a similar matching process. The best examples of this are found in the control of physical processes such as growth. The growth of a child is a very regular and organized process; it is also self-stabilizing or target-seeking (Tanner, 1970), so that if the child's weight is depressed after illness or malnutrition, weight gain will subsequently occur more rapidly until the child catches up to where he or she would have been. Various control mechanisms have been suggested for such catch-up effects (for example, Tanner, 1970; Bateson, 1976). Essentially, they involve a negative feedback loop of the type found in many biological systems: any variation due to the environment is compared to a reference value, in this case specifying the ideal outcome of growth, and discrepancies are corrected by appropriate action, such as by eating more or less. Similar catch-up effects have been observed in the case of intellectual development, again suggesting some form of internal reference value.

Most features of psychological development are more complex than these examples, and many psychologists now agree that notions of overriding control by either the social environment or the biological organism are often too simple to account for the complexities. Thus many writers on psychological development now stress the notion of an *interaction* or continuous interplay between biology and the environment (for example, Danziger, 1971; Schaffer, 1974; Lewis, 1975).

Although the interactionist position is not particularly amenable to commonsense description, it can be more readily described in terms of a model of development. The main-effect models which we have described so far view the controlling influence as being either external or internal. In contrast, one interactionist model sees the controlling influence as residing neither within the individual nor in the outside world (Bowers, 1973; Bateson, 1976; Archer and Lloyd, 1975). The outcome is therefore difficult to specify from knowledge of either environmental or biological factors alone. A far greater variety of possible outcomes can occur than with either type of main-effect model. But this particular point raises a major difficulty when the interactionist model is applied to the development of psychological gender differences. Although there is a great deal of inconsistency in some of the research findings, many gender-related characteristics do show a measure of consistency in their outcome. Examples include aggression, spatial ability, mathematical and verbal ability (Maccoby and Jacklin, 1974), and gender differences in major interests and occupational choice. It would seem, therefore, that this form of interactionist model might only fit gender differences which tend to be inconsistent from one study to another. Where there is more consistency, it fits less well.

Are such consistencies better explained by a main-effect model? Many gender differences can be viewed as a result of the socialization process, as we have indicated in this and other chapters. But we have also emphasized that development involves an interaction or continuous interplay between the child and the environment, and this aspect is absent from the socialization main-effect model. How can we reconcile these two aspects? This can be done partly by realizing that the term 'interactionist' is often used in two senses, one referring to any approach which recognizes the two-way interplay between the child and environment, and the other – a more specialized meaning – referring to those cases where there is no overriding control on development from within the organism or from the environment. The interactionist model which we have just described is of the second type. To account for consistencies in gender development, we require a model which involves both the notion of control and the principle of interaction used in the sense of interplay between organism and environment. We now outline such a model, derived from Bateson (1976), and argue that it is the most appropriate one for describing the development of many gender differences.

The essential feature of Bateson's model is that the constant interplay of organism and environment leads to the establishment of an internal controlling influence on development. In effect, what happens is that the organism is born with the capacity to control its own development, as in the maturational main-effect model, but that it has no fixed control mechanism until it interacts with its environment, the exact nature of the control mechanism being determined by that environment. Bateson (1976) suggests that many behavioural systems, such as imprinting (Sluckin, 1972), are of this type. He does not refer to human gender role learning, but the model would appear to fit this process – or rather, it would fit the cognitive developmental account of it.

The individual comes into the world with no set notion of what male and female are, but develops this classification process at about two years of age; subsequently this is elaborated and used as a way of making sense of the social world and of guiding action. Precisely what characteristics the child will use for distinguishing between appropriate and inappropriate action for his or her gender will depend on cultural influences. Hence the *content* of the internal reference value, the gender role concept, depends on external influences; but the existence of the potential for classifying and acting on the basis of categories such as male or female is something which is part of the human biological make-up. In this way, human beings possess the intellectual equipment for incorporating aspects of their culture into a particular way of viewing the world, one which emphasizes differences between categories. One might almost say that people are 'programmed' to look at the social world in terms of differences, and that gender provides the most readily available material for this programme to act upon. The construction of this internal gender reference system occurs gradually throughout development without the child being consciously aware of it. Eventually, he or she comes to regard their own culturally induced variety of gender differences as equivalent to the natural order of things. In other words, nurture becomes second nature.

It is our opinion that environmental influences are very important for understanding gender differences (and we would largely disregard the biological explanations mentioned earlier). Nevertheless, the socialization process occurs in an interactive way, and standards of masculinity and femininity become incorporated into the mental fabric at an early age. It is scarcely surprising that they become very difficult to change later on.

CHAPTER 10

Social Change and the Future

Sex or Gender: Does it Matter?

In the preceding nine chapters we have tried to maintain a clear distinction between sex and gender. We have used sex in biological contexts, while we have employed the term gender to denote a socially derived distinction between people. It is time to consider whether this precise usage produces better understanding or whether it is primarily a bit of academic pedantry.

Practically the distinction matters little. Most people class themselves and are categorized by others as the gender congruent with their biological sex. Nonetheless, we have seen that in Omani society certain people who are biologically male choose to define themselves as *Xanith*, a social category which one anthropologist has described as a third gender. In our own society we have become aware in recent years of people who believe themselves to be living in physical bodies which contradict their psychological and socially determined gender group. These transsexuals seek surgery to transform their bodies and to remove the stigmata of the wrong 'sex'.

Emphasizing the social construction of genders allows us to pursue possibilities for change in a number of directions. On the one hand, we can contemplate the gradual blurring of distinctions in the roles and activities of men and women towards a unisex or androgynous position which need only be tempered by the few constraints of human reproduction. On the other hand, we can consider the possibility that comparison and differentiation are essential aspects of social organization and that biological sex provides a convenient symbol around which to construct social categories or gender groups.

Sandra Bem has contemplated the consequences of her goal of an androgynous society. She has recently suggested that if a society were to give meaning to behaviour in a manner which ignored the gender of the actor, the very notions of masculinity and femininity would cease to have significance (Bem, 1979). In so far as we can specify the limits of masculinity and femininity, we are presently able to measure androgyny. Sex-typed people describe their behaviour in terms of stereotypes or commonsense beliefs, but androgynous individuals espouse aspects of both masculine and feminine behaviour. These considerations led Bem to conclude that 'when andryogyny becomes a reality, the *concept* of androgyny will have been transcended'.

We believe that the androgynous society will not become a reality. Some form of group differentiation seems essential to human social organization. Although it can be argued that the basis of social stratification need not be biological sex – it could be age, for example – we believe that gender will continue to be an important basis for social comparison. There are many sources of support for this position, which we call the gender view. Social stratification based on age is possible; it does occur in some societies, but it is arbitrary and cumbersome. Age is a continuous dimension and cut-off points must be selected and marked. To a limited degree, rites of passage such as initiation at puberty perform such functions. On the other hand, sex is easily seen as a dichotomous variable, and in most cases identification as either male or female is made with no difficulty. These considerations provide a partial account for the virtually universal presence of gender as a principle of social organization.

Taking the argument a step further, it is difficult to imagine a completely androgynous society. In discussing infantile sexuality and gender identity, we noted that awareness of one's gender develops very early and is essential to the construction of a sense of self. In turn, it is difficult to imagine an individual functioning adequately in society as we understand it without a firm sense of self. This early gender awareness aids the child in organizing the social world and reflects his understanding of it. Gender awareness arises not only from infants' experiences of their bodies but through interaction with adults in their society who are themselves moulded by their membership in gender groups. As we proposed in the last chapter, nurture becomes second nature and gender identity becomes an important schema in mental life (Bem, 1981).

In adopting the gender view, we think of genders as social groups and we can consider them in terms of social psychological theories of intergroup relations. Glynis Breakwell (1979) uses this body of theory to analyse the women's movement. She views women as members of the social group 'woman' and sees their social identity as deriving from group membership and reflecting the social value of the group. This value reflects the differentiation of the gender groups from one another. In the case of the group 'woman', it stands in contrast to the group 'man' and derives its value from that comparison. As we have noted many times, the category 'woman' suffers in the comparison, and this leads us to consider whether it need always be so.

The Gender View: Intergroup Relations and Social Change

We have so far outlined two views of gender which have different implications for the possibility of change. One, which is called the androgyny view, emphasizes the similarities between human beings and assumes that we could choose not to distinguish people by gender. The second, which we call the gender view, emphasizes differences between the gender groups and assumes that categorization by gender is fundamental to a person's self-concept. This is a view adopted at the end of Chapter 9 and in the previous section.

In the next three sections we use the framework of intergroup relations theory to consider social change. Firstly, we look at the inequality of power between the gender groups and ask whether this necessarily leads to conflict. Secondly, we examine what it means to belong to a gender group and the consequences of making the requirements for membership less obligatory. Finally, we consider the ways in which the gender concepts of women undervalue their achievements and restrict their potential.

Do Men Always Have More Power than Women?

Breakwell's analysis of gender in terms of intergroup relations theory does not explicitly address the issue of the inevitability of inequality between men and women. Breakwell initially infers inequality from attempts by women, as individuals or organized groups, to bring about social change to alter their position relative to men. Later on she explicitly rejects the idea that men and women are merely different but not unequal as an ideology which prevents women from changing their position; this she calls 'the grand illusion'.

In apparent contrast to Breakwell's view is that of Rogers (1978) which we considered in Chapter 5. She considers that inequality is not an inevitable consequence of there being two gender groups. She argues that inequality will exist under circumstances where the two groups differ in their behaviour but do not see one another as fundamentally different in aims and values – that is, ideological differentiation. Where there is ideological differentiation as well as behavioural differentiation, Rogers asserts that the two gender groups can see each other as different and interdependent rather than as unequal and in conflict. Rogers argues that the position of women in traditional Islamic societies is of this nature. Her interpretation differs from that of many anthropologists, however, and the material on Islamic societies is clearly open to different interpretations.

Rosenblatt and Cunningham (1976) have used cross-cultural evidence to develop an argument which is intermediate between the views of Rogers and Breakwell. They note that in most societies male activities have higher status and that men dominate the economic life of most communities, but they emphasize the importance of distinguishing public and private power. Noting that private power is often held by women, they argue, as does Rogers, that in many societies the worlds of men and women are so different that the higher public status of men is irrelevant to the question of whether women see themselves as having less power. They argue that a woman's status, feelings and reputation are concerned with her relations with other women and not how she is seen in relation to the world of men. Accordingly, the self-perceived status of women will not be less than that of men.

The Rosenblatt and Cunningham analysis highlights a crucial issue in deciding between the views of Rogers and Breakwell: how do we define power? Do we take the views of women themselves or do we take an outside observer's analysis of the position of women in that society? The first option, the one adopted by Rogers and to some extent by Rosenblatt and Cunningham, is open to the criticism that the views of certain women may be misleading. They may believe that they are different but not unequal because men have encouraged them to do so in order to subjugate them and keep them contented. The second option, that of Breakwell, is open to a different kind of criticism, that of an American or European ethnocentrism in the analysis of power. We have already noted in Chapter 5 that power is notoriously difficult to define and that any observer brings a particular cultural bias to the choice of status and power indicators. Thus both these criticisms raise fundamental issues and result in a dilemma which will continue to produce arguments.

Acknowledging that there are potential problems in transferring our own conceptions of power to other societies, we would nevertheless argue that a wholly subjective view of power is inadequate: slaves cannot obtain power simply by being contented with their social position relative to other slaves. We agree, along with Breakwell, that inequality is independent of whether or not a disadvantaged group perceives that inequality. She suggests that conflict is inevitable if members of the less powerful group experience dissatisfaction with their position and perceive that they are less powerful. The outcome of this dissatisfaction and conflict depends on the degree of social mobility that group membership permits. If there is little opportunity to move out of the lower-status group, then the members of that group will attempt collectively to change the social position of their group. If movement out of the group is readily available, there will be emphasis on individual change. If individual women feel that they can maintain their identities and at the same time relinquish traditional feminine characteristics by adopting masculine roles and behaviour, they can in a sense change their group membership. It has been argued that throughout history individual women have achieved positively valued identities this way (Williams and Giles, 1978). This is an option which is only open to a few women who are prepared to, and are able to, abandon those feminine characteristics which may be crucial to the identity of most women. For the majority, change of this sort would be unacceptable. Instead, more collective action which would benefit the majority of women is urged by those of a feminist outlook.

What are the possible forms that social change can take? One approach is for women to seek membership in the more powerful masculine groups and become, for instance, tractor drivers and neurosurgeons. A second involves changing the values ascribed to the existing characteristics of lower-status group members with related changes in intergroup relations. A third entails fundamental changes in group structures. We consider these strategies in the next two sections.

What are the Requirements for Belonging to a Gender Group?

In this section we consider the first strategy for social change; attempting to gain membership of the male gender group. In the last section we stated that individual women, because of the rigidity of membership requirements, can only gain membership of male groups with some difficulty. This leads us to ask what the requirements are and how rigidly they are enforced.

Male and female gender concepts provide prescriptions for gender group membership. To be fully accepted as a man, one must act, look and feel like a man. Although there is an overall consensus as to what this entails, there is also considerable variation within particular societies. In group relations theory, men and women are seen as distinct 'conceptual groups' as opposed to 'concrete groups'. The latter are more formalized in terms of goals and entry requirements, while conceptual groups do not meet for an overt purpose or have specific entry requirements.

Breakwell uses the notion of a conceptual group in analysing the position of women. The social group 'woman' exists in many different forms both as a social entity and in terms of the criteria for group membership. Breakwell argues that various standards are imposed from outside – that is, by men – in deciding what it means to be a woman, and these are often incompatible with individual women's conceptions of themselves. Women will therefore see themselves as marginal to their gender group – that is, they are neither affiliated to it nor free of it. Breakwell goes on to argue that marginal individuals will be dissatisfied with their position and will wish to change it. Both types of analysis – that based on intergroup inequality and that based on marginality – predict pressure for social change.

Breakwell outlines the various strategies for change open to someone who is in a marginal position. The first is to expand the criteria for group membership so as to include the marginal individual. This would entail lessening the obligatory nature of gender concepts. In this way a woman would still feel part of the social world of women even if she chose to pursue a career instead of having a family, or if she lived in a homosexual relationship. Similarly, a man who was a househusband or in a homosexual relationship would still feel and be accepted as part of the social world of men. At present we would expect all of these people to feel excluded from full acceptance by their gender group. Because of their marginal position, they will also find it difficult to alter the criteria for group membership so as to enable them to become accepted. In such cases, social change has to come from an alternative direction. One common strategy is to affiliate with like-minded individuals and to press for social change through collective action. The difficulty with this strategy is that the new group may remain marginal or be accepted only in restricted circles and not by the majority of the gender group.

In this respect, the more the women's movement is identified with marginal women, such as lesbians and Marxists, the less will be its influence on widening the criteria for group membership. Even the wider influence of broader-based feminism has largely affected only the habits of an educated elite and may not be transmitted to the cultural mainstream of society. Nevertheless, individual women will obtain a positive self-concept by belonging to a marginal group: it is more satisfactory to be a member of a marginal group than to be an isolated individual.

The gender view predicts that even if gender concepts were made much more flexible so that marginal individuals were able to become affiliated to their gender group, the majority of people will still opt to belong to one gender group or the other. Most will opt for their sex-appropriate gender role, but a few individuals, convinced that they really belong to the opposite gender group, will want to adopt their life-style and appearance.

But do we mean that change will be restricted to making gender concepts more flexible? This is only one avenue of change which we can derive from the analysis of intergroup relations. There are two other possibilities, which we consider in the next section.

Revaluation of Gender Relations and Structural Change

In this section we consider two further forms of social change which can be derived from intergroup relations theory. If members of a group view their own characteristics as undervalued, they can try to alter the values ascribed to them and to their behaviour. Similarly, if they view their potential as being underdeveloped, they can seek to change the existing social order. Both these methods of achieving change involve altered self-perception by members of the group, but they depend for their ultimate success on members of the dominant group acknowledging these changes.

We first consider how the values of women's achievements and characteristics may be increased. Until comparatively recently the activities of women and their artistic and scientific achievements have been neglected. This imbalance is beginning to be redressed by books on the place of women in history (for example, Power, 1975) and on their artistic achievements (for example, Moers, 1978; Petersen and Wilson, 1978; Perry, 1979). In the biological and social sciences, many topics of interest to women have been neglected or viewed from a male standpoint. There is now more interest in these subjects. In psychology, the subjects of pregnancy, childbirth and the menopause have recently been discovered as legitimate areas of research (for example, Bardwick, 1971; Sherman, 1971; Macfarlane, 1977; Paige, 1973). In sociology, too, there are now studies of housework and childbirth which seek to increase the value of these activities (Oakley, 1974; 1979).

Penelope Leach (1979) argues that child care is greatly undervalued in our society, and she advocates a new approach to parenthood which would recognize and reward it as an important and high-status activity. Among the measures which she suggests are paying mothers to stay at home and look after their young children. Alice Rossi advocates a more cooperative approach to counteract the social isolation felt by many mothers and their children. Both Leach and Rossi accept that child care is a woman's role, and their solutions for social change are to aid women in performing this role and to accord value to its enactment. Their writings provide a sharp contrast to the prevailing spirit of the women's movement in Britain and North America, which aims to enable women to escape from child care and to concentrate on activities outside the home.

Whether or not we agree that women should have primary responsibility for children, how easy would it be to change the status of the role of housewife and mother? In Chapter 8 we considered research which suggested that a loss of status occurred when an occupation changed from being mainly male to mainly female. An increase occurs when men undertake the same activity and this may be reflected in language: thus 'cook' becomes 'chef'. In some occupations which used to be predominantly female and lower-paid, an influx of men has occurred when pay was increased. In addition, men come to occupy the higher-status positions within these occupations, for example in primary schools, teaching and nursing. It is therefore possible that a sudden increase in the pay and status of child care might result in attracting men, particularly as the higher-paid organizers of women's activities. This would, of course, be quite the opposite of Leach's and Rossi's intentions.

There are therefore two dilemmas in adopting a strategy for social change based on increasing the status of the child care role: first, whether concentrating on this strategy will be to the detriment of widening women's occupational choices; and secondly, whether it would simply attract more men who would organize women.

A second strategy for social change is to concentrate on the development of women's unrealized potential in order to alter the existing social structure. In Chapters 2 and 8 we noted that women leave full-time education before men, and that their attainments in higher education are likely to be lower than those of men. Fewer women embark on occupational training, and women tend to take up unskilled, low-status and repetitive jobs.

It is probably too soon to tell whether the trends of the 1970s, showing more women in education and training (Blackstone, 1978), will be maintained so that more women realize their educational potential. In employment, media publicity tends to concentrate on a few cases of women entering stereotypically male occupations, and hence it may be misleading in reflecting overall trends. Despite the equal opportunities legislation in the United Kingdom, there are still powerful influences which discourage women from trying to succeed in the masculine world of work.

Sport provides a particularly clear example of the underdevelopment of women's potential. In Chapter 3 we noted that although, on average, the physical potential of women for various sports activities is lower than that of men, the gap between the performance of men and women in athletic events has narrowed in recent years. Professional sport is becoming less exclusively a male preserve. In Chapter 4 we considered the denial and underdevelopment of women's capacity for sexual enjoyment. Studies of female sexuality, such as *The Hite Report*, seek to overcome female inhibitions and to encourage more women to seek sexual activity and to develop the capacity for fulfilment.

A final example of women engaging in activities beyond the bounds of the traditional feminine role and stereotype is the area of aggression, though many would hesitate to refer to this as unrealized potential. Aggression can mean either assertiveness or fighting and violence, as we mentioned in Chapter 5. Assertiveness is often regarded as being necessary to compete effectively with men in their social world. Although few would regard violence as a positive characteristic, there are some women who are prepared to engage in traditional masculine activities such as professional boxing and wrestling, political terrorism and violent crime. Changes may occur in the structure of the army and other services as women carry arms.

These examples represent various ways in which women seek to develop their potential and redefine the limits of what has traditionally been seen as feminine. The extent of the future development of women's potential in these areas will depend on the future flexibility and definition of gender concepts. If women can engage in activities which were exclusively masculine and still feel that they are feminine, the potential for change will be far more extensive than at present. This depends partly on the attitude of men to women who engage in once traditional masculine activities. The more that men come to accept women who seek to develop their potential beyond the boundaries of their traditional gender concepts, the more that women will see that such development need not conflict with a positive self-image.

Implications of the Gender View for the Future

We have used intergroup relations theory to consider the implications for social change in gender concepts. This is one way to explore the possible course of future events. Another way to predict the future is by extrapolation from the present: it is assumed that current trends have an impetus which will carry them into the future. In this manner, it is predicted that more women will enter higher education and the work force, will participate in sports and will commit violent crimes in the future.

We are sceptical about the possibility of accurate predictions based solely on an analysis of the possibilities for social change derived from intergroup relations theory, or on projections from current changes in gender constructs. Both focus only on sources of change directly re-lated to gender concepts, and do not adequately recognize that the futures of women and men are embedded in a larger society. Changes in this larger society are likely to have greater consequences for the future of women and men than current changes in gender concepts.

It is difficult to predict the course of wider changes in society which will affect gender role changes. Predictions about the numbers of women in the labour force must take account of the absolute numbers of jobs. If these are decreasing, it will be less likely that more women will enter the labour force in the future. During this century in the United Kingdom unemployment and changes in work requirements resulting from war have been associated with more widespread changes in occupational gender roles than have changes in social attitudes towards gender concepts. An example of wider societal trends affecting the occupational roles of women is recruitment in the United States Army. Owing to a shortage of available male recruits since the abolition of conscription, the Pentagon has reconsidered an earlier policy and decided to recruit more women and to allow them combat roles. The military planners intend to almost double the proportion of enlisted women during the five years from 1978 to 1983 (Davidson, 1978).

The Pentagon plans covered only a five-year period. We now turn to an attempt made to predict changes in child-rearing and family life over a longer period. Lois Hoffman (1977) identified several trends which she assumed would be maintained and affect the future. The first was that motherhood would continue to occupy a smaller proportion of a woman's life, and the second was that maternal employment would become increasingly common. The first of these was based on the expectation of a declining birth rate and longer life expectancy, and the second on full employment. In the 1980s both of these assumptions are being called into question and illustrate the problems in making accurate predictions. Although at the time that Hoffman was writing the birth rate was declining in both Britain and the United States, there are recent signs that this trend is not continuing. Similarly, rising unemployment calls into question the assumption that more women with children will continue to work outside the home. Other developments – for example, in medical technology – may produce further complications which will make prediction even more difficult.

Given these uncertainties in prediction based on extrapolation from the present, we finally turn to some more imaginative visions of the future. We offer two examples. The first is George Orwell's *Nineteen Eighty-Four*, in which the author describes his vision of the structure of a society of the future; it is this wider society combined with Orwell's own assumptions about gender roles that contribute to his conception of future roles and the relations of women and men. The second is a fantasy offered by the social psychologist Marie Jahoda (1975) on the possible future relations of women and men. In this case, she concentrates on gender relations without situating them in a wider social context.

Orwell's *Nineteen Eighty-Four* was written before the women's movement of the 1960s had stimulated analysis and consciousness of gender roles. It reflects many assumptions about gender roles which may have been acceptable in British society in the 1940s. The leader, Big Brother, and most of the soldiers and heroes of the party are men. Boys and men were socialized to play an active heroic role. The early childhood of a model but fictitious citizen, Comrade Ogilvy, entailed the following: at the age of three he had refused all toys except a drum, a sub-machine gun, and a model helicopter, and at six he joined the Spies – an organization designed to make children watch their parents for signs of unorthodoxy. It was the women who were conditioned to reject their sexual feelings and to remain chaste, since men's sex instincts were held to be less controllable than those of women.

Many aspects of the relationships between women and men portrayed in the novel are very different from those of Britain in the 1940s. In the world of Newspeak and Thoughtcrime, gender roles are seen as incidental to the overall control of people's lives and habits by the party. Socialization is aimed at producing loyal party members and at preventing any loyalties which it cannot control. Emotional attachments between child and parent are discouraged. So too is eroticism, and the authorities try to remove pleasure from the sexual act: 'Sexual intercourse was to be looked on as a slightly disgusting minor operation, like having an enema.'

In Orwell's vision of the future, sexuality is denigrated and gender concepts are exaggerated in directions which would help the state to achieve its ends. Marie Jahoda's scheme is aimed at providing the individual with a more satisfactory erotic life. To achieve this end she makes some radical proposals.

Marie Jahoda is frank in admitting that her fantasy is outrageous and not easily implemented. Having considered both the benefits and the limitations of the two-gender family – parents and their children – she proposes a new form of three-generational family. It would consist of three adults, either two men and one woman or two women and one man. A young girl would first marry a middle-aged man and through him learn about sexuality and perhaps produce children. In middle age she might take a second husband, a young man whom she would initiate into the sexual culture. In her old age the by now middle-aged man could take a second, young wife and produce children of his own. So the cycle would evolve, giving age and sexual experience new meanings. Jahoda's fantasy is exciting to contemplate, since it challenges such fundamental values as monogamous marriage and age in relation to sexual partners and it almost touches the Oedipal taboo, that universal principle of human social organization.

This fantasy permits us to see clearly the values that it challenges, but less imaginative schemes often encourage us to forget an important consequence of social change. In choosing a new solution to an old problem – for example, caring for the young communally as it is done in the *kibbutzim* – we are also choosing not to do something, in this case to encourage the development of family life. Change involves giving up old ways as well as adopting new ones.

Given the importance of gender in individuals' self-concepts, it seems inevitable that social change will come about slowly and perhaps painfully. Were a society able to provide meaningful freedom of choice in domains such as education, child care and careers, individuals would still experience difficulty in exercising this freedom. The return to an emphasis on the nuclear family in *kibbutzim* is an indication of the difficulties to be encountered in bringing major change to gender concepts (Tiger and Shepher, 1975). We are not counselling the maintenance of the *status quo*; but rather, we are trying to approach the question of change with awareness of the difficulties both in predicting the course of social history and in implementing proposals once they have been developed.

References

Ainsworth, M. D. S. 1965. Further research into the adverse effects of maternal deprivation. In J. Bowlby, *Child Care and the Growth of Love* (2nd edn). Harmondsworth: Penguin.

Alcock, J. 1975. *Animal Behavior: An Evolutionary Approach*. Sunderland (Mass.): Sinauer.

Alther, L. 1977. *Kinflicks*. Harmondsworth: Penguin.

American Psychiatric Association. 1968. *Diagnostic and Statistical Manual*.

Anastasi, A. 1958. *Differential Psychology* (3rd edn). New York: Macmillan.

Anon. 1970. Effects of sexual activity on beard growth in man. *Nature*, 30: 869–70.

Archer, J. 1971. Sex differences in emotional behaviour: a reply to Gray and Buffery. *Acta Psychologica*, 35:415–29.

Archer, J. 1973. Tests for emotionality in rats and mice: a review. *Animal Behaviour*, 21:205–35.

Archer, J. 1975. Rodent sex differences in emotional and related behaviour. *Behavioral Biology*, 14:451–79.

Archer, J. 1976a. Biological explanations of psychological sex differences. In B. B. Lloyd and J. Archer (eds.), *Exploring Sex Differences*. London and New York: Academic Press.

Archer, J. 1976b. The organization of aggression and fear in vertebrates. In P. P. G. Bateson and P. Klopfer (eds.), *Perspectives in Ethology 2*. New York: Plenum.

Archer, J. 1979. *Animals Under Stress*. London: Edward Arnold.

Archer, J. and Lloyd, B. B. 1975. Sex differences: biological and social interactions. In R. Lewin (ed.), *Child Alive*. London: Temple Smith.

Archer, J. and Westeman, K. 1981. Sex differences in the aggressive behaviour of school children. *British Journal of Social and Clinical Psychology*, 20:31–6.

Ardener, E. 1972. Belief and the problem of women. In J. La Fontaine (ed.), *The Interpretation of Ritual*. London: Tavistock.

Ardrey, R. 1967. *The Territorial Imperative*. London: Collins.

Bandura, A., Ross, D. and Ross, S. A. 1961. Transmission of aggression through imitation of aggressive models. *Journal of Abnormal Social Psychology*, 63: 575–82.

Bardwick, J. M. 1971. *Psychology of Women: A Study of Bio-Cultural Conflicts*. New York: Harper and Row.

Barkley, R. A., Ullman, D. G., Otto, L. and Brecht, J. M. 1977. The effects of sex-typing and sex appropriateness of modelled behavior on children's imitation. *Child Development*, 48:721–5.

Baron, R. A. 1977. *Human Aggression*. New York: Plenum.

Barry, W. A. 1970. Marriage research and conflict: an integrative review. *Psychological Bulletin*, 73:41–54.

Bart, P. B. 1971. Depression in middle-aged women. In V. Cornick and B. K. Moran (eds.), *Women in Sexist Society*. New York: Basic Books.

Bateson, P. P. G. 1976. Rules and reciprocity in development. In P. P. G. Bateson and R. A. Hinde (eds.), *Growing Points in Ethology*. Cambridge: Cambridge University Press.

Bayley, N. and Oden, M. 1955. The maintenance of intellectual ability in gifted adults. *Journal of Gerontology*, 10:91–101.

Bayley, N. and Schaefer, E. S. 1964. Correlations of maternal and child behaviors with the development of mental abilities: data from the Berkeley Growth Study. *Monographs of the Society for Research in Child Development*, 29, serial no. 97.

Beach, F. A. 1966. Review of *The Human Sexual Response* by W. H. Masters and V. E. Johnson. *Scientific American*, 215(2):107–10.

Beck, A. T. and Greenberg, R. L. 1974. Cognitive therapy with depressed women. In V. Franks and B. Vasanti (eds.), *Women in Therapy*. New York: Brunner-Mazel.

Bem, S. L. 1974. The measurement of psychological androgyny. *Journal of Consulting and Clinical Psychology*, 42:155–62.

Bem, S. L. 1979. Theory and measurement of androgyny: a reply to the Redhazur–Tenbaum and Locksley–Colten critiques. *Journal of Personality and Social Psychology*, 37:1047–54.

Bem, S. L. 1981. Gender Schema theory: a cognitive account of sex typing. *Psychological Review*, 88:354–64.

Best, D. L., Williams, J. E., Cloud, J. M., Davis, S. W., Robertson, L. S., Edwards, J. R., Giles, H. and Fowles, J. 1977. Development of sex-trait stereotypes among young children in the United States, England, and Ireland. *Child Development*, 48:1375–84.

Bibring, E. The mechanism of depression. 1953. In P. Greenacre (ed.), *Affective Disorders*. New York: International Universities Press.

Biller H. B. 1976. Paternal deprivation and sex role development. In M. E. Lamb (ed.), *The Role of the Father in Child Development*. New York: Wiley.

Birke, L. and Best, S. 1980. The tyrannical womb: menstruation, menopause and science. In Brighton Women and Science Collective (ed.), *Alice Through the Microscope: The Power of Science Over Women's Lives*. London: Virago.

Birns, B. 1976. The emergence and socialization of sex differences in the earliest years. *Merrill-Palmer Quarterly*, 22:229–54.

Blackstone, T. 1978. Success or failure? *The Times Higher Educational Supplement*, 8 September:11.

Block, J. H. 1976a. Debatable conclusions about sex differences. *Contemporary Psychology*, 21:517–22.

Block, J. H. 1976b. Issues, problems and pitfalls in assessing sex differences: a critical review of *The Psychology of Sex Differences*. *Merrill-Palmer Quarterly*, 22:283–308.

Blum, J. E., Fosshage, J. L. and Jarvik, L. F. 1972. Intellectual changes and sex differences in octogenarians: a twenty-year longitudinal study of ageing. *Developmental Psychology*, 7:178–87.

Blurton-Jones, N. G. 1972. Categories of child-child interaction. In N. Blurton-Jones (ed.), *Ethological Studies of Child Behaviour*. London: Cambridge University Press.

Blurton-Jones, N. G. and Konner, M. J. 1973. Sex differences in the behaviour of London and Bushman children. In R. P. Michael and J. H. Crook (eds.), *Comparative Ecology and Behaviour of Primates*. London and New York: Academic Press.

Bowers, K. S. 1973. Situationism in psychology: an analysis and critique. *Psychological Review*, 80:307–36.

Bowlby, J. 1951. *Maternal Care and Mental Health*. Geneva: World Health Organization.

Bowlby, J. 1969. *Attachment and Loss* (vol. I). London: Hogarth Press.

Brackbill, Y. and Schroder, K. 1980. Circumcision, gender differences and neo-natal behaviour: an update. *Developmental Psychobiology*, 13:607–14.

Brain, M. 1978. Transsexualism in Oman (correspondence). *Man* 13:322–3.

Breakwell, G. 1979. Woman: group and identity? *Women's Studies International Quarterly*, 2:9–17.

Breen, D. 1975. *The Birth of a First Child: Towards an Understanding of Femininity*. London: Tavistock.

Brimer, M. A. 1969. Sex differences in listening comprehension. *Journal of Research and Develpment in Education*, 3:72–9.

Broverman, I. K., Broverman, D. M., Clarkson, F. E., Rosenkrantz, P. S. and Vogel S. R. 1970. Sex role stereotypes and clinical judgments of mental health. *Journal of Consulting and Clinical Psychology*, 34:1–7.

Broverman, D. M., Klaiber, E. L., Kobayashi, Y. and Vogel, W. 1968. Roles of activation and inhibition in sex differences in cognitive abilities. *Psychological Review*, 75:23–50.

Brown, G. W. and Harris, T. 1978. *Social Origins of Depression: A Study of Psychiatric Disorder in Women*. London: Tavistock.

Bryan, J. W. and Luria, Z. 1978. Sex-role learning: a test of the selective atten-tion hypothesis. *Child Development*, 49:13–23.

Buffery, A. W. H. and Gray, J. A. 1972. Sex differences in the development of spatial and linguistic skills. In C. Ounsted and D. C. Taylor (eds.), *Gender Differences: Their Ontogeny and Significance*. London: Churchill.

Burns, R. B. 1977. Male and female perceptions of their own and the other sex. *British Journal of Social and Clinical Psychology*, 16:213–20.

Burnstyn, J. N. 1971. Brain and intellect: science applied to a social issue 1860–1875. *XII* Congrès International d'Histoire des Sciences, 9:13–16.

Cerullo, M., Stacy, J. and Breines, W. 1977–8. Alice Rossi's sociobiology and anti-feminist backlash. *Berkeley Journal of Sociology*, 22:167–77.

Chang, Jolan. 1977. *The Tao of Love and Sex: The Ancient Chinese Way to Ecstasy*. London: Wildwood House.

Chesler, P. 1972. *Women and Madness*. New York: Doubleday and Co.

Chodorow, N. 1978. *The Reproduction of Mothering*. Berkeley and Los Angeles: University of California Press.

Clancy, K. and Gove W. 1974. Sex differences in mental illness: an analysis of response bias in self-reports. *American Journal of Sociology*, 80:205–16.

Clarke, A. E. and Ruble, D. N. 1978. Young adolescents' beliefs concerning menstruation. *Child Development*, 49:231–4.

Clarke-Stewart, K. A. 1977. The father's impact on mother and child. SRCD meetings New Orleans, March.

Coates, S. 1974. Sex differences in field independence among preschool children. In R. C. Friedman and R. M. Richart (eds.), *Sex Differences in Behavior*. New York: Wiley.

Coltheart, M., Hull, E. and Slater, D. 1975. Sex differences in imagery and reading *Nature*, 253:438–40.

Cowley, J. E., Levitui, T. E. and Quinn, R. P. 1973. Seven deadly half-truths about women. *Psychology Today*, 6:94–6.

Crook, J. H. 1972. Sexual selection, dimorphism and social organization in the primates. In B. Campbell (ed.), *Sexual Selection and the Descent of Man*. Chicago: Aldine.

Dalton, K. 1969. *The Menstrual Cycle*. Harmondsworth: Penguin

Dalton, K. 1971. Prospective study into puerperal depression. *British Journal of Psychiatry*, 689–92.

Dalton, K. 1979. *Once a Month*. London: Fontana. 112:771–4.

Daly, M. 1978. Cost of mating. *American Naturalist*, 112:771–4.

Danziger, K. 1971. *Socialization*. Harmondsworth: Penguin.

Darwin, C. 1871. *The Descent of Man, and Selection in Relation to Sex* (1901 edn). London: John Murray.

Davidson, C. 1978. US armed forces to use womanpower. *The Times*, 21 July.

Davidson, T. 1977. Wifebeating: a recurring phenomenon throughout history. In M. Roy (ed.), *Battered Women: a Psychological Study of Domestic Violence*. New York: Van Nostrand.

Davis, J. M. 1973. Imitation: a review and critique. In P. P. G. Bateson and P. Klopfer (eds.), *Perspectives in Ethology*. New York: Plenum.

Dawkins, R. and Carlisle, T. R. 1976. Parental investment, mate selection and a fallacy. *Nature*, 262:131–3.

Dawson, J. L. M. 1972. Effects of sex hormones on cognitive style in rats and men. *Behavior Genetics*, 2:21–42.

Deaux, K. 1976a. Sex: a perspective on the attribution process. In J. H. Harvey, W. J. Ickes and R. F. Kidd (eds.), *New Directions in Attribution Research*, vol. 1. New York: Wiley.

Deaux, K. 1976b. *The Behavior of Women and Men*. Monterey, California: Brooks-Cole.

Deaux, K. 1977. Sex differences. In T. Blass (ed.), *Personality Variables in Social Behavior*. New York: Halsted Press.

Decarie, T. G., Goulet, J., Brossard, M. D., Rafman, S. and Shaffran, R. 1974. *The Infant's Reaction to Strangers*. Translated by Diamanti, J. New York: International Universities Press, Inc.

Defries, J. C., Johnson, R. C., Kuse, A. R., McClearn, G. E., Polovina, J., Vandenberg, S. G. and Wilson, J. R. 1979. Familial resemblance for specific cognitive abilities. *Behavior Genetics*, 9:23–43.

Deleuze, G. and Guattari, F. 1976. *Anti-Oedipus: Capitalism and Schizophrenia*. Translated by R. Hunley *et al.* New York: Viking.

Department of Health and Social Services. 1977. *Health and Personal Social Statistics for England*.

Depp, F. C. 1976. Violent behaviour patterns on psychiatric wards. *Aggressive Behavior*, 2:295–306.

Deutsch, H. 1945. *The Psychology of Women*. New York: Grune and Stratton.

DeVries, R. 1969. Constancy of generic identity in the years three to six. *Monographs of Society for Research in Child Development*, no. 127, vol. 34 (3).

Doering, C. H., Brodie, H. K. H., Kraemer, H., Becker, H. and Hamburg, D. A. 1974. Plasma testosterone levels and psychologic measures in men over a 2-month period. In R. C. Friedman and R. M. Richart (eds.), *Sex Differences in Behavior*. New York: Wiley.

Doise, W. 1978. *Groups and Individuals: Explanations in Social Psychology*. Cambridge: Cambridge University Press.

Dorner, G., Rohde, W., Stahl, F., Krell, L. and Masius, W. G. 1975. A neuro-endocrine predisposition for homosexuality in men. *Archives of Sexual Behaviour*, 4:1–8.

Douglas, J. D. 1967. *The Social Meanings of Suicide*. Princeton, New Jersey: Princeton University Press.

Durett, M. E. 1959. The relationship of early infant regulation and later behavior in play interviews. *Child Development*, 30:211–16.

Ebert, P. D. and Hyde, J. S. 1976. Selection for agonistic behavior in wild female *Mus musculus. Behavior Genetics*, 6:291–304.

Ehrhardt, A. A. and Baker, S. W. 1974. Fetal androgens, human central nervous system differentiation, and behaviour sex differences. In R. C. Friedman and R. M. Richart (eds.), *Sex Differences in Behavior*. New York: Wiley.

Ehrenkranz, J., Bliss, E. and Sheard, M. H. 1974. Plasma testosterone: correlation with aggressive behavior and social dominance in men. *Psychosomatic Medicine*, 36:469–75.

El-Badry, M. A. 1969. Higher female than male mortality in some countries of South Asia: a digest. *American Statistical Association Journal*, 64:1234–44.

Ellis, L. J. and Bentler, P. M. 1973. Traditional sex-determined role standards and sex stereotypes. *Journal of Personality and Social Psychology*, 25:28–34.

Ellman, M. 1968. *Thinking about Women*. New York: Harcourt, Brace and World, Inc.

Eme, R. F. 1979. Sex differences in childhood psychopathology: a review. *Psychological Bulletin*, 86:574–95.

Fagot, B. I. 1977. Consequences of moderate cross-gender behavior in preschool children. *Child Development*, 48:902–7.

Fairweather, H. 1976. Sex differences in cognition. *Cognition*, 4:231–80.

Ferri, E. 1976. *Growing Up in a One-Parent Family*. Windsor: National Foundation for Educational Research.

Feshbach, S. 1970. Aggression. In P. H. Mussen (ed.), *Carmichael's Manual of Child Psychology*. New York: Wiley.

Fling, S. and Manosevitz, M. 1972. Sex-typing in nursery-school children's play interests. *Developmental Psychology*, 7:146–52.

Flor-Henry, P. 1974. Psychosis, neurosis and epilepsy. *British Journal of Psychiatry*, 124:144–50.

Foucault, M. 1979. *The History of Sexuality*. London: Allen Lane.

Fox, C. A., Ismail, A. A., Love, D. N., Kirkham, K. E. and Loraine, J. A. 1972. Studies on the relationship between plasma testosterone levels and human sexual activity. *Journal of Endocrinology*, 52:51–8.

Fox, N. 1977. Attachment of *kibbutz* infants to mother and *metapelet*. *Child Development*, 48:1228–39.

Frank, F. 1957. The causality of microtine cycles in Germany. *Journal of Wildlife Management*, 21:113–212.

Frazier, S. H. and Carr, A. C. 1967. Phobic Reactions. In A. M. Freedman and H. I. Kaplan, *Comprehensive Textbook of Psychiatry*. Baltimore: Williams and Wilkins Co.

Freedman, D. G. 1964. A biological view of man's social behavior. In W. Etkin (ed.), *Social Behavior from Fish to Man*. Chicago: Chicago University Press.

French, M. 1978. *The Women's Room*. London: Deutsch.

Freud, S. 1905. *Three Essays on the Theory of Sexuality*, vol. 7, standard edition. London: Hogarth Press, 1953.

Freud, S. 1917 (1915). *Mourning and Melancholia*, vol. 14, standard edition. London: Hogarth Press, 1957.

Freud, S. 1923. *The Ego and the Id*, vol. 19, standard edition. London: Hogarth Press, 1961.

Freud, S. 1924. *The Dissolution of the Oedipus Complex*, vol. 19, standard edition. London: Hogarth Press, 1961.

Freud, S. 1925. *Some Psychical Consequences of the Anatomical Distinction between the Sexes*, vol. 19, standard edition. London: Hogarth Press, 1961.

Freud, S. 1931. *Female Sexuality*, vol. 21, standard edition. London: Hogarth Press, 1961.

Freud, S. 1940. *An Outline of Psychoanalysis*, vol. 23, standard edition. London: Hogarth Press, 1964.

Frodi, A., Macaulay, J. and Thome, P. R. 1977. Are women always less aggressive than men? A review of the experimental literature. *Psychological Bulletin*, 84:634–60.

Gagnon, J. H. and Simon, W. 1973. *Sexual Conduct: The Social Sources of Human Sexuality*. Chicago: Aldine.

Galenson, E. and Roiphe, H. 1977. Some suggested revisions concerning early female devvvelopment. In H. P. Blum (ed.), *Female Psychology: Contemporary Psychoanalytic Views*. New York: International Universities Press.

Garai, J. E. 1970. Sex differences in mental health. *Genetic Psychology Monographs*, 81:123–42.

Garai, J. E., and Scheinfeld, A. 1968. Sex differences in mental and behavioral traits. *Genetic Psychology Monographs*, 77:169–299.

Garvey, C. 1977. *Play*. London: Open Books/Fontana.

Gavron, H. 1966. *The Captive Housewife: Conflict of Housebound Mothers*. London: Routledge and Kegan Paul.

Gelles, R. J. 1972. *The Violent Home*. Beverly Hills and London: Sage.

General Household Survey. 1976. Office of Population Censuses and Social Surveys; Survey Division.

Ghiselin, M. T. 1974. *The Economy of Nature and the Evolution of Sex*. Berkeley and Los Angeles: University of California Press.

Gillie, O. and Weitz, M. 1978. HRT research: little and late. *Sunday Times*, 24 September.

Glucksmann, A. 1974. Sexual dimorphism in mammals. *Biological Review*, 49:423–75.

Goldberg, P. A. 1968. Are women prejudiced against women? *Transaction*, 5:28–30.

Goldberg, S. 1973. *The Inevitability of Patriarchy*. New York: Morrow.

Gough, H. G. and Heilbrun, A. B. 1965. *Adjective Checklist Manual*. Palo Alto, California: Consulting Psychologists' Press.

Gould, S. J. 1978. Women's brains. *New Scientist*, 80:364–6.

Gove, W. R. Sex, marital status and suicide. *Journal of Health and Social Behavior*, 1972. 13:204–13.

Gove, W. R. and Tudor, J. F. 1972. Adult sex roles and mental illness. *American Journal of Sociology*, 78:812–35.

Goy, R. W. 1968. Organizing effects of androgen on the behaviour of rhesus monkeys. In R. P. Michael (ed.), *Endocrinology and Human Behaviour*. Oxford: Oxford University Press.

Gray, J. A. 1971a. Sex differences in emotional behaviour in mammals including Man: endocrine bases. *Acta Psychologica*, 35:29–46.

Gray, J. A. 1971b. *The Psychology of Fear and Stress*. London: Weidenfeld and Nicolson.

Gray, J. A. and Buffery, A. W. H. 1971. Sex differences in emotional and cognitive behaviour in mammals including Man: adaptive and neural bases. *Acta Psychologica*, 35:89–111.

Gray, J. A. and Drewett, R. F. 1977. The genetics and development of sex differences. In R. B. Cattell and R. M. Dreger (eds.), *Handbook of Modern Personality Theory*. New York: Halsted Press.

Hamburg, D. A. and Lunde, D. T. 1967. Sex hormones in the development of sex differences in human behaviour. In E. E. Maccoby (ed.), *The Development of Sex Differences*. London: Tavistock.

Hargreaves, D. 1976. What are little boys and girls made of? *New Society*, 37:542–4.

Hargreaves, D. 1977. Sex roles in divergent thinking. *British Journal of Educational Psychology*, 47:25–32.

Harlow, H. 1958. The nature of love. *American Psychologist*, 13:673–85.

Harris, L. J. 1978. Sex differences in spatial ability: possible environmental, genetic and neurological factors. In M. Kinsbourne (ed.), *Asymmetrical Function of the Brain*. Cambridge: Cambridge University Press.

Hartnett, O. 1978. Sex-role stereotyping at work. In J. Chetwynd and O. Hartnett (eds.), *The Sex-role System*. London: Routledge and Kegan Paul.

Heilbrun, A. B. 1965. An empirical test of the modelling theory of sex-role learning. *Child Development*, 36:789–99.

Heim, A. 1970. *Intelligence and Personality*. Harmondsworth: Penguin.

Heiman, J. R. 1975. The physiology of erotica: Women's sexual arousal. *Psychology Today*, April: 90–94.

Henley, N. M. 1977. *Body Politics, Power, Sex and Non Verbal Communication*. Englewood Cliffs: Prentice-Hall.

Herbert, J. 1976. Hormonal basis of sex differences in rats, monkeys and humans. *New Scientist*, 70:284–6.

Hersov, L. 1977. Adoption. In M. Rutter and L. Hersov (eds.), *Child Psychiatry*. Oxford: Blackwell Scientific Publications.

Hetherington, E. M. 1965. A developmental study of the effects of sex of the dominant parent on sex-role preference, identification and imitation in children. *Journal of Personality and Social Psychology*, 2:188–94.

Hill, J. 1978. The psychological impact of unemployment. *New Society*, 43:118–20.

Hite, S. 1976. *The Hite Report*. New York: Macmillan.

Hocquenghem, G. 1978. *Homosexual Desire*. Translated by D. Dangoor. London: Allison and Busby.

Hoffman, L. W. 1977. Changes in family roles, socialization, and sex differences. *American Psychologist*, 32:644–57.

Horney, K. 1924. On the genesis of the castration complex in women. *International Journal of Psychoanalysis*, V:50–65.

Hutt, C. 1972a. *Males and Females*. Harmondsworth: Penguin.

Hutt, C. 1972b. Sexual dimorphism: its significance in human development. In F. J. Monks, W. W. Hartup and J. de Wit (eds.), *Determinants of Behavioral Development*. New York and London: Academic Press.

Hyde, J. S. 1979. *Understanding Human Sexuality*. New York: McGraw-Hill.

Hyde, J. S., Rosenberg, B. G. and Behrman, J. A. 1977. Tomboyism. *Psychology of Women Quarterly*, 2:73–5.

Ingham, J. G. and Miller, P. McC. 1976. The concept of prevalence applied to psychiatric disorders and symptoms. *Psychological Medicine*, 6:217–25.

Jacobson, M. B. and Effertz, J. 1974. Sex roles and leadership: perceptions of the leaders and the led. *Organizational Behavior and Human Performance*, 12:383–96.

Jahoda, M. 1975. Technicalities and fantasy about men and women. *Futures: the Journal of Forecasting and Planning*, 7:414–19.

Janiger, O., Riffenburgh, R. and Kersh, R. 1972. Cross-cultural study of premenstrual symptoms. *Psychosomatics*, 13:226–35.

Jenni, D. A. 1974. Evolution of polyandry in birds. *American Zoologist*, 129–44.

Jewell, P. A. 1976. Selection for reproductive success. In C. R. Austin and R. V. Short (eds.), *Reproduction in Mammals, 6: The Evolution of Reproduction*. Cambridge: Cambridge University Press.

Johnson, R. N. 1972. *Aggression in Man and Animals*. Philadelphia: Saunders.

Jost, A. 1972. A new look at the mechanisms controlling sex differentiation in mammals. *John Hopkins Medical Journal*, 130:38–53.

Jourard, S. M. 1964. *The Transparent Self: Self-disclosure and Well-being*. Princeton: D. Van Nostrand.

Kagan, J. 1978. Sex differences in the human infant. In T. E. McGill, D. A. Dewsbury and B. D. Sachs (eds.), *Sex and Behavior: Status and Prospects*. New York: Plenum Press.

Kagan, J. and Moss, H. A. 1962. *Birth to Maturity*. New York: Wiley.

Kamin, L. J. 1978. Sex differences in susceptibility of IQ to environmental influence. *Child Development*, 49:517–18.

Kangas, J. and Bradway, K. 1971. Intelligence at middle age: a thirty-eight year follow-up. *Developmental Psychology*, 5:333–7.

Katchadourian, H. A. and Lunde, D. T. 1975. *Fundamentals of Human Sexuality*. New York: Holt, Rinehart and Winston.

Katongole, C., Naftolin, F. and Short, R. V. 1971. Relationship between blood levels of luteinizing hormone and testosterone in bulls, and the effects of sexual stimulation. *Journal of Endocrinology*, 50:457–60.

Katz, D. and Braly, K. W. 1935. Racial prejudice and racial stereotypes. *Journal of Abnormal and Social Psychology*, 30:175–93.

Keating, F. 1978. Ladies didn't run until 1928: now they face the sex test hurdle. *Guardian*, 3 August.

Kessler, S. J. and McKenna, W. 1978. *Gender: An Ethnomethodological Approach*. New York: Wiley.

Kinsey, A. C., Pomeroy, W. B. and Martin, C. E. 1948. *Sexual Behavior in the Human Male*. Philadelphia: W. B. Saunders.

Kinsey, A. C., Pomeroy, W. B., Martin, C. E. and Gebhard, P. H. 1953. *Sexual Behavior in the Human Female*. Philadelphia: W. B. Saunders.

Kipnis, D. M. 1976. Intelligence, occupational status, and achievement orientation. In B. B. Lloyd and J. Archer (eds.), *Exploring Sex Differences*. London and New York: Academic Press.

Klaus, M. H. and Kennell, J. H. 1976. *Maternal-Infant Bonding*. Saint Louis: C. V. Mosby Co.

Knorr, D., Bidlingmaier, F., Butenandt, O., Fendel, H. and Ehrt-Wehle, R. 1974. Plasma testosterone in male puberty: I. Physiology of plasma testosterone. *Acta Endocrinologica*, 75:181–94.

Kohlberg, L. 1966. A cognitive developmental analysis of children's sex role concepts and attitudes. In E. E. Maccoby (ed.), *The Development of Sex Differences*. Stanford, CA: Stanford University Press.

Kolakowski, D. and Malina, R. M. 1974. Spatial ability, throwing accuracy and man's hunting heritage. *Nature*, 251:410–12.

Komarovsky, M. 1950. Functional analysis of sex roles. *American Sociological Review*, 15:508–16.

Kotelchuck, M. 1976. The infant's relationship to the father: experimental evidence. In M. Lamb, *The Role of the Father in Child Development*. New York: Wiley.

Kreuz, L. E. and Rose, R. M. 1972. Assessment of aggressive behavior and plasma testosterone in a young criminal population. *Psychosomatic Medicine*, 34:321–32.

Kuhn, D., Nash, S. C. and Bruchan, L. 1978. Sex role concepts of two- and three-year-olds. *Child Development*, 49:445–51.

Lacan, J. 1966. *The Signification of the Phallus Ecrits*. Paris: Editions de Senil, 1966. *Ecrits: A Selection*. Translated by A. Sheridan. London: Tavistock 1977.

Laing, R. D. 1967. *The Politics of Experience*. Harmondsworth: Penguin.

Lamb, M. E. 1976. *The Role of the Father in Child Development*. New York: Wiley.

Lamb, M. E. 1977a. Father-infant and mother-infant interaction in the first year of life. *Child Development*, 48:167–81.

Lamb, M. E. 1977b. The development of mother-infant and father-infant attachments in the second year of life. *Developmental Psychology*, 13:637–48.

Lambert, H. H. 1978. Biology and equality: a perspective on sex differences. *Signs: Journal of Women in Culture and Society*, 4:97–117.

Lambert, L. and Hart, S. 1976. Who needs a father? *New Society*, 8 July.

Lawick-Goodall, J. van. 1971. *In the Shadow of Man*. London: Collins.

Leach, P. 1979. *Who Cares?* Harmondsworth: Penguin.

Lehrke, R. G. 1978. Sex linkage: a biological basis for greater male variability in intelligence. In R. T. Osborne, C. E. Noble, and N. Weyl (eds.), *Human Variation: The Biopsychology of Age, Race and Sex*. New York: Academic Press.

Levine, A. and Crumrine, J. 1975. Women and the fear of success: a problem in replication. *American Journal of Sociology*, 80:964–74.

Levy, J. 1969. Possible basis for the evolution of lateral specialization of the human brain. *Nature*, 224:614–15.

Lewis, M. 1975. Early sex differences in the human: studies of socio-emotional development. *Archives of Sexual Behavior*, 4:329–35.

Lipshitz, S. 1978. Women and psychiatry. In J. Chetwynd and O. Hartnett (eds.), *The Sex-role System*. London: Routledge and Kegan Paul.

Litman, G. K. 1978. Clinical aspects of sex-role stereotyping. In J. Chetwynd and O. Hartnett (eds.), *The Sex-role System*. London: Routledge and Kegan Paul.

Lloyd B. B. 1976. Social responsibility and research on sex differences. In B. B. Lloyd and J. Archer (eds.), *Exploring Sex Differences*. London and New York: Academic Press.

Locke, B. Z. and Gardner, E. A. 1969. Psychiatric disorders among the patients of general practitioners and internists. *Public Health Report*, 84:167–73.

Lorenz, K. 1966. *On Aggression*. New York: Harcourt, Brace and World.

Lukes, S. 1975. *Power: A Radical View*. London: Macmillan.

Maccoby, E. E. and Jacklin, C. N. 1974. *The Psychology of Sex Differences*. Stanford, California: Stanford University Press.

Macfarlane, A. 1977. *The Psychology of Childbirth*. London: Open Books/Fontana.

McGee, M. G. 1979. Human spatial abilities: psychometric studies and environmental, genetic, hormonal and neurological influences. *Psychological Bulletin*, 86:889–918.

McGlone, J. and Davidson, W. 1973. The relation between cerebral speech laterality and spatial ability with special reference to sex and hand preference. *Neuropsychologia*, 11:105–13.

McGuinness, D. 1976. Sex differences in the organization of perception and cognition. In B. B. Lloyd and J. Archer (eds.), *Exploring Sex Differences*. London and New York: Academic Press.

Mack, J. 1976. Children half-alone. *New Society*, 7 October: 6–8.

Mackie, L. and Pattullo, P. 1977. *Women at Work*. London: Tavistock.

Madigan, F. C. 1957. Are sex mortality differentials biologically caused? *Milbank Memorial Fund Quarterly*, 35:202–23.

Manual of the International Statistical Classification of Diseases, Injuries and Causes of Death. 1967. Geneva: World Health Organization.

Martin, M. K. and Voorhies, B. 1975. *The Female of the Species*. New York and London: Macmillan.

Mason, J. W., Tolson, W. W., Robinson, J. A., Brady, J. V., Tolliver, G. A. and Johnson, T. A. 1969. Urinary androsterone, etiocholanolone, and dehydroepiandrosterone responses to 72-hour avoidance sessions in the monkey. *Psychosomatic Medicine*, 30:710–20.

Masters, W. H. and Johnson, V. E. 1966. *Human Sexual Response*. Boston: Little, Brown and Co.

Masters, W. H. and Johnson, V. E. 1970. *Human Sexual Inadequacy*. Boston: Little, Brown and Co.

Masters, W. H. and Johnson, V. E. 1979. *Homosexuality in Perspective*. Boston: Little, Brown and Co.

Maynard Smith, J. 1971. What use is sex? *Journal of Theoretical Biology*, 30:319–35.

Mayo, P. 1976. Sex differences in psychopathology. In B. Lloyd and J. Archer (eds.), *Exploring Sex Differences*. London: Academic Press.

Mead, M. 1935. *Sex and Temperament in Three Primitive Societies*. London: Routledge and Kegan Paul.

Mead, M. 1950. *Male and Female*. Harmondsworth: Penguin.

Megargee, G. 1969. Influence of sex roles on the manifestation of leadership. *Journal of Applied Psychology*, 53:377–82.

Meyer-Bahlberg, H. F. L., Boon, D. A., Shama, M. and Edwards, J. A. 1974. Aggressiveness and testosterone measures in man. *Psychosomatic Medicine*, 36:269–74.

Mischel, W. 1966. A social learning view of sex differences. In E. E. Maccoby (ed.), *The Development of Sex Differences*. Stanford, CA: Stanford University Press.

Mischel, W. 1970. Sex-typing and socialization. In P. H. Mussen (ed.), *Carmichael's Manual of Child Psychology*, vol. 2 (3rd edn). New York: Wiley.

Mitchell, J. 1974. *Psychoanalysis and Feminism*. London: Allen Lane.

Mitchell, J. and Oakley, A. 1976. *The Rights and Wrongs of Women*. Harmondsworth: Penguin.

Mittwoch, U. 1973. *Genetics of Sex Differentiation*. New York and London: Academic Press.

Moers, E. 1978. *Literary Women*. London: The Women's Press.

Money, J. and Ehrhardt, A. A. 1972. *Man and Woman, Boy and Girl*. Baltimore and London: Johns Hopkins University Press.

Money, J., Hampson, J. G. and Hampson, J. L. 1957. Imprinting and the establishment of gender role. *Archives of Neurology and Psychiatry*, 77:333–6.

Moos, R. H., Kopell, B. S., Melges, F. T., Yalom, I. D., Lunde, D. T., Clayton, R. B. and Hamburg, D. 1969. Fluctuations in symptoms and moods during the menstrual cycle. *Journal of Psychosomatic Research*, 13:37–44.

Morgan, E. 1972. *The Descent of Woman*. London: Souvenir Press.

Morgan, P. 1975. *Child Care: Sense and Fable*. London: Temple-Smith.

Morgan, G. A. and Ricciuti, H. N. 1969. Infant's response to strangers during the first year. In B. M. Foss (ed.), *Determinants of Infant Behaviour*, vol. 4. London: Methuen.

Morris, D. 1967. *The Naked Ape*. London: Jonathan Cape.

Morris, J. 1974. *Conundrum*. London: Faber and Faber.

Murphy, R. J. L. 1980. Sex differences in GCE examination results and entry statistics. Paper presented at Sex Differentiation and Schooling Conference, Cambridge, 2–5 January.

Napier, J. 1971. *The Roots of Mankind*. London: Allen and Unwin.

Nemeth, C. 1973. A critical analysis of research utilizing the Prisoners' Dilemma paradigm for the study of bargaining. In L. Berkowitz (ed.), *Advances in Experimental Social Psychology*, vol. VI. New York: Academic Press.

New Earnings Survey. 1978. Government Statistical Service, Department of Employment. London: HMSO.

Newson, J. and Newson, E. 1968. *Four Years Old in an Urban Community.* London: Allen and Unwin.

Oakley, A. 1974. *Housewife.* London: Allen Lane.

Oakley, A. 1979. *Becoming a Mother.* Oxford: Martin Robertson.

Oetzel, R. M. 1966. Annotated Bibliography. In E. E. Maccoby (ed.), *The Development of Sex Differences.* London: Tavistock.

Ohno, S. 1976. The development of sexual reproduction. In C. R. Austin and R. V. Short (eds.), *Reproduction in Mammals, 6: The Evolution of Reproduction.* Cambridge: Cambridge University Press.

O'Leary, V. E. 1974. Some attitudinal barriers to occupational aspirations in women. *Psychological Bulletin,* 81:809–26.

Olioff, M. and Stewart, J. 1978. Sex differences in the play behaviour of prepubescent rats. *Physiology and Behavior,* 20:113–15.

Orwell, G. 1949. *Nineteen Eighty-Four.* London: Secker and Warburg.

Ounsted, C. and Taylor, D. C. 1972. The Y chromosome message: a point of view. In C. Ounsted and D. C. Taylor (eds.), *Gender Differences: Their Ontogeny and Significance.* London: Churchill.

Paige, K. E. 1973. Women learn to sing the menstrual blues. *Psychology Today,* 7:41–6.

Parke, R. D. 1979. Perspectives on father-infant interaction. In J. D. Osofsky (ed.), *Handbook of Infancy.* New York: Wiley.

Parke, R. D. and Sawin, D. B. 1977. The family in early infancy: social interactional and attitudinal analysis. Paper SCRD, New Orleans. Reported in Parke, 1979.

Parker, G. A., Baker, R. R. and Smith, V. G. F. 1972. The origin and evolution of gamete dimorphism and the male-female phenomenon. *Journal of Theoretical Biology,* 36:529–53.

Parkes, C. M. 1975. *Bereavement: Studies of Grief in Adult Life.* Harmondsworth: Penguin.

Parlee, M. B. 1973. The premenstrual syndrome. *Psychological Bulletin,* 80:454–65.

Parsons, J. E., Ruble, D. N., Hodges, K. L. and Small, A. W. 1976. Cognitive-developmental factors in emerging sex differences in achievement-related expectancies. *Journal of Social Issues,* 32:47–61.

Parsons, T. and Bales, R. F. 1955. *Family, Socialization, and Interaction Process.* Glencoe: Free Press.

Payne, A. P. and Swanson, H. H. 1970. Agonistic behaviour between pairs of the same and opposite sex in a neutral observation area. *Behaviour,* 36:259–69.

Perry, G. 1979. *Paula Modersohn-Becker.* London: Women's Press.

Persky, H., Smith, K. D. and Basu, G. K. 1971. Relation of psychologic measures of aggression and hostility to testosterone production in man. *Psychosomatic Medicine,* 33:265–77.

Petersen, K. and Wilson, J. J. 1978. *Women Artists.* London: The Women's Press.

Phillips, D. and Segal, B. 1969. Sexual status and psychiatric symptoms. *American Sociological Review*, 34:58–72.

Phoenix, C. H. 1974. Prenatal testosterone in the nonhuman primate and its consequences for behaviour. In R. C. Friedman and R. M. Richart (eds.), *Sex Differences in Behavior*. New York: Wiley.

Polatnick, M. 1973. Why men don't rear children: a power analysis. *Berkeley Journal of Sociology*, 45–85.

Population Trends. 1977. Office of population censuses and surveys. London: HMSO.

Power, E. 1975. *Medieval Women*. Cambridge: Cambridge University Press.

Purvis, K. and Haynes, N. B. 1974. Short-term effects of copulation, human chorionic gonadotrophin injection and non-tactile association with a female on testosterone levels in the male rat. *Journal of Endocrinology*, 60:429–39.

Quadagno, D. M., Briscoe, R. and Quadagno, J. S. 1977. Effect of perinatal gonadal hormones on selected nonsexual behaviour patterns: a critical assessment of the human and nonhuman literature. *Psychological Bulletin*, 84:62–80.

Rachman, S. 1978. *Courage and Fearfulness*. San Francisco: Freeman.

Rada, R. T., Kellner, R. and Winslow, W. W. 1976. Plasma testosterone and aggressive behavior. *Psychosomatics*, 17:138–42.

Ralls, K. 1976. Mammals in which females are larger than males. *Quarterly Review of Biology*, 51:245–76.

Ralls, K. 1978. When bigger is best. *New Scientist*, 77:360–63.

Rebelsky, F. and Hanks, C. 1971. Fathers' verbal interaction with infants in the first three months of life. *Child Development*, 42:63–8.

Reeves, A. C. 1971. Children with surrogate parents: cases seen in analytic therapy and an aetiological hypothesis. *British Journal of Medical Psychology*, 44:155–71.

Reinisch, J. M. 1976. Effects of prenatal hormone exposure on physical and psychological development in humans and animals: with a note on the state of the field. In E. J. Sachar (ed.), *Hormones, Behavior and Psychopathology*. New York: Raven Press.

Rendina, I. and Dickersheid, J. D. 1976. Father involvement with first-born infants. *Family Coordinator*, 25:373–9.

Resko, J. A. 1975. Foetal hormones and their effect on the differentiation of the CNS in primates. *Federation Proceedings*, 34:1650–55.

Rheingold, H. and Cook, K. 1975. The contents of boys' and girls' rooms as an index of parents' behavior. *Child Development*, 46:459–63.

Richards, M. P. M., Bernal, J. F. and Brackbill, Y. 1976. Early behavioral differences: gender or circumcision? *Developmental Psychobiology*, 9:89–95.

Robinson, J. R. and Converse, P. E. 1978. Summary of the US Time Use Survey, 30 May 1966. Quoted in I. H. Frieze, J. E. Parsons, P. B. Johnson, D. N. Ruble and G. L. Zellman, *Women and Sex Roles*. New York: Norton.

Rogers, S. C. 1978. Woman's Place: A critical review of anthropological theory. *Comparative Studies in Society and History*, 20:123–62.

Rosaldo, M. Z. and L. Lamphere (eds.). 1974. *Woman, Culture and Society*. Stanford: Stanford University Press.

Rose, R. M., Gordon, T. P. and Bernstein, I. S. 1972. Plasma testosterone levels in male rhesus: influences of sexual and social stimuli. *Science*, 178:643–5.

Rose, S. P. R. and Rose, H. 1974. 'Do not adjust your mind, there is a fault in reality' – ideology in neurobiology. *Cognition*, 2:479–502.

Rosenblatt, P. C. and Cunningham, M. R. 1976. Sex differences in cross-cultural perspective. In B. B. Lloyd and J. Archer (eds.), *Exploring Sex Differences*. London and New York: Academic Press.

Rosenblatt, P. C., Walsh, R. P. and Jackson, D. A. 1976. *Grief and Mourning in Cross-Cultural Perspective*. New Haven: Human Relations Area File Press.

Rosenkrantz, P. S., Vogel, S. R., Bee, H., Broverman, I. K. and Broverman, D. M. 1968. Sex role stereotypes and self-concepts in college students. *Journal of Consulting and Clinical Psychology*, 32:287–95.

Rossi, A. S. 1964. Equality between the sexes: an immodest proposal. *Daedalus*, 93:607–52.

Rossi, A. S. 1977. A biosocial perspective on parenting. *Daedalus*, 106:1–31.

Roy, M. 1977. A survey of 150 cases. In M. Roy (ed.), *Battered Women: A Psychosociological Study of Domestic Violence*. New York: Van Nostrand.

Rutter, M. 1972. *Maternal Deprivation Reassessed*. Harmondsworth: Penguin.

Rutter, M. 1979. Maternal deprivation 1972–1978. New findings, new concepts, new approaches. *Child Development*, 50:283–305.

Sahlins, M. 1977. *The Use and Abuse of Biology*. London: Tavistock.

Schaar, K. 1974. Suicide rate among women psychologists. *APA Monitor 5*, 1:10.

Schafer, R. 1977. Problems in Freud's psychology of women. In H. P. Blum (ed.), *Female Psychology: Contemporary Psychoanalytic Views*. New York: International Universities Press, Inc.

Schaffer, H. R. and Emerson, P. 1964. *The Development of Attachments in Infancy*. Monographs of the Society for Research in Child Development, 29.

Schaffer, H. R. 1974. Early social behaviour and the study of reciprocity. *Bulletin of the British Psychological Society*, 27:209–16.

Schonberg, W. B., Costango, D. J. and Carpenter, R. S. 1976. Menstrual cycle: phases and reaction to frustration. *Psychological Record*, 26:321–5.

Secord, P. F. and Backman, C. W. 1964. *Social Psychology*. New York: McGraw Hill.

Selander, R. K. 1972. Sexual selection and dimorphism in birds. In B. Campbell (ed.), *Sexual Selection and the Descent of Man*. Chicago: Aldine.

Seligman, M. E. P. 1975. *Helplessness: On Depression, Development and Death*. San Francisco: W. H. Freeman.

Serbin, L. A., O'Leary, K. D., Kent, R. N. and Tonick, I. J. 1973. A comparison of teacher response to the preacademic problems and problem behaviour of boys and girls. *Child Development*, 44:796–804.

Shapiro, B. H., Goldman, A. S., Bongiovanni, A. M. and Marino, J. M. 1976. Neonatal progesterone and feminine sexual development. *Nature*, 264: 795–6.

Sharman, G. B. 1976. Evolution of viviparity in mammals. In C. R. Austin and R. V. Short (eds.), *Reproduction in Mammals, 6: The Evolution of Reproduction*. Cambridge: Cambridge University Press.

Shepherd, G. 1978. The Omani *Xanith*, (correspondence). *Man*, 13:663–5.

Shepherd, M., Cooper, B., Brown, A. C. and Kalton, G. W. 1966. *Psychiatric Illness in General Practice*. London: Oxford University Press.

Sherfey, M. J. 1973. *The Nature and Evolution of Female Sexuality*. New York: Vintage Books.

Sherman, J. A. 1967. Problems of sex differences in space perception and aspects of intellectual functioning. *Psychological Review*, 74:290–99.

Sherman, J. A. 1971. *On the Psychology of Women*. Springfield: Charles C. Thomas.

Sherman, J. A. 1978. *Sex-related Cognitive Differences: An Essay on Theory and Evidence*. Springfield: Charles C. Thomas.

Short, R. 1976. The origin of species. In C. R. Austin and R. V. Short (eds.), *Reproduction in Mammals, 6: The Evolution of Reproduction*. Cambridge: Cambridge University Press.

Siann, G. 1977. Sex differences in spatial ability in children: its bearing on theories accounting for sex differences in spatial ability in adults. Unpublished doctoral dissertation, University of Edinburgh.

Simpson, J. L. 1976. *Disorders of Sexual Differentiation*. New York: Academic Press.

Slocum, S. 1975. Woman the gatherer: male bias in anthropology. In R. Reiter (ed.), *Toward an Anthropology of Women*. New York: Monthly Review Press.

Sluckin, W. 1972. *Imprinting and Early Learning* (2nd edn). London: Methuen.

Sluckin, W. (ed.). 1979. *Fear in Animals and Man*. Wokingham: Van Nostrand Reinhold.

Smith, C. and Lloyd, B. B. 1978. Maternal behaviour and perceived sex of infant. *Child Development*, 49:1263–5.

Smith, P. K. 1980. Shared care of young children: alternative models to monotropism. *Merrill–Palmer Quarterly*, 26:371–90.

Smith, P. K. and Connolly, K. 1972. Patterns of play and social interaction in preschool children. In N. G. Blurton–Jones (ed.), *Ethological Studies of Child Behaviour*. London: Cambridge University Press.

Smith, P. K. and Green, M. 1975. Aggressive behavior in English nurseries and play groups: sex differences and response of adults. *Child Development*, 46: 211–14.

Social Trends. 1977 and 1979. Central Statistics Office, London: HMSO, Nos. 8 and 9.

Sommer, B. 1973. The effect of menstruation on cognitive and perceptual-motor behavior: a review. *Psychosomatic Medicine*, 35:515–34.

Speltz, M. L. and Bernstein, D. A. 1976. Sex differences in fearfulness: verbal report, overt avoidance and demand characteristics. *Journal of Behaviour Therapy and Experimental Psychiatry*, 7:117–22.

Spence, J. T., Helmreich, R. and Stapp, J. 1975. Ratings of self and peers on sex role attributes and their relation to self-esteem and conceptions of masculinity and femininity. *Journal of Personality and Social Psychology*, 32:29–39.

Stafford, R. E. 1961. Sex differences in spatial visualization as evidence of sex-linked inheritance. *Perceptual and Motor Skills*, 13:428.

Stassinopoulos, A. 1972. *The Female Woman*. London: Davis–Poynter.

Statistical Abstracts of the USA. 1978. Washington, DC: US Government Printing Office.

Steinmetz, S. K. 1977. Wifebeating, husbandbeating: a comparison of the use of physical violence between spouses to resolve marital fights. In M. Roy (ed.), *Battered Women: A Psychological Study of Domestic Violence*. New York: Van Nostrand.

Stengel, E. 1964. *Suicide and Attempted Suicide*. London: Penguin, 1964. Revised Edition, 1970.

Stoll, C. S. 1978. *Female and Male: Socialization, Social Roles and Social Structure*. Dubugue: Willian C. Brown.

Swanson, H. H. 1973. Sex differences in the agonistic behaviour of the Mongolian gerbil. *Journal of Endocrinology*, 57:38–9.

Symonds, A. 1971. Phobias after marriage: women's declaration of independence. *American Journal of Psychoanalysis*, 31:144–52.

Szasz, T. S. 1970. *The Manufacture of Madness*. New York: Harper and Row.

Tanner, J. M. 1970. Physical growth. In P. H. Mussen (ed.), *Carmichael's Manual of Child Psychology*, vol. 1. New York and London: Wiley.

Tanner, J. M. 1978. *Foetus Into Man*. London: Open Books.

Tavris, C. and Offir, C. 1977. *The Longest War: Sex Differences in Perspective*. New York: Harcourt, Brace and Jovanovich.

Tennes, K. M. and Lampl, E. E. 1964. Stranger and separation anxiety. *Journal of Mental and Nervous Diseases*, 139:247–54.

The National Commission on Marihuana and Drug Abuse. 1973. *Drug Use in America*. Washington, DC: US Government Printing Office.

Thompson, R. J., Jr. and Lozes, J. 1976. Female gang delinquency. *Corrective and Social Psychiatry*, 22:1–5

Tiger, L. 1970. The possible biological origins of sexual discrimination. *Impact of Science on Society*, 20:29–45.

Tiger, L. and Shepher, J. 1975. *Women in the Kibbutz*. New York and London: Harcourt, Brace and Jovanovich.

Tizard, B. and Hodges, J. 1978. The effect of early institutional rearing on the development of eight-year-old children. *Journal of Child Psychology and Psychiatry*, 19:99–118.

Touhey, J. C. 1974. Effects of additional women professionals on ratings of occupational prestige and desirability. *Journal of Personality and Social Psychology*, 29:86–9.

244 *Sex and Gender*

Tresemer, D. W. 1975. Measuring 'sex differences'. *Sociological Inquiry*, 45:29-32.

Tresemer, D. W. 1977. *Fear of Success*. New York: Plenum.

Trivers, R. L. 1972. Parental investment and sexual selection. In B. Campbell (ed.), *Sexual Selection and the Descent of Man*. Chicago: Aldine.

Tucker, D. M. 1976. Sex differences in hemispheric specialization for synthetic visuospatial functions. *Neuropsychologica*, 14:447-54.

Ullian, D. Z. 1976. The development of conceptions of masculinity and femininity. In B. B. Lloyd and J. Archer (eds.), *Exploring Sex Differences*. London and New York: Academic Press.

Vernon, P. E. 1969. *Intelligence and Cultural Environment*. London: Methuen.

Vila, J. and Beech, H. R. 1978. Vulnerability and defensive reactions in relation to the human menstrual cycle. *British Journal of Social and Clinical Psychology*, 17:93-100.

Waddington, C. H. 1977. *Tools for Thought*. London: Jonathan Cape.

Waldon, I. 1976. Why do women live longer than men (part 1). *Journal of Human Stress*, 2:2-13.

Walum, L. R. 1977. *The Dynamics of Sex and Gender: A Sociological Perspective*. Chicago: Rand McNally.

Washburn, S. L. and Lancaster, C. S. 1968. The evolution of hunting. In R. B. Lee and I. DeVore (eds.), *Man the Hunter*. Chicago: Aldine.

Weeks, J. 1978. Movements of affirmation: sexual meanings and homosexual identities. British Sociological Association Conference, University of Sussex.

Weissman, M. M. and Klerman, G. L. 1977. Sex differences and the epidemiology of depression. *Archives of General Psychiatry*, 34:98-111.

Whiting, B. and Edwards, C. P. 1973. Cross-cultural analysis of sex differences in the behaviour of children aged 3 through 11. *Journal of Social Psychology*, 91:171-88.

Whitlock, F. A. 1973. Suicide in England and Wales. Part 1: The county boroughs. *Psychological Medicine*, 3:350-65.

Wikan, U. 1977. Man becomes woman: transsexualism in Oman as a key to gender roles. *Man*, 12:304-19.

Wikan, U. 1978. The Omani *Xanith* (correspondence). *Man*, 13:667-71.

Williams, G. C. 1975. *Sex and Evolution*. Princeton: Princeton University Press.

Williams, J. and Giles, H. 1978. The changing status of women in society: an intergroup perspective. In H. Tajfel (ed.), *Differentiation Between Social Groups*. New York: Academic Press.

Williams, J. E. and Bennett, S. M. 1975. The definition of sex stereotypes via the adjective check list. *Sex Roles*, 1:327-37.

Williams, J. H. 1977. *Psychology of Women*. New York: Norton and Co.

Wilson, J. R. and Vandenberg, S. G. 1978. Sex differences in cognition: evidence from the Hawai family study. In T. E. McGill, D. A. Dewsbury and B. D. Sachs (eds.), *Sex and Behavior: Status and Prospects*. New York: Plenum Press.

Witelson, S. F. 1976. Sex and the single hemisphere: specialization of the right hemisphere for spacial processing. *Science*, 193:425–7.

Witkin, H. A. 1967. A cognitive-style approach to cross-cultural research. *International Journal of Psychology*, 2:233–50.

Witkin, H. A., Dyk, R. B., Paterson, H. F., Goodenough, D. R. and Karp, S. A. 1962. *Psychological Differentiation*. New York: Wiley.

Wittig, M. A. and Petersen, A. C. (eds.), 1979. *Sex Related Differences in Cognitive Functioning*. New York: Academic Press.

Wolkind, S. and Rutter, M. 1973. Children who have been 'in care' – an epidemiological study. *Journal of Child Psychology and Psychiatry*, 14:97–105.

Woman's Own. 4 February 1978. IPC Magazines.

Wyer, R. S. and Malinowski, C. 1972. Effects of sex and achievement level upon individualism and competitiveness in social interaction. *Journal of Experimental Social Psychology*, 8:303–14.

Author Index

This index of authors cited in the text includes only those whose work is listed in the References. Other authors can be found in the General Index.

Numbers in *italics* indicate (a) pages in the text where the author referred to is not specifically named but is included in an '*et al.*' reference, or (b) pages in the References where the author referred to is cited within the entry of another author.

General Index

accidents, and the menstrual cycle, 134
achievement
  in women, 136, 219–22
  occupational, 188, 196–7
  motivation, 194–7
adolescents
  mental testing of, 35
  sexuality of, 82
  violence by, 108
  gender role concepts of, 208
  see also puberty
adoption, 164, 165
adrenal glands, 60
  androgen secretion by, 62, 64
  see also adrenogenital syndrome
adrenogenital syndrome (AGS), 68–9
ageing
  in relation to menopause, 65
  see also old age
aggression
  animal: evolution of, 54–5; sex differences in, 112–14, 133; seasonal variation in, 113
  human: gender stereotypes about, 39ff., 102–3, 107, 119–20; evolution of, 56; in adults, 102–3, 106–12, 114–20; definition of, 103–4; in children, 104–6, 118–19; verbal, 104, 105–6; physical, 105–6, 108–12, 117–20; prosocial, 105; laboratory studies of 106–7; 'real life' studies, 107–12, 117, 119–20; theories of, 112–20; and fear, 129; socialization theory of, 202
  see also conflict; violence; power
alcohol
  and domestic violence, 110
  and fear, 130
  poisoning, in relation to psychoses, 140
alcoholism
  gender differences, 141, 146
androgens, 59
  adrenal, 62, 64

  in Klinefelter's syndrome, 67
  in testicular feminizing syndrome, 68
  in adrenogenital syndrome, 68–9
  see also testosterone
androgyny, 213–14, 215
anger, see aggression; violence
Anthias squamipinnis, see red fish
anti-psychiatry, 139
antlers, 51, 112
anxiety, 132–3
  about aggressive feelings, 107
  clinical, 132–3
  premenstrual, 134ff.
  menopausal, 137
  separation, 162
apprenticeships, 29, 176
  see also occupations, training for
arithmetic, performance in, 34
  in children from single-parent families, 169
  and parental visits to school, 171
Arlott, John, 129
armed forces, recruitment of women in, 117, 222–3
aspirations, occupational, 193–7
athletics, see sport
Atlas, Charles, 75
attachment, 161–8
  to mother, 163–4
  to father, 164, 169
  to metaplot, 164
  to many caretakers, 165–6
  gender differences in, 167–8
attribution studies, 189–90, 193

Badminton, 73
bank clerks, 188
Barr body, 48
beards
  evolutionary origin of, 56
  hormonal influences on, 70–71

Also published by Penguins

HUMAN SEXUAL RELATIONS
Edited by Mike Brake

As sexual beings we are caught up in ideologies, roles and identities which owe much to a structured definition of sexual power.

Surrounded by myths and taboos, human sexuality has always been the subject of intense debate in religion, philosophy and the arts and an area of conflict in everyday life.

Aimed at readers who would like to think socially about experiences we have been taught to keep private, this reader in human sexuality also represents an exciting foray into new territory for the sociologist. Traditionally a discipline that has held aloof from the psycho/political areas, sociology is changing and *Human Sexual Relations* offers an excellent and thought-provoking example of this new wave of thinking.

From Georg Simmel and Max Weber to Simone de Beauvoir and Michel Foucault, the contributors here explore the dialectic relation between sexual definitions prescribed by society, how the individual interprets these, how sexuality is affected by the arts and what the effect of the various liberation movements has been on modern sexuality.

THE HISTORY OF SEXUALITY
Volume One: An Introduction
Michel Foucault

Why has there been such an explosion of discussion about sex in the West since the seventeenth century?

In this, the first of a six-volume history of sexuality, Michel Foucault offers an exploration of why we feel compelled to analyse and discuss sex, and of the social mechanisms that cause us to direct the question of what we are to what our sexuality is.

'Foucault is at his polemical best. He brilliantly succeeds in turning commonplaces on their heads (or sides), permitting us to see that, like any notion that has become a part of conventional wisdom, they can be viewed in at least two ways ... I cannot ... do justice to the wealth of insights, original conceptualizations and provocative ideas which Foucault provides' – Hayden White in *The Times Literary Supplement*

THE FEMININE MYSTIQUE
Betty Friedan

First published in the sixties *The Feminine Mystique* still remains a powerful and illuminating analysis of the position of women in Western society.

'Brilliantly researched, passionately argued book – a time-bomb flung into the Mom-and-Apple-Pie image ... Out of the debris of that shattered ideal, the Woman's Liberation Movement was born' – Ann Leslie

'A controversial polemic' – *New Statesman*

'Fascinating' – *Guardian*

'Intelligently argued and persuasively written' – *Listener*

'Densely researched study' – *Evening Standard*

'An angry thoroughly documented book' – *Life*

THE SCEPTICAL FEMINIST
A Philosophical Enquiry
Janet Radcliffe Richards

In this important and original study, Janet Radcliffe Richards demonstrates with incisive, systematic and often unexpected arguments the precise nature of the injustice women suffer, and exposes the fallacious arguments by which it has been justified. Her analysis leads her to considerable criticism of many commonly held feminist views, but from it emerges the outline of a new and more powerful feminism which sacrifices neither rationality nor radicalism.

'Intellectually sober and politically practical, yet gay, witty and dashing at the same time ... It's a model of how to write a book on *any* topic; on a contentious subject like this *it's a triumph*' – *Sunday Times*

Also published by Penguins

WOMEN, SEX AND PORNOGRAPHY
Beatrice Faust

Pornography is a topic that produces feverish responses, but women's reactions until now have been left unexamined. Even the responses of the women's movement have been contradictory. In this major new work, Beatrice Faust discusses the psychology of sexual differences and how they relate to differences in the sexual and erotic styles of men and women and the influence of culture.

In a frank and polemical analysis, Beatrice Faust explores the enormous social implications of these sexual differences, from novels, films and fashion to social behaviour patterns – and rape. She argues that pornography is neither pro- nor anti-woman. But it certainly presents a misleading view of woman's sexuality, and the solution is not censorship but sex education through bona fide erotica and the recognition of differences between male and female sexuality.

THE WISE WOUND
Menstruation and Everywoman
Penelope Shuttle and Peter Redgrave

Menstruation – blessing or curse? This book tackles a subject that has been forbidden for centuries.

It is the first study of its kind, and in unveiling taboos both ancient and modern, it will change the way women – and men – view themselves.

'An important, brave and exciting exploration into territory that belongs to all of us, and nobody could read it without a sense of discovery' – Margaret Drabble in the *Listener*

'Peter Redgrave and Penelope Shuttle have researched their subject with unerring diligence ... It could bring about a major change in our understanding of the sexes' – *Psychology Today*

'An Aladdin's cave of scientific, psychological and anthropological insights ... all quite irresistible' – *Observer*

Also published by Penguins

PSYCHOANALYSIS AND FEMINISM
Juliet Mitchell

The author of the widely acclaimed *Woman's Estate* here reassesses Freudian psychoanalysis in an attempt to develop an understanding of the psychology of femininity and the ideological oppression of women.

Analysing sexuality, femininity and the family as they are treated in the works of Freud, Reich and Laing, she demonstrates that Freud's theories have much to offer women in the understanding of their sexuality, and compares him to Reich and Laing, whose contributions to the feminist cause, in her opinion, are less radical and more ephemeral.

'Juliet Mitchell has risked accusations of apostasy from her fellow feminists. Her book not only challenges orthodox feminism, however, it defies the conventions of social thought in the English-speaking countries ... *Psychoanalysis and Feminism* is a brave and important book, and its influence will not be confined to feminists' – *New York Review of Books*

TOWARDS A NEW PSYCHOLOGY OF WOMEN
Jean Baker Miller

Every so often a book appears that overshadows any other on the subject. *Toward a New Psychology of Women* is one of those books. Dr Jean Baker Miller draws on her years of experience as a psychoanalyst and her insight as a woman, as she expresses with clarity and compassion her ideas on women and their future in the world.

She argues that the psychological development of both sexes has been distorted by an 'inequality of framework'. As a result, the qualities that women possess in abundance – tenderness, cooperativeness, unselfishness – have been consistently devalued as characteristics of a subordinate sex, and women have endorsed this attitude. In fact, as the author points out, these qualities are sources of enormous strength and must be used as such; and she goes on to specify how these assets can be used to change women's lives.